New Frontiers in Entrepreneurship

INTERNATIONAL STUDIES IN ENTREPRENEURSHIP

Series Editors:

Zoltan J. Acs
Geroge Manson University
Fairfox, VA, USA

David B. Audretsch
Indiana University
Bloomington, IN, USA

For other titles published in this series, go to
www.springer.com/series/6149

David B. Audretsch · Giovanni Battista Dagnino
Rosario Faraci · Robert E. Hoskisson
Editors

New Frontiers in Entrepreneurship

Recognizing, Seizing, and Executing Opportunities

Springer

Editors
David B. Audretsch
Max Planck Institute of Economics
Jena, Thuringia
Germany
and
Indiana University
Bloomington, IN
USA

Rosario Faraci
University of Catania
Catania
Italy
faraci@unict.it

Giovanni Battista Dagnino
University of Catania
Catania
Italy
dagnino@unict.it

Robert E. Hoskisson
Rice University
Houston, TX
USA
robert.hoskisson@rice.edu

ISBN 978-1-4419-0057-9 e-ISBN 978-1-4419-0058-6
DOI 10.1007/978-1-4419-0058-6
Springer New York Dordrecht Heidelberg London

Library of Congress Control Number: 2009933114

Printed on acid-free paper

Springer is part of Springer Science+Business Media (www.springer.com)

Contents

Contributors

Jonathan D. Arthurs
Washington State University, Pullman, WA, USA

David B. Audretsch
Max Planck Institute of Economics, Jena, Thuringia, Germany;
Indiana University, Bloomington, IN, USA

Fabio Bertoni
Polytechnic of Milan, Milano, Italy

Massimo G. Colombo
Polytechnic of Milan, Milano, Italy

Ken Colwell
Drexel University, Philadelphia, PA, USA

Diego D'Adda
Polytechnic of Milan, Milano, Italy

Giovanni Battista Dagnino
University of Catania, Catania, Italy

Thomas Dalziel
University of Cincinnati, Cincinnati, OH, USA

Donna M. DeCarolis
Drexel University, Philadelphia, PA, USA

Rosario Faraci
University of Catania, Catania, Italy

Paola Giuri
University of Bologna, Bologna, Italy

Luca Grilli
Polytechnic of Milan, Milano, Italy

Robert E. Hoskisson
Rice University, Houston, TX, USA

Hicheon Kim
Korea University, Seoul, Korea

Suresh Kotha
University of Washington, Seattle, WA, USA

Sergio G. Lazzarini
Ibmec São Paulo, São Paulo, Brazil

Luis F. Mesquita
Arizona State University, Phoenix, AZ, USA

Corey Phelps
University of Washington, Seattle, WA. USA

Richard Reed
Washington State University, Pullman, WA, USA

Francesco Rullani
Copenhagen Business School, Copenhagen, Denmark

Mario Sorrentino
Second University of Naples, Naples, Italy

Susan F. Storrud-Barnes
Cleveland State University, Cleveland, OH, USA

Salvatore Torrisi
University of Bologna, Bologna, Italy

Anu Wadhwa
Ecole Polytechnique Fédérale de Lausanne, Lausanne, Vaud, Switzerland

Robert E. White
Iowa State University, Ames, IA, USA

Daphne Yiu
Chinese University of Hong Kong, Hong Kong

Chapter 1
Introduction

David B. Audrestch, Giovanni Battista Dagnino, Rosario Faraci, and Robert E. Hoskisson

Moving from the received state of the art, this book presents and discusses a variety of attractive recent developments and achievements in entrepreneurship research. In more detail, it makes a systematic analysis of both theory and practice associated with the current evolving contours of "strategic entrepreneurship" intended as a new tradition in management and a field of study per se. This book intentionally encompasses four distinct domains: the nurturing of governance mechanisms and arrangements, the mobilization of capital, the activation of learning and innovation loops, and the role of open innovation in new entrepreneurial organizations.

Research on entrepreneurship and entrepreneurial processes has met greatest success at the dawn of this new millennium, stretching its frontiers from a peripheral subfield of management studies into one of the most relevant spheres of strategic management. Coined roughly a decade ago, the term "strategic entrepreneurship" joins together the insights of both entrepreneurship and strategic management and explores the overlap between the two (Hitt et al. 2001).

The decision to follow this integrative line of enquiry rested on the conviction that a chasm exists at the intersection of entrepreneurship and strategic management. In 2007, the *Strategic Entrepreneurship Journal*, an entirely new and ambitious scholarly journal was launched with the exact intention to fill this gap and to cultivate the "natural relationship" between strategic management and entrepreneurship (Schendel and Hitt 2007). Understandably, the inauguration of a new journal has ignited a great amount of enthusiasm and passionate effort from various academic parts directed to expand and solidify the examination of what is generally felt as an attractive interface to inspect.

In this regard, Venkataraman and Sarasvathy (2001) used a metaphor based on William Shakespeare's celebrated drama *Romeo and Juliet*. They suggested that

D.B. Audrestch (✉)
Max Planck Institute of Economics and Indiana University, Bloomington, IN, USA

G.B. Dagnino and R. Faraci
University of Catania, Catania, Italy

R.E. Hoskisson
Jones Graduate School of Business, Rice University, 6100 Main Street, Houston, TX 77005

D.B. Audretsch et al. (eds.), *New Frontiers in Entrepreneurship: Recognizing, Seizing, and Executing, Opportunities*, International Studies in Enterpreneurship,
DOI 10.1007/978-1-4419-0058-6_1,

strategic management research that does not integrate an entrepreneurial perspective is like "the balcony without Romeo." They also argued that entrepreneurship research without integration of a strategic perspective is like "Romeo without a balcony." In the words of Venkataraman and Sarasvathy, entrepreneurial action is the "Romeo on the balcony."

As a nod to the current debate, we have decided to name this book "*New Frontiers in Entrepreneurship*" as we endeavour to underscore the importance of two closely related themes: (1) connecting developments in entrepreneurship to current strategy thinking and practice, and (2) generating new and innovative ways to cultivate and advance entrepreneurship and entrepreneurial processes. Consequently, the subtitle "*Recognizing, Seizing and Executing Opportunities*" refers to the fact that – as Shane (2003) has submitted – entrepreneurship is scanning, capturing and profiting from opportunity. Ultimately what is important to an entrepreneur is achieving and coagulating the ability to understand the determinants of the raising of a new opportunity (or a set of opportunities), sense, and catch it in a well-timed fashion to make profit (Teece 2007).

Accordingly, this volume is primarily directed to raise and discuss a bouquet of new and creative ideas that are – and will reasonably be – key in entrepreneurship investigation. Because it raises several aspects relevant to entrepreneurial consultancy and practice, this book is expected to provide entrepreneurial practice a valuable guiding light and a nautical compass to navigate with more confidence in the years to come as well.

Like a pivotal lighthouse embedded in a forceful sea-rock, the ten chapters contained within argue about the nature and boundaries of central issues currently stretching the boundaries of entrepreneurship research and practice (e.g., different technological platforms and paces including open source, different avenues of finance for new ventures, sources of exploratory learning and entrepreneurial innovation, as well as novel governance issues and mechanisms). We have asked 26 authors, all strategic contributors and much-admired scholars in the field, to flesh out what, in their opinions are the new frontiers in the entrepreneurial field of study and to assess their own inner potential to push them forward so as to revolutionize our way of thinking. On this fertile ground and in the remainder of this introductory chapter, we further explain our rationale for this book, and present and discuss the new frontiers in entrepreneurial scrutiny that, collectively, we will unpack.

1.1 Our Objective

Entrepreneurial processes are essentially driven by the desire to start a new venture, or to reinvent or radically transform an existing company. Entrepreneurs and entrepreneurial managers seek to shape the future of their businesses by visualizing and implementing new imaginative ventures and models. The desired outcome is organizational genesis, growth and rejuvenation underpinned by new competitive advantages leading to new profitable opportunities.

On this fertile ground, this volume seeks to accomplish the following goals:

1. To identify new conceptual frameworks and models to foster research in entrepreneurship leading to the genesis of new ventures and the rejuvenation of existing firms and businesses;
2. To reflect on advances in entrepreneurship research vis-à-vis practical experiences with entrepreneurship financing and new ventures;
3. To experiment with innovative entrepreneurship analytical techniques and methods that encourage the firm's and the new venture's strategic guidance, governance and evolution (e.g., the lenses supplied by Gibrat law-type dynamic panel data model and the use of structural equation methods).

This book displays an additional original flavor borne of the following. First, it is one of the outcomes of the Strategic Management Society Special Conference held at the University of Catania, Italy, on May 23, 24, and 25, 2007, which bore the same name ("New Frontiers in Entrepreneurship") and was aimed to foster cutting-edge studies in entrepreneurship. The Catania conference was organized into 32 sessions; i.e., 5 plenary sessions and 27 parallel sessions with roughly 140 presenters. Second, since gathering in the SMS venue to discuss new advancements in entrepreneurship and reflect on previous accomplishments and breakdowns with fresh conceptual and new empirical approaches, business consultants, entrepreneurs, and academics have all taken an active part in connecting the key threads and subsequently, have given life to this grassroots endeavor. Third, we take advantage of the fact that each single contributor to the book has a unique economic and managerial qualification that consents him/her to play an active role in the development of new knowledge and practice at the crossroads of entrepreneurship and strategy. This circumstance seems particularly favorable as it provides intriguing opportunities to spark dialogue across the various groups of people involved in entrepreneurial issues while simultaneously fostering entrepreneurial research and practice. In other words, because the book's original design comes from and encourages continuous interactions among academics, entrepreneurs and other business people and consultants, it has the potential to contribute new ideas, ventures and models that intermingle solid conceptual theory with practical relevance thereby infusing fresh blood to practising entrepreneurs, entrepreneurial managers, consultants and scholars. Because its cradle was a widely attended international conference that brought for the first time an initiative cosponsored by the Strategic Management Society, the book covers a variety of topics at the pourous border of entrepreneurship and strategy, such as the four we summarized earlier. In the next section, we give an outline of each of the ten chapters offered in this book.

1.2 New Frontiers in Strategic Entrepreneurship: The Ten Chapters

The ten chapters contained in this book collectively represent an intriguing map of some of the directions that current entrepreneurship research has lately started to forge thereby tracing a path toward an increased amalgamation of the boundaries of entrepreneurship and strategy. To promote our understanding of the sources of wealth creation in current fast-paced evolving business environments, the contributors use a mix of traditional and new theoretical approaches. In particular, they constitute pioneering contributions to entrepreneurship that are theoretically and methodologically sound and strategically relevant to future research. The essays comprised in this volume collectively lay down the groundwork for significantly pushing forward the frontiers of investigation and practical understanding of entrepreneurship and entrepreneurial action.

As specifically concerns new frontiers in entrepreneurship, we can account for pushing the boundaries in the flourishing bouquet of issues that follow:

1. Governance mechanisms at the basis of rising entrepreneurship
2. International entrepreneurship and entrepreneurship in emerging economies
3. The intercontinental comparison of studies on entrepreneurship
4. Financing mechanisms and devices for new ventures
5. The mechanisms underlying processes of learning and innovation within and by new ventures
6. The role and function of open innovation as concerns the rising of nascent entrepreneurship
7. The road toward the fully fledged affirmation of the entrepreneurial society

Along the lines outlined heretofore, we have decided to partition the book into four main sections each dedicated to contribute a definite topic: Part One is devoted to the relationships between corporate governance and entrepreneurship; Part Two relates to the mobilization of capital for fostering new entrepreneurship; Part Three concerns the interaction among learning processes, innovation and entrepreneurship; finally, Part Four addresses the issue of the potential connection between open innovation and the rising of new entrepreneurship.

Chapter Two, written by Dalziel, White, Arthurs, and Hoskisson, submits that, while the process of pursuing an initial public offering (IPO) provides new capital with which new ventures might pursue significant opportunities, research suggests that many IPO firms decrease in value subsequent to the new offering. Using an agency perspective, Dalziel et al. argue that the IPO process itself may not only raise direct governance costs due to increased monitoring and bonding, but may also create a distraction for managers who need to remain focused on the strategy in order to effective use the large infusion of capital from the IPO. Likewise, governance participants, especially board members, will be distracted by the work necessary to take the firm public and, as such, not be focused on the strategic monitoring necessary to continue firm viability. This lack of monitoring may allow managerial opportunism to be more prevalent, especially given the large amount of capital that may be available for managers once the IPO is completed. Accordingly, Dalziel et al. argue that excessive governance costs may be associated with the IPO process and subsequent IPO firm performance.

Chapter Three, by Mesquita and Lazzarini, integrates the resource-base view, transaction cost economics, and institutional theory to model how collaboration efforts among small and medium-sided enterprises (SMEs) immersed in weak infrastructure and institutional environments help them achieve a host of collective efficiencies and greater access to global markets. Using a survey database from 232 Argentinian furniture SMEs, Mesquita and Lazzarini found that, while vertical ties yield manufacturing productivity along the supply chain, horizontal ties enable the access to collective resources and joint product innovation. These collective efficiencies in turn serve as competitive currencies for SMEs to access global markets.

Chapter Four, by Hoskisson, Yiu, and Kim, is the only one in this original collection of papers directly deriven from previously published work. It draws on institutional economics to examine how institutional congruence between capital and labor markets influences corporate governance systems, which, in turn, create differences in national corporate innovation and entrepreneurship systems and subsequently global competitiveness. Hoskisson et al. argue that such institutional congruence cultivates two ideal corporate governance systems. The first ideal type is the market-based system with transactional capital and external labor markets. This corporate governance system facilitates more explorative and revolutionary innovations. The second ideal type is the relationship-based governance system with relational capital and internal labor markets. This system facilitates more exploitative and evolutionary innovations. Finally, Hoskisson et al. present a few intriguing implications that their congruence model suggests for global competitiveness, high-tech management, and public policy regarding national innovations systems.

Chapter Five, by David Audrestch, argues that, over the course of the past six decades, the role of entrepreneurship in society has changed dramatically. During the solid and sustained economic boom subsequent to World War II, the importance of entrepreneurship and small business seemed to fade away. However, beginning in the late 1970s and gaining momentum since that time, entrepreneurship has become the engine of economic and social development throughout the world. Audrestch's purpose in this chapter is to explain the emergence of what he has termed *The Entrepreneurial Society* and why its development is important (Audrestch 2007). In particular, this chapter traces the evolution of the engine of economic growth and development from physical capital during the postwar era, to knowledge capital and, more recently, to entrepreneurship capital. The chapter concludes by suggesting that public policy has shifted its focus toward promoting entrepreneurship as an important key to economic growth, employment creation and competitiveness in globally linked markets.

Chapter Six, by Dagnino, Faraci, and Sorrentino, discusses various aspects of the multifaceted relation between entrepreneurs seeking to finance their early-stage projects and the business angels providing equity. In particular, Dagnino et al. underscore the rationale for the emergence of the business angel networks in order to optimize search costs and identity good matches between supply and demand for funds. While business angel networks have found their tickets for admission in many European countries, US angel groups (or spontaneous investor associations) are far more developed. On the ground of a 5-year panel data survey extracted from the European Business Angel Network (EBAN), Dagnino et al. investigate in depth the intricacies and inefficiencies related to the action of the business angels networks in Continental Europe and juxtapose them to the Anglo-Saxon experience.

The rationale of the chapter lays in the condition that, despite the important role recognized to outside equity in financing and fostering innovative entrepreneurial firms (i.e., entrepreneurial start-ups), relatively little is actually known about the key characteristics of the different fund providers involved either in a temporal perspective (diverse stages of the early firm's life) or in a industry perspective (specialized equity investors). While business angels and venture capitalists are relatively common and welcome companions of entrepreneurs, various kinds of circumstances need to be coordinated and accomplished in order to establish and govern these relationships in a way that is beneficial to all the parties.

Chapter Seven, by Bertoni, Colombo, D'Adda, and Grilli, draws on the financial literature as it claims that venture capital (VC) financing spurs the growth of new technology-based firms (NTBFs). First, VC investors allegedly have superior scouting capabilities so that they are able to provide great hidden value firms with the financing they would otherwise be unable to obtain. Second, they provide monitoring and coaching services to portfolio companies. Third, VC financing has a "certification" effect that makes it easier for the portfolio firms to obtain support from third parties. The aim of Bertoni et al. is to test whether VC financing has a positive effect on the subsequent growth of sales and employment of portfolio companies by taking into account the actual willingness of the NTBF to receive equity financing. Bertoni et al. take into account a 10-year longitudinal dataset of 215 Italian NTBFs, most of which are privately held. To capture the effects of VC financing on the subsequent growth of firms, Bertoni et al. estimated an augmented Gibrat law-type dynamic panel data model. The results support the view that VC financing spurs firm growth.

Chapter Eight, by Wadhwa, Phelps, and Kotha, examines how corporate venture capital (CVC), or direct minority equity investments made by established companies in privately held start-ups, has become an important strategic tool for large companies. In particular, firms often pursue CVC investing as a way to learn about novel technologies. Although CVC investments are inherently exploratory and have been found to enhance the investing firm's innovation, research has yet to establish whether CVC investing leads to the development of exploratory innovations (i.e., innovations that embody knowledge that differs from knowledge used by the firm in prior innovation efforts). In this paper, Wadhwa et al. explore the conditions under which CVC investments lead to the creation of exploratory knowledge by corporate investors. Building on insights from the recombinatory search and interorganizational learning literatures, they argue that the characteristics of an investing firm's portfolio of startups will enhance its creation of exploratory knowledge. Using longitudinal data on a panel of 40 telecommunications equipment manufacturers, Wadhwa et al. submit that investing firms produce more exploratory knowledge when their portfolios include startups that are moderately diverse, mature, and possess codified technological knowledge.

Chapter Nine, by Colwell and DeCarolis, applies the concept of capability lifecycles to new and adolescent technology ventures so as to propose and test a model of the sources of heterogeneous knowledge capabilities that impact innovation. Colwell and DeCarolis suggest that the characteristics of the top management of these ventures impacts business-university alliance formation; a critical knowledge capability that affects innovation. Building on prior research, Colwell and DeCarolis also examine the source of firm specific knowledge by way of geographical munificence. The results suggest there are paths to knowledge capability development and innovation and that key individuals and not merely being in the right location are critical in building collaborative relationships.

Chapter Ten, by Giuri, Rullani, and Torrisi, investigates the emergence of entrepreneurs and their skill profiles in the open source software (OSS) community. Giuri et al. test the hypothesis that entrepreneurs carrying out complex multi-task activities have more balanced skill sets when compared with individuals who are less involved in project management activities. Giuri et al.'s empirical analysis employs the SourceForge dataset containing information on 77,039 individuals working in 54,229 OSS projects. They estimate and order logit models to predict the likelihood that an individual is a project founder or manager. The results obtained support their main hypothesis.

In Chapter Eleven, the last, Reed and Storrud-Barnes look at the consequences of entrepreneurs who decided to tap into the "intellectual economy" by using open innovation and, thus, relinquished their property rights. Open innovation transcends R&D consortia and open licensing and copyleft work that has accompanied the open source development of computer code. Open innovation occurs when a new product or service is designed by an individual or several individuals that come together in an Internet-based, innovation community. Like the people involved in open sourcing, they are not paid for their efforts but, instead, have other motives such as personal need or, simply, the pleasure of being creative. Open innovations in computer hardware are utilized by large firms like IBM and Sun Microsystems, as well by smaller firms in clothes design, cell phones, and white goods. Reed and Storrud-Barnes ultimate that conceptual contention is an "open systems strategy" whereby firms reveal proprietary knowledge to others in the industry, in a low-tech environment to encourage new entrants many of which are smaller, more adaptable, specialized entrepreneurial firms who are better able to cope with the open-systems approach.

References

Audrestch DB (2007) The Entrepreneurial Society. Oxford University Press, Oxford

Hitt MA, Ireland D, Camp SM, Sexton DL (2001) Guest editors' introduction to the special issue strategic entrepreneurship: entrepreneurial strategies for wealth creation. Strategic Manage J, *22*(Special Issue):479–491

Schendel D, Hitt MA (2007) Comments from the editors: introduction to volume 1. Strategic Entrep J 1(1):1–6

Shane S (2003) A general theory of entrepreneurship: the individual-opportunity nexus. Edward Elgar, Cheltenham, UK

Teece DJ (2007) Explicating dynamic capabilities: the nature and microfoundations of (sustainable) enterprise performance. Strategic Manage J 28(13):1319–1350

Venkataraman S, Sarasvathy SD (2001) Strategy and entrepreneurship: outlines of an untold story. In: Hitt MA, Freeman E, Harrison JS (eds) Handbook of strategic management. Blackwell, Oxford

Part I
Corporate Governance and Entrepreneurship

Chapter 2
Initially Distracted: The Influence of Boards on Agency Costs in Initial Public Offering (IPO) Firms

Thomas Dalziel, Robert E. White, Jonathan D. Arthurs, and Robert E. Hoskisson

Abstract While the process of pursuing an initial public offering (IPO) provides new capital with which new ventures might pursue significant opportunities, research suggests that many IPO firms decrease in value subsequent to the new offering. Using an agency perspective, we argue that the IPO process itself may not only raise direct governance costs (due to increased monitoring and bonding), but may also create a distraction for managers who need to remain focused on the strategy to effectively use a large infusion of capital from the IPO. Likewise, we argue that governance participants, especially board members, will be distracted by the work necessary to take the firm public and, as such, may not be focused on the strategic monitoring necessary for continued firm's viability. This lack of monitoring may also allow managerial opportunism to be more prevalent, especially given the large amount of capital available to managers once the IPO is completed. Accordingly, we argue that excessive governance costs (both direct and indirect) may be associated with the IPO process and subsequent IPO firm performance.

T. Dalziel (✉)
Department of Management, College of Business, University of Cincinnati, P.O. Box 210165, Cincinnati, OH45221-0165, USA
e-mail: dalziet@ucmail.uc.edu

R.E. White
Department of Management, College of Business, Iowa State University, 2350 Gerdin Business Building, Ames, IA, 50011–1350

J.D. Arthurs
Department of Management and Operations, College of Business, Washington State University, P.O. Box 644736, Pullman, WA, 99164-4736, USA

R.E. Hoskisson
Jones Graduate School of Business, Rice University, 6100 Main Street, MS–531, Houston, TX 77005

D.B. Audretsch et al. (eds.), *New Frontiers in Entrepreneurship: Recognizing, Seizing, and Executing, Opportunities*, International Studies in Enterpreneurship, DOI 10.1007/978-1-4419-0058-6_2, © Springer Science+Business Media, LLC 2010

While the precise degree is difficult to ascertain, the presence of long-run underperformance in IPO firms has been well documented. Ritter and Welch (2002) endorse two explanations of this trend. The first is that the most optimistic investors purchase IPO stocks first and that, over time, as the company gains a track record or as information asymmetries decrease, opinions regarding the actual value of the stock converge toward the mean and the stock price falls (Miller 1977). The second is that IPOs appear in waves, such that highly successful IPOs incite a large number of unprepared followers that perform poorly, thereby dampening the average performance of IPO firms (Schultz 2001).

While these and the other extant rationales discussed below provide some important insights, they do not fully explain the occurrence of underperformance in IPO firms in the years immediately following the launch of their public stock. In this chapter, we adopt an agency theory lens to examine the corporate governance changes that occur at the time of IPOs and the subsequent effects of these changes in contributing to long-run IPO firm underperformance. Our contribution focuses on suggesting that excessive governance costs, both direct (monitoring and bonding) and indirect (through the distraction of managers and board members), may significantly contribute to the lack of

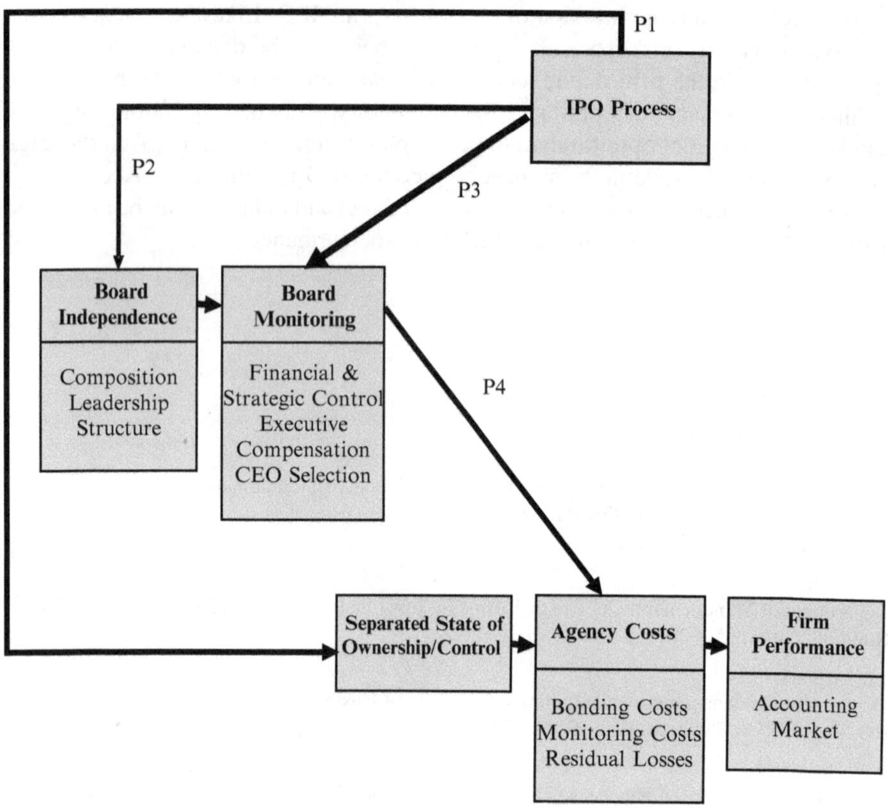

Fig. 2.1 The effect of IPOs on agency costs

long-run performance by newly publicly traded firms. Thus, as we suggest in Fig. 2.1, excessive agency costs may be a critical aspect contributing to low performing IPO firms and even firm failure. This is interesting in that, in theory, the IPO process[1] should allow for improved monitoring and public scrutiny of firms with future potential.

We begin our study with a summary of the tenets of agency theory and the monitoring function of corporate boards. Next, we review studies of the relationship between boards and IPO firm performance. We discuss factors which lead to IPOs and the effect the decision to go public has on board composition and structure. We show how these changes incite board monitoring of IPO-related issues which, although helpful to the IPO process itself, distracts board members from monitoring the core operations of the firm and sidetracks senior managers away from these core operations. We demonstrate how the IPO process produces distractions at the expense of other important issues thus aggrevating the potential for opportunistic behavior by top managers.

One of the contributions to theory that arises from this study pertains to the notion of bounded rationality, a key assumption of agency theory (Eisenhardt 1989), which reflects the fact that, when faced with complexity and uncertainty, human actors are limited in their ability to process and manage information (Simon 1957). The bounded rationality assumption suggests that complexity and uncertainty make it difficult for owners to foresee future contingencies and to form contracts with agents that will maximize the interests of the firm. In traditional agency theory treatments, boards of directors are proposed as a remedy to this problem because they are able to actively monitor the agents, exert pressure, modify incentives, and more fully align agent behavior with principals' interests.

In contrast to this logic, we build upon the assumption of bounded rationality to suggest that the board may also inadvertently contribute to agency costs around the time of major strategic processes (e.g., IPOs). We argue that the complex and rigorous nature of going public distracts the board from other issues within the firm. Owing to bounded rationality and constraints on the time and attention of directors, the board cannot monitor the non-IPO-related activities of the firm as effectively. Top executives may be similarly distracted by the IPO and thus somewhat limited in their ability to supervise the non-IPO-related functions. Accordingly, the problem of distraction can extend throughout the organizational hierarchy as managers involved in the IPO neglect other important duties, opening the door to agent shirking and opportunism at multiple organizational levels. Thus, our work reinterprets the implications of a critical assumption of agency theory and simultaneously spotlights some of the costs of going public which have received less attention in extant research and which can inform owners and other practitioners of the pitfalls they may encounter as they take their companies public.

[1] The IPO process (as mentioned in Fig. 2.1) begins with the decision to take the firm public and ends with value stabilizing efforts (e.g., creating a market in the new public stock, providing liquidity to exiting investors) after the stock issue. See Ellis et al. (1999) for a helpful examination of this process.

2.1 Literature Review

2.1.1 Agency Theory and Boards of Directors

We begin with a review of agency theory assertions with particular emphasis on the role of corporate boards of directors. Agency theorists treat the firm as a nexus of contracts between owners, employees, creditors, and others. Agency theory advocates (a) efficiency as a means to improve firm performance, and (b) the use of governance mechanisms to manage agency costs as the primary means of improving efficiency (Eisenhardt 1989; Fama and Jensen 1983). The theory also contends that agency costs arise in corporations where owners delegate control to agents (Berle and Means 1932; Jensen and Meckling 1976).

These agency costs include bonding and monitoring costs and residual losses (Jensen and Meckling 1976). Bonding costs are incurred to tie the interests of agents to those of principals and include costs associated with executive employment contracts, explicit bonding against malfeasance, and performance-based executive compensation (Williamson 1988). Monitoring costs are costs incurred to supervise and control the agents and include costs associated with conducting board meetings and recruiting and remunerating directors (e.g., annual retainers, committee retainers and meeting fees, as well as stock compensation in the form of shares and options).

Agency theory contends these (bonding and monitoring) costs are justifiable to the degree they prevent more significant "residual losses," defined as losses from unchecked agent opportunism and the divergence of principal and agent interests. Myriad examples of residual losses exist, including the costs of agents shirking their duties, embezzling or misusing company funds, and consuming excessive perquisites.

Owing to the significant potential of such costs to harm owners, agency theorists emphasize the importance of boards of directors to curb residual losses and enhance firm performance by "monitoring" or "controlling" agent behavior (Hillman and Dalziel 2003; Zahra and Pearce 1989), creating and enforcing budget restrictions and operating rules (Jensen and Meckling 1976), and overseeing strategy implementation (Rindova 1999). As part of their monitoring function, boards have the responsibility of selecting, bonding, evaluating, compensating and replacing top of executives (Conyon and Peck 1998; Pitcher et al. 2000) who are in turn responsible for managing the organization. Because boards of directors sit at the apex of the organization, the decisions and priorities of corporate boards can have a direct effect on top managers and a trickle-down effect throughout the entire control structure or hierarchy of the organization.

2.1.2 Boards and IPO Performance

Given the potential of boards to control top executives and influence the strategy and thus performance of firms, it is not surprising that researchers studying IPOs have considered the influence of corporate boards on IPO firm performance. The agency literature on this topic has been dominated by a focus on two measures of board independence: (a) board composition (e.g., the ratio of outside to total directors) and (b) board leadership structure (i.e., division of the CEO and board chair positions).

Studies examining the link between board composition at the time of the IPO and initial stock performance have yielded equivocal results (see Table 2.1 for a summary). Some researchers find that the percentage of outside directors is positively associated with initial underpricing[2] (Certo et al. 2001) and the percentage of insiders is negatively associated with initial underpricing (Arthurs et al. 2008). Conversely, many others find that the percentage of outsiders is positively associated with higher initial stock returns (Howton et al. 2001) and initial firm value (Roosenboom and van der Goot 2005), and negatively associated with underpricing of the initial offering (Chahine and Filatotchev 2008).

Whatever benefit there may be to independent board composition at the time of the IPO, it seems to wear off in the years following the IPO. In fact, researchers find inside (rather than outside) director participation on the board is positively related

Table 2.1 Board composition and structure and IPO firm performance

Antecedent	Outcome	Finding	Authors
% of inside directors	Initial underpricing	–R.	Arthurs et al. (2008)
% of independent outside directors	Initial underpricing	+R.	Certo et al. (2001)
Separate (nondual) CEO/ Chair leadership structure		N.S.	
% of independent directors	Initial underpricing	–R.	Chahine and Filatotchev (2008)
% of nonaffiliated outside directors	Initial stock returns	+R.	Howton et al. 2001
CEO/Chair duality		N.S.	
% of independent directors	Initial IPO firm value	+R.	Roosenboom and van der Goot (2005)
Outside director control	5-year post-IPO operating performance	N.S.	Balatbat et al. (2004)
Separate (nondual) CEO/ Chair leadership structure		+R.	
Outside director presence	IPO firm survival	N.S.	Howton (2006)
Increases in the % of outside directors	Time to post-IPO operating profitability	–R.	Jain et al. (2008)
Original TMT board participation	2-year post-IPO stock performance	+ R.	Kroll et al. (2007)
Post-IPO division of CEO/ Chair positions	3-year post-IPO stock performance	+ R.	Li and Naughton (2007)

N.S. = No support for a significant relationship between the antecedent and the outcome
+R. = Evidence that the antecedent is positively related to the outcome
–R. = Evidence that the antecedent is negatively related to the outcome

[2] Underpricing is the difference between the initial market price of the offering (e.g., at the end of the first day of trading) and the stock price set by the IPO firm managers and their underwriter.

to 2-year post-IPO stock performance (Kroll et al. 2007). Studies predicting post-IPO operating performance also support this view. For example, Cox proportional hazard models reveal that higher percentages of outside directors lengthen the time it takes for unprofitable Internet IPOs to achieve profitability (Jain et al. 2008). These findings are tempered by other research which reports no significant relationship between outside directors and post-IPO operating performance (Balatbat et al. 2004) and survival (Howton 2006). In sum, studies reveal that independent board composition is not a reliable predictor of long-run IPO firm performance.

Investigations of independent board leadership structures and IPO firm performance also create a perplexing picture. Researchers find that an independent (separated) CEO/Chair leadership structure is not significantly related to initial underpricing (Certo et al. 2001) and, similarly, that CEO/Chair duality is not significantly related to initial-day stock returns (Howton et al. 2001). In the years following the initial offering, however, it seems that nondual structures may enhance IPO firm operating performance (Balatbat et al. 2004) and stock performance (Li and Naughton 2007).

Together, these studies underscore the complexity of the relationship between board independence and the performance of IPO firms. Nondual leadership structures – which do not seem to help initially – may have long-term benefits, whereas independent board composition – which sometimes appear to generate value initially – decline in importance and may even dampen post-IPO performance.

Scholars have tried to explain the long-run underperformance of IPO firms using a variety of perspectives (see Ritter and Welch (2002) for a helpful review of such explanations). One agency theory explanation is that after the firm has gone public and received the associated injection of funds, agents mismanage the newly received IPO funds and thereby produce negative performance consequences (Howton et al. 2001). While such an explanation is consistent with the preceding findings that independent leadership structures add value post-IPO (e.g., by reducing the CEO's control of IPO funds), it does not explain the (nonsignificant and negative) findings related to outside directors and post-IPO performance.

In this chapter, we attempt to address this issue by providing additional reasoning grounded in agency theory. We more fully interpret the bounded rationality assumption and demonstrate how boards are subject to human limits and become caught up in the demands of taking a firm public. We argue that the decision to go public gives rise to changes in board composition and structure, thereby directly producing agency costs, and that these changes tend to increase board monitoring activities in preparation for the firm to go public. We contend, however, that going public may also produce indirect governance costs as well. That is, the demands of going public may distract the board, and consequently top managers and agents at the other levels of the organization, from their primary purpose of running the organization, inadvertently opening a window for increased agent opportunism and residual losses which dampen firm performance. Thus, board monitoring produces both direct and indirect agency costs. As such, we contribute to agency theory by demonstrating how (boundedly rational) boards can contribute to the very same agency costs they were meant to reduce.

2.2 Theory Development

Numerous factors incite private firms to go public. For example, private firms that perform well or are likely to in the future, experience pressure to go public from venture capitalists and other powerful owners (e.g., angel investors) (Gulati and Higgins 2003; McBain and Krause 1989). To the extent public equity investors demand investment opportunities, these entities also lure firms into public equity markets. The need for additional financial capital, the economic outlook, and several other factors may also prompt firms to engage in the IPO process (see Prasad et al. (1995) for a detailed summary of such factors).

When a firm goes public, venture capitalists, angels, and other early owners can exit or reduce their interests in the firm. For example, founders may view the IPO as a chance to relinquish the responsibilities of control and cash in on firm value. Though some founder CEOs may prefer to maintain as much control and ownership as possible (Nelson 2003), there are disincentives for this decision as some researchers find that managers retaining equity this increases underpricing or the amount of money "left on the table" in the IPO (Daily et al. 2003).

Like founders, VCs, in search of a strong return on investment within a relatively short time period (e.g., 5 years) (Zider 1998), often view the IPO as a critical step that moves them closer to recouping their initial investment and any associated returns (Sanders and Boivie 2004). The same is true for family members and other private informal investors who are critically interested in harvesting their investments and who often view the IPO as a means to this end (Prasad et al. 1995).

The sale of equity by owners such as these results in an increase in the degree of separation of ownership and control for the firm. For example, when founders and owner-managers sell their interests in the firm to public equity holders with no management duties, the degree of separation increases because generally, public equity holders have no direct day-to-day involvement with the firm, exert very limited control by voting on only a narrow array of issues presented to them by managers and boards of directors, or may even lack significant voting rights (e.g., nonvoting or restricted shareholders).

Similarly, when VCs sell their ownership stakes to public equity holders at the time of an IPO, the degree of separation of ownership and control widens. Though VCs may not officially "manage" the organization, they can be unusually active in controlling the firm's strategy and operations by participating on the firm's board or through placement of managers in key positions (Fried et al. 1998). Likewise, family members and other early investors don't manage the firm, but they often have strong ties with managers and can exert a degree of control through them (Gomez-Mejia et al. 2001). Accordingly, we suggest that, in the absence of other factors, the exit of any of these owners will likely result in a transition to a more elevated state of separation between those that own and those that control the firm.

Conversly there are also cases where all of the pre-IPO owners maintain their ownership and control of the organization (e.g., founder-managers continue in their management duties, and no pre-IPO equity holdings are sold). However, even in these cases, IPOs still involve outsiders who acquire new public equity holdings in the firm. These new equity holders include investment banks, institutional investors, and many private individuals (Lewellen 2006). As many of these new owners will not share the control of the organization to the same degree as pre-IPO owners, these equity purchases are nonetheless likely to increase the degree of separation between principals and agents of the firm.

In view of these arguments, we formally propose:

Proposition 1: The transition from being privately held to publicly traded via an initial public offering (IPO) will be positively related to a more separated state of ownership and control.

Because IPOs are associated with the separation of ownership and control, investors like to receive assurances that the potential for agency problems in the firm is being mitigated by board governance (Certo et al. 2001). Accordingly, we contend the decision to move a firm into the public equity markets will also be associated with changes in board composition and board leadership structure.

There are numerous reasons why the onset of an IPO influences board composition. For example, firms seeking financial resources often appoint outside directors (Pfeffer 1972), particularly those from the financial community (Stearns and Mizruchi 1993), to the board. Outside "support specialist" directors, including investment bankers, may join the board to facilitate firm access to capital markets (Hillman et al. 2000). Similarly, as a firm goes public, it is subject to powerful investors who can influence who sits on the board (Luoma and Goodstein 1999). Influential investors (i.e., investment banks, institutional investors, large block shareholders) and other stakeholder groups most often focus on increasing board independence in view of curbing agent opportunism (Davis and Thompson 1994; McConnell and Servaes 1990). In fact, in their efforts to influence board effectiveness and protoect their interests, owners may even appoint their own representatives to the board. In addition, when firms conduct an IPO and become listed on an exchange, they become subject to regulators and stock exchange guidelines stipulating that independent outside board members chair or sit on key board committees such as the nomination, compensation and audit committees. Accordingly, we submit:

Proposition 2a: The transition from being privately held to publicly traded via an initial public offering (IPO) will be positively related to changes in board composition, such that boards will be more independent after the decision to go public.

In addition to board composition, the decision to go public may also change the board leadership structure. CEO/Chair duality is common in pre-IPO firms as they are often CEO-centric. Pressure from investment bankers, potential investors and regulators (e.g., the US Securities and Exchange Commission) often lead to more independent boards with divided leadership structures (Certo et al. 2001) upto and potentially including the displacement of the founder who chaired the board and simultaneously acted as chief executive. The argument for such action is that separating the CEO/Chair position will improve governance and that replacing founders with "professional" managers and directors, who are better-suited to the challenges associated with leading public corporations (Fischer and Pollock 2004), may in some cases substantially increase the value of the firm (Arcand 2004).

Together, these preferences for new management and independent boards may increase the likelihood that a new CEO will be appointed from outside the firm and that this new CEO will not chair the board of directors. Even in cases where the founder-CEO is not replaced with a professional outsider, researchers find the founders are less likely to chair the board post-IPO (Nelson 2003). This may be because a divided leadership structure can reduce the potential for conflicts of interest and may increase the odds of vigilant board monitoring. In keeping with this logic, researchers find divided board leadership structures are positively associated with post-listing firm performance (Balatbat et al. 2004; Li and Naughton 2007). Accordingly, we contend IPOs may lead to the separation of dual leadership structures. Thus, we propose:

> Proposition 2b: The transition from being privately held to publicly traded via an initial public offering (IPO) will be positively related to changes in board leadership structure such that duality will be less common after the decision to go public.

From an agency perspective, board independence (in composition and structure) is the primary antecedent of board monitoring. The relationships between board independence and monitoring have been examined extensively so we do not explicate them here. (See Johnson et al. 1996; Zahra and Pearce 1989 for reviews.)[3] We do, however, direct our attention to the influence of the IPO process on board monitoring.

Though board monitoring may occur continuously (e.g., scrutinizing the latest accounting documents, ongoing comparison of financial targets with current performance, monitoring strategic plans and implementation), IPOs create additional opportunities for monitoring. With the decision to go public, board procedures often become increasingly formalized and the duties of directors are liable to increase (Welbourne and Andrews 1996). Boards assume fiduciary responsibility for a larger asset base. They must comply with the formal dictates of regulators. They may be required to participate in more frequent meetings, particularly if they employ strategic controls to monitor management (Beekun et al. 1998). The board may also need to participate in the firm's IPO road show and in communicating the firm's intended direction to potential investors and other stakeholders as the firm enters the public spotlight (Pollock and Rindova 2003). Boards often need to be involved in crafting and approving the company prospectus because it is their fiduciary duty to ensure that when the firm issues its securities, there are no material misrepresentations or omissions in the registration statement. Litigation involving directors who fail to fulfill this duty provides an incentive for directors to actively participate in their monitoring function around the time of an IPO (Altschul 1986).

[3] Given the challenge of gaining access to board members and boardrooms, it is worth noting, however, that many studies use firm performance in place of actual measures of monitoring behaviors. See Gulati and Westphal (1999) and Huse et al. (2005)) for recent exceptions.

In addition, the board may need to add members to its ranks in order to satisfy potential investors or regulators, a task which has become more daunting owing to the heightening of director liability due to the Sarbanes-Oxley Act of 2002 (Scherpenseel 2004). After the firm has selected an underwriter, boards need to monitor the actions of bankers who tend to underprice IPOs and may do so at the expense of the initial shareholders in an attempt to generate loyalty among their syndicate banks and clients (Prasad et al. 1995). After the issue, boards continue to monitor underwriters to encourage them to follow through in creating a market in the new stock by trading shares and providing liquidity to investors. Similarly, boards may also have to weigh the benefits and determine the nature of antitakeover provisions when going public, as incumbent managers often push for them (Daines and Klausner 2001) despite the fact that takeover defenses can damage IPO firm value (Roosenboom and van der Goot 2005). These supplementary tasks associated with IPOs provide boards with the increased need to monitor. Accordingly, we suggest:

Proposition 3: The transition from being privately held to publicly traded via an initial public offering (IPO) will be positively related to board monitoring, such that board monitoring will be higher after the decision to go public than before.

Given these and other monitoring activities around the time of the IPO, we predict higher bonding and monitoring costs. For example, boards often replace the CEO before the IPO (Daily and Dalton 1992) and engage in executive compensation negotiations to bond the new executives' interests with those of the owners. Renegotiating the CEO employment contract (with an incumbent executive or a new arrival) at the time of the IPO often leads to higher bonding costs. Supporting this view, researchers find higher executive compensation is likely when the founder CEO is replaced by a professional (He 2005; Wasserman 2006).

Owing to the risky nature of IPO firms, investors like to see evidence that executives' interests are aligned with their own or that adequate bonding has been arranged (Sanders and Boivie 2004). Accordingly, researchers find that, at the time of the IPO, boards often implement incentive (or "pay-for-performance") compensation schemes (Allcock and Pass 2006), which reward executives handsomely if the firm performs well. Also, because the asset base (size) of the firm increases at the time of the IPO and because executive compensation is positively associated with firm size (Barkema and Gomez-Mejia 1998), boards and owners may need to reconfigure compensation plans in order to pay executives of IPO firms competitively.

In addition to using compensation to tie executives' interests to those of shareholders, firms commonly increase director and officer insurance policies around the time of IPOs, at significant cost (Towers 2007). Thus, they engage in extensive bonding to (a) avert agent actions that could harm shareholders, and (b) insure against, or provide remuneration in the face of, such actions. In view of these arguments, we submit:

Proposition 4a: Board monitoring activity at the time of an IPO will be positively associated with bonding costs, such that bonding costs will be higher after the decision to go public than before.

While we expect the board activities during the IPO to have an influence on bonding costs, we also anticipate board monitoring costs to increase. As demonstrated above, the IPO provides the board with a significant amount of additional work and liability, which may easily justify an increase in their compensation. In addition, because the board itself is responsible for setting top executive compensation (Baysinger and Hoskisson 1990), the issue of remuneration will often become salient to the board around the time of the IPO. Since boards are empowered to adjust their own compensation as well as that of top executives (Dalton and Daily 2001), we anticipate that, justifiability, salience and empowerment may all lead to increases in board compensation.

The need for accountability may also prompt changes in board compensation, though the potential impact of these changes is less certain. For example, market pressures may prompt a board to use operational or financial controls to motivate its members or prompt board members to accept lower compensation when the board is staffed with higher percentages of insiders (Boyd 1994). Board members may be required to participate in meetings to maximize their pay, or director compensation may be more tightly coupled with firm performance outcomes (Kosnik 1990), which may increase the upper and lower limits of board compensation. Accordingly, we contend that IPOs may lead to numerous changes in board compensation.

In sum, because environmental pressures (Pfeffer 1972) favor increases in the number of directors at the time of the IPO and because board compensation (an important monitoring cost) is the aggregate of director compensation, we expect the costs of remunerating directors will increase with the IPO. Owing to the increased demands on the board to meet and monitor brought on by the decision to go public and the rest of the IPO process which were discussed previously, the costs of operating the board are also likely to increase. These include the costs of travel, food, and accommodations for board meetings, as well as the time and expense associated with preparing documentation and reports for such meetings, among others. In all, we expect the decision to go public will be positively associated with higher monitoring costs. This view is bolstered by the fact that the same people (i.e., board members) who engage in these additional meetings and monitoring activities are responsible for allocating funds for monitoring and adjusting their own compensation. Accordingly, we formally submit:

> Proposition 4b: Board monitoring activity at the time of an IPO will be positively associated with board monitoring costs, such that board monitoring costs will be higher after the decision to go public than before.

In the preceding propositions we have argued the decision to go public gives rise to increases in board monitoring activities and in associated bonding and monitoring costs. We now turn our attention to the influence of increased monitoring activities on residual losses. Agency theorists traditionally argue that the costs of bonding and monitoring are justifiable to the degree they prevent residual losses (Jensen and Meckling 1976). Thus, if boards shirk their duties and do not monitor sufficiently, the opportunistic behavior of agents will lead to harmful residual losses (Fama and Jensen 1983).

It is our contention that, in the context of IPOs, this view may be overly simplistic. That is, a board of directors may be actively engaged in performing monitoring duties (related to the IPO), yet still overlook important aspects of ongoing firm functioning, and thereby open the way to agent opportunism. We note that this suggestion is (a) completely in harmony with agency logic, which places limits on human reasoning and capacity (i.e., bounded rationality) (Eisenhardt 1989), and (b) seems most likely if the board is involved in monitoring important strategic decisions (such as those associated with IPOs) and their implementations. To illustrate our argument, we review the aspects of the IPO process and board involvement therein.

Firms typically do not decide to go public overnight. In fact, the decision to go public is often part of a larger series of strategic decisions and events that involve the board and senior executives. For example, IPOs are used as a vehicle to facilitate the privatization of government-owned firms (Gu 2003). They are pursued by large corporations including those whose entrepreneurial endeavors lead to equity carve-out and lettered stock IPOs.[4] In diversified firms, spinoffs (Bergh et al. 2008), which result in a piece of the corporation breaking off through a new offering (IPO), are sometimes evaluated as an alternative to selloffs (Kingstone et al. 2002); whereas in small firms, IPOs provide an alternative to debt financing, alliances, and mergers, through which the focal firm might otherwise gain access to needed capital.

While the decision to go public requires a great deal of board involvement, that choice only initiates more work for directors. The boards of successful IPO firms engage in extensive preparations for the initial offering including changing executive and employee compensation schemes, developing antitakeover provisions, adjusting accounting and reporting systems, improving strategic planning systems and investor relations capabilities and policies, selecting an underwriter, and courting prospective investors (Ellis et al. 1999). Board member and executive owners must decide how much stock to retain and when they will cash in their stakes after the required lockup period (Daily et al. 2003). They often replace top executives and debate the merits and drawbacks of issuing warrants (How and Howe 2001) and dual-class shares (Amoako-Adu and Smith 2001) in the offering.

Researchers find these preparations take up to 18 months to accomplish and, accordingly, describe the IPO process as an "ordeal" or a "rite of passage" rather than a mere transaction (Champion 1999, p. 17). For this reason, some senior executives have avoided the IPO process altogether. For example, Supply Dynamics (a supply chain aggregation firm which services the global airline manufacturing industry) was recently sold by Trevor Stansbury to O'Neal Steel (a $2.3 B metals service company). While benefiting from the resources O'Neal could provide, Supply Dynamics has retained its management team and operates independently as a subsidiary of O'Neal. In a recent interview we conducted, Stansbury explained why this transaction was preferable to an IPO: "If we were to have invested the time and resources required to go public, it would have invariably meant a major

---

[4] Equity carve-outs and the issuance of lettered stocks are common elements of corporate entrepreneurship strategies. In equity carve-outs, the parent corporation takes a subsidiary public by creating a new legal entity and often retains a controlling interest in the new IPO firm. In the case of lettered stocks (also referred to as tracking stocks or targeted stocks) no new entity is formed, but the parent uses an IPO to issue new stocks in a subsidiary or division so that it can be "targeted" by investors and tracked by analysts separately from the parent firm (Frank 2001).

distraction and a loss of focus. As a growing SME, we could not afford to take our eyes off the ball" (personal interview, June 2008). While the IPO may be the preferred alternative for many firms, it is nevertheless a labor-intensive process, which has only become more demanding since the passing of Sarbanes-Oxley and similar legislation around the world.

Because of the time and effort involved in taking a firm public, board meetings can become consumed in reviewing IPO-related agenda items and progress. Directors and some top executives (e.g., those responsible for the finance, accounting, and legal functions) are also likely to be distracted with preparations for and involvement in the IPO. While board members and some top managers may be anxiously engaged in preparing and taking the firm public, other senior executives and agents at the other levels of the organization are less likely to have equally demanding roles in the IPO process and remain responsible for the ongoing operations of the firm. To the extent boards are focused on making the IPO a success, they may be less available to monitor the normal operations of the business and less likely to deter agent opportunism, to the extent it exists. Because IPO preparations span an extensive period of time (Champion 1999), board members and senior executives can be distracted for extended periods. Neglect of other areas and issues in the firm can lead to opportunity costs and open the door to agent opportunism, which can go unchecked while directors and officers are engaged in the IPO process.

The case of myCFO Inc., a financial services company which serviced the Silicon Valley elite, provides a helpful illustration (Waldman 2007). The firm's founding owners and board members included James Barksdale, James Clark, and John Doerr (all founders of Netscape Communications), John Chambers of Cisco Systems Inc., and Thomas Jermoluk, past chairman of Excite@Home, among other notables. Signs of trouble emerged as early as 1999, when accountants at myCFO Inc., began showing concerns about the "tax elimination" products that were a lucrative area of the business. One such tax shelter, known by the acronym "Cards", allowed clients to shelter $50–100 MM from tax liability with a foreign debt mechanism. Kevin McAuliffe, a myCFO accountant, raised concerns about such shelters to the board and top executives including CEO Art Shaw during the period in which myCFO was preparing to go public. Unfortunately, excitement about the firm's possible IPO was all-consuming and his concerns fell on deaf ears. While the board and senior executives deliberated over the IPO, the US Internal Revenue Service declared that Cards were improper tax shelters. Subsequently, numerous tax-fraud indictments were made against myCFO employees and the assets of the company were sold in 2002 to the Bank of Montreal and others.

Cases such as this reveal that because preparing for an IPO is so intense, it can distract the board from adequately monitoring other operations in the run-up to the IPO. They also suggest that directors may hesitate to adequately monitor or scrutinize profitable strategies and products around the time of the IPO because they don't want to turn up something that could threaten the success of the IPO and the personal benefits they stand to receive through the IPO-related appreciation of their stock and options.

We further contend that agency problems may persist during and after the IPO as well. When a firm goes public, significant attention is focused on the planned allocation and use of the new IPO funds. Goals and projections are shared with analysts, media representatives, and potential investors to build excitement around the new issue (Ellis et al. 1999). Once the firm receives the injection of capital, top managers must be ready to move forward with their plans; which often involve capital investments, including property, plant, and equipment purchases and upgrades, debt repayment, domestic and international market expansion, workforce growth, investments in innovation, and corporate acquisitions, among others. All of these activities need to be monitored to ensure that the executives do not misuse IPO funds.

The importance of post-IPO monitoring is illustrated by recent IPO scandals where board monitoring was lacking. For example, the Betonsports IPO, in which IPO funds were used to acquire online sports gambling entities operating illegally in the US, resulted in racketeering and fraud charges against senior company officials (Pimlott 2007). Monitoring was also problematic during the eChapman.com IPO, in which senior officers, including CEO Nathan A. Chapman, were accused of using IPO funds for personal use (e.g., home financing, gifts for significant others) and received extensive fines and jail time for defrauding a state pension fund (Jarboe 2004).

To avoid scandals such as these, it is imperative that board members actively monitor the agents responsible for the disposition of IPO funds. Not surprisingly, this is a daunting challenge for busy directors, many of whom are chief executives of outside companies (Useem 1993) and have already committed their time and resources preparing the company to go public. In view of the demands placed on board members in the run up to the IPO, the post-IPO push for expansion may simply be overwhelming. Even if directors manage to stay on top of post-IPO growth, it is easy to conceive of scenarios in which agency problems pertaining to the core business are neglected by the board.

To illustrate, suppose a corporate board pushes for cost reductions and the Vice President (VP) of Operations responds by implementing new efficiency metrics. However, as the prospect of going public takes root and IPO preparations begin, no one may ask for a progress update. As the VP attempts to report back to the board on the progress being made (or the lack thereof), IPO-related agenda items repeatedly take precedence. When the VP asks for funds to expend in pursuit of the sought-after efficiencies, the board refuses on the grounds that expenses must be delayed in order to strengthen the income statement around the time of the IPO. The VP of Operations soon realizes that efficiency is not a top priority and is less likely to endorse and supervise the new metrics. To the extent apathy, shirking, and other forms of opportunism go unchecked at higher levels of the organization, awareness of such activities and replication of them throughout the organization begin to occur (Carr and Brower 1996).

Unfortunately, when the firm receives the large infusion of funds from the IPO, these and other agency problems also occur. The attention of the board and top executives now center on spending the new capital (e.g., building a new manufacturing plant or funding a geographic expansion) and so the manufacturing inefficiencies may be allowed to persist, and agent apathy and opportunism can become ingrained. At the same time, owing to the size of the injection of capital, the board is likely to encourage top managers to move forward promptly with pre-IPO plans for growth since utilizing the newly received capital is necessary for the firm to generate adequate returns for investors. Unfortunately, these plans may not be optimal because they were conceived before the IPO, at a point in time when the amount of capital the IPO would generate could only be roughly estimated. Accordingly, pressure from a board that is striving to fulfill its monitoring function may inadvertently prompt executives to prematurely move forward with projects that are not as well conceived as they could be. Thus, a well-intentioned board working for investors may push executives to act inefficiently. Sadly, experimental research suggests that executives may be particularly susceptible to escalation of commitment at this intermediate stage of the implementation (He and Mittal 2007) when the IPO has yielded funds that must now be used.

In summary, the real-world examples and scenarios reviewed above emphasize the demands IPOs place on directors and the challenge of effectively monitoring the IPO process. While an IPO may be the best course of action in many cases, we contend the demands on boards in preparing for an IPO and dealing with its aftereffects create numerous distractions and burdens that deter them from effectively monitoring both the core operations of the firm and the use of new funds obtained from the IPO. We expect this to result in agency costs and poorer operating performance in the years immediately following the IPO, when IPO funds are being used to implement dramatic growth-oriented changes. Formally stated:

> Proposition 4c: Board monitoring activity related to the IPO will be positively associated with residual losses related to distractions away from the core activities of the firm and the inefficient use of IPO funds.

2.3 Discussion and Conclusion

This chapter provides an alternative explanation to the underperformance of IPO firms in the years immediately following the listing. Our rationale for this troubling phenomenon differs from those currently available in the literature. It is grounded in agency theory and rests upon the assumption that, like senior executives, who are the traditional objects of agency theory criticisms, directors are also fallible human actors who are limited by bounded rationality and time constraints (Hambrick et al. 2005). As Baird and Rasmussen (2007: 924, 928) aptly note, a firm's directors "are part-timers. They have day jobs.... [D]irectors do not curtail their other activities once they join the board. Because they are part-timers, there are real limits on how much time they can invest in... the affairs of the corporation.... Part-time directors cannot be full-time police officers." We contend that, when faced with the rigors of taking a firm public and then monitoring the use of new IPO funds, boards of directors are likely to focus their limited time on IPO-related monitoring, such that they routinely overlook matters pertaining to the more stable ongoing operations of the firm. In effect, IPO-related decisions and events create distractions that deter the directors from governing the firm holistically.

In addition to the distractions, many directors are newly appointed at the time of an IPO and may not sufficiently understand firm operations to make the highest quality decisions. Likewise, often there are CEO changes in IPO firms as entrepreneurs step down, making room for more professional managers. As such, there may be several changes in both the management and monitoring functions of the IPO firm. We suggest these and other chaotic changes associated with taking a firm public open the door to distractions which lead to the neglect of core operations, shirking and other forms of agent opportunism and lead to residual losses which damage firm performance. Our logic that other categories of agency costs – namely bonding and monitoring costs – increase with the IPO as well, thereby creating further direct and indirect costs, also contributes to the explanation of IPO firm underperformance noted earlier.

Our observations regarding the role of boards in IPOs suggest firms moving toward the public equity markets may be wise to consider ways to minimize the effect of the distraction that the IPO process typically entails and to concomitantly develop ways to ensure that other monitoring is not neglected. Our analysis would counter-intuitively discourage IPO firms from staffing their board with directors maintaining several other directorships as these additional directorships may only distract directors further. Instead of staffing the board with individuals serving on several other boards, it may be preferable to staff the board with individuals who have personally gone through an initial public offering (as either a manager or a director). Experience with the IPO process among board members is likely to be particularly valuable for IPO firms seeking to reduce agency costs and recent research finds this to be true (e.g., Arthurs et al. 2008). Furthermore, it appears that board member experience with other new ventures may be invaluable as well (Arthurs et al. 2009). However, we should note that recent changes, particularly those enacted by Sarbanes-Oxley in the US and similar governance legislation in other parts the world, may limit the availability of experienced board members as the liability, requirements, and associated headaches for directors increase their reticence to serve on new boards. Accordingly, Sarbanes-Oxley and similar legislation may have the unintended effect of reducing the effectiveness of boards, particularly those of new ventures preparing for their IPO. We believe that important opportunities exist for scholars to use our ideas as a means to predict the outcomes associated with IPOs, particularly by comparing the impact of Sarbanes-Oxley legislation on the effectiveness of IPO-era firms.

While we have focused on IPOs, we believe much of our logic applies to other significant strategic processes as well, including large mergers, joint ventures, and privatizations; any of which may be sufficiently complex and time consuming to press the limits of a board's capacity. The importance here is that the introduction of a transition in an organization's legal form, a large change in firm capital structure, or some other significant firm event outside the course of normal operations introduces enormous distractions for directors who would otherwise be involved in monitoring the normal activity of the firm. When these change processes extend over a long period of time, our analysis would indicate that agency costs (both the direct costs of monitoring activities and the indirect costs of managerial and board distraction, as well as agent opportunism) can increase, rapidly undermining firm performance.

In conclusion, we have sought to explain why IPO firms may experience poor performance subsequent to going public. While there is little consensus among scholars for explanations of this poor performance, we have developed arguments using agency theory to explain why monitoring may diminish through the IPO process itself. And we have argued that this may lead to longer term problems given the massive influx of capital at the time of the IPO. In particular, we have identified how the IPO process not only increases the separation between ownership and control, but also creates a distraction and a drain on attention limiting the ability of directors to monitor normal operations. Our analysis points to the need for boards to develop coping strategies such as the appointment of directors with experience with the IPO process itself to ensure that the IPO process does not give rise to agency problems.

References

Allcock D, Pass C (2006) Executive incentive pay strategies in entrepreneurial UK initial public offering companies: an empirical study. Corporate Governance 6:148–161

Altschul JS (1986) Corporate directors' liability in the US. Int Fin Law Rev 5:33–35

Amoako-Adu B, Smith BF (2001) Dual class firms: capitalization, ownership structure and recapitalization back into single class. J Banking Finance 25:1083–111

Arcand J-P (2004) Institutional and strategic implications of founder-CEO transitions in firms issuing initial public offerings. Department of Management, Concordia University, Montreal, Canada

Arthurs JD, Busenitz LW, Hoskisson RE, Johnson RA (2009) Firm-specific human capital and governance in IPO firms: addressing agency and resource dependence concerns. Entrep Theory Pract, 33:845–865

Arthurs JD, Hoskisson RE, Busenitz LW, Johnson RA (2008) Managerial agents watching other agents: multiple agency conflicts regarding underpricing in IPO firms. Acad Manage J 51:277–94

Baird DG, Rasmussen RK (2007) The prime directive. U Cinci Law Rev 75:921–941

Balatbat MCA, Taylor SL, Walter TS (2004) Corporate governance, insider ownership and operating performance of Australian initial public offerings. Acc Fin 44:299–328

Barkema HG, Gomez-Mejia LR (1998) Managerial compensation and firm performance: a general research framework. Acad Manage J 41:135–145

Baysinger B, Hoskisson RE (1990) The composition of boards of directors and strategic control: effects on corporate strategy. Acad Manage Rev 15:72–87

Beekun RI, Stedham Y, Young GJ (1998) Board characteristics, managerial controls and corporate strategy: a study of U.S. hospitals. J Manage 24:3–19

Bergh DD, Johnson RA, Dewitt R (2008) Restructuring through spin-off or sell-off: transforming information asymmetries into financial gain. Strategic Manage J 29:133–148

Berle A, Means G (1932) The modern corporation and private property. Macmillan, New York

Boyd B (1994) Board control and CEO compensation. Strategic Manage J 15:335–344

Carr JB, Brower RS. (1996) Principal-agent as an explanation of nonsanctioned organizational behaviors: is the theory useful? Academy of Management Proceedings 323–327

Certo ST, Daily CM, Dalton DR (2001) Signaling firm value through board structure: an investigation of initial public offerings. Entrep Theory Prac, Winter:33–50
Chahine S, Filatotchev I (2008) The effects of information disclosure and board independence on IPO discount. J Small Bus Manage 46:219–241
Champion D (1999) Entrepreneurship (initial public offerings). Harvard Bus Rev 77:17
Conyon MJ, Peck SI (1998) Board control, remuneration committees, and top management compensation. Acad Manage J 41:146–157
Daily CM, Certo ST, Dalton DR, Roengpitya R (2003) IPO underpricing: a meta-analysis and research synthesis. Entrep Theory Pract 27:271–295
Daily CM, Dalton DR (1992) Financial performance of founder-managed versus professionally managed small corporations. J Small Bus Manage 2:25–34
Daines R, Klausner M (2001) Do IPO charters maximize firm value? Antitakeover protection in IPOs. J Law Econ Organ 17:83–120
Dalton DR, Daily CM (2001) Director stock compensation: an invitation to a conspicuous conflict of interest? Bus Ethics Quart 11:89–108
Davis GF, Thompson TA (1994) A social movement perspective on corporate control. Admin Sci Quart 39:141–173
Eisenhardt KM (1989) Agency theory: an assessment and review. Acad Manage Rev 14:57–74
Ellis K, Michaely R, O'Hara M (1999) A guide to the initial public offering process. Corp Fin Rev 3:14–18
Fama EF, Jensen MC (1983) Separation of ownership and control. J Law Econ 26:301–323
Fischer HM, Pollock TG (2004) Effects of social capital and power on surviving transformational change: the case of initial public offerings. Acad Manage J 47:463–481
Frank KE (2001) Making sense out of spin-offs, tracking stock, and equity carve-outs. Strategic Fin 83:38–43
Fried VH, Bruton GD, Hisrich RD (1998) Strategy and the board of directors in venture capital-backed firms. J Bus Venturing 13:493–503
Gomez-Mejia LR, Nunez-Nickel M, Gutierrez I (2001) Role of family ties in agency contracts. Acad Manage J 44:81–95
Gu AY (2003) State ownership, firm size, and IPO performance: evidence from Chinese "A" share issues. Am Bus Rev 21:101–112
Gulati R, Higgins MC (2003) Which ties matter when? The contingent effects of interorganizational partnerships in IPO success. Strategic Manage J 24:127–144
Gulati R, Westphal JD (1999) Cooperative or controlling? The effects of CEO-board relations and the content of interlocks on the formation of joint ventures. Admin Sci Quart 44:473–505
Hambrick DC, Finkelstein S, Mooney AC (2005) Executives sometimes lose it, just like the rest of us. Acad Manage Rev 30:503–508
He L (2005) An integrated system of corporate governance: regulation, internal control and managerial attributes. University of Pennsylvania, Philadelphia, PA
He X, Mittal V (2007) The effect of decision risk and project stage on escalation of commitment. Organ Behav Hum Dec 103:225–237
Hillman A, Cannella A, Paetzold R (2000) The resource dependence role of corporate directors: strategic adaptation of board composition in response to environmental change. J Manage Stud 37:325–256
Hillman A, Dalziel T (2003) Boards of directors and firm performance: integrating agency and resource dependence perspectives. Acad Manage Rev 28:383–415
How JCY, Howe JS (2001) Warrants in initial public offerings: empirical evidence. J Bus 74:433–457
Howton SD, Howton SW, Olson GT (2001) Board ownership and IPO returns. J Econ Fin 25:100–114
Howton SW (2006) Effect of governance characteristics on the state of the firm after an initial public offering. Fin Rev 41:419–433
Huse M, Minichilli A, Schoning M (2005) Corporate boards as assets for operating in the new Europe: the value of process-oriented boardroom dynamics. Org Dyn 34:285–297

Jain BA, Jayaraman N, Kini O (2008) The path-to-profitability of Internet IPO firms. J Bus Venturing 23:165–194
Jarboe KJ (2004) Chapman defense opens with praise from board member. Daily Record, Jul 20:1
Jensen M, Meckling W (1976) Theory of the firm: managerial behavior, agency costs and ownership structure. J Finan Econ 3:305–360
Johnson JL, Daily CM, Ellstrand AE (1996) Boards of directors: a review and research agenda. J Manage 22:409–438
Kingstone M, Scott T, Walkington L (2002) The BT demerger – Lessons for UK structures. Int Tax Rev 13:13–23
Kosnik RD (1990) Effects of board demography and directors' incentives on corporate greenmail decisions. Acad Manage J 33:129–150
Kroll M, Walters BA, Le SA (2007) The impact of board composition and top management team ownership structure on post-IPO performance in young entrepreneurial firms. Acad Manage J 50:1198–1216
Lewellen K (2006) Risk, reputation and IPO price support. J Fin 61:613–653
Li L, Naughton T (2007) Going public with good governance: evidence from China. Corp Gov 15:1190–1202
Luoma P, Goodstein J (1999) Stakeholders and corporate boards: institutional influences on board composition and structure. Acad Manage J 42:553–563
McBain ML, Krause DS (1989) Going public: the impact of insiders' holdings on the price of initial public offerings. J Bus Venturing 4:419–428
McConnell J, Servaes H (1990) Additional evidence on equity ownership and corporate value. J Finan Econ 37:595–612
Miller EM (1977) Risk, uncertainty, and divergence of opinion. J Fin 32:1151–1168
Nelson T (2003) The persistence of founder influence: management, ownership, and performance effects at initial public offering. Strategic Manage J 24:707–724
Pfeffer J (1972) Size and composition of corporate boards of directors: the organization and its environment. Admin Sci Quart 17:218–229
Pimlott, D (2007) Betonsports fugitives are targeted. Financial Times, Apr 11:20
Pitcher P, Chreim S, Kisfalvi V (2000) CEO succession research: methodological bridges over troubled waters. Strategic Manage J 21:625–648
Pollock TG, Rindova VP (2003) Media legitimation effects in the market for initial public offerings. Acad Manage J 46:631–642
Prasad D, Vozikis GS, Bruton GD, Merikas A (1995) 'Harvesting' through initial public offerings (IPOs): the implications of underpricing for the small firm. Entrep Theory Pract 20:1042–2587
Rindova VP (1999) What corporate boards have to do with strategy: a cognitive perspective. J Manage Stud 36:953–975
Ritter JR, Welch I (2002) A review of IPO activity, pricing, and allocations. J Fin 57:1795–1828
Roosenboom P, van der Goot T (2005) The effect of ownership and control on market valuation: evidence from initial public offerings in the Netherlands. Int Rev Finan Anal 14:43–59
Sanders WG, Boivie S (2004) Sorting things out: valuation of new firms in uncertain markets. Strategic Manage J 25:167–186
Scherpenseel C (2004) The ever-changing landscape of corporate governance. Strategic Fin 86:49–51
Schultz PH (2001) Pseudo market timing and the long-run underperformance of IPOs. University of Notre Dame, Notre Dame, IN
Simon HA (1957) Models of man: Social and rational; Mathematical essays on rational human behavior in society setting. Wiley, New York
Stearns L, Mizruchi M (1993) Board composition and corporate financing: the impact of financial institution representation on borrowing. Acad Manage J 36:603–618
Towers Perrin (2007) Directors and officers liability survey of insurance purchasing and claims trends
Useem M (1993) The inner circle. Oxford University Press, Oxford

Waldman P (2007) House of 'Cards': fling with tax shelters haunts Silicon Valley. Wall St J, Mar 6: A.1
Wasserman A (2006) Stewarts, agents, and the founder discount: executive compensation in new ventures. Acad Manage J 49:960–976
Welbourne TM, Andrews AO (1996) Predicting the performance of initial public offerings: should human resource management be in the equation? Acad Manage J 39:891–919
Williamson OE (1988) Corporate finance and corporate governance. J Fin 43(3):567–591
Zahra SA, Pearce JA (1989) Boards of directors and corporate financial performance: a review and integrative model. J Manage 15:291–334
Zider B (1998) How venture capital works. Harvard Bus Rev 76:131–139

Chapter 3
Horizontal and Vertical Relationships in Developing Economies: Implications for SMEs' Access to Global Markets[1]

Luiz F. Mesquita and Sergio G. Lazzarini

Abstract We integrate resource-based-view, transaction-cost economics, and institutional theory to model how collaboration efforts among SMEs immersed in weak infrastructure and institutional environments help them achieve a host of collective efficiencies and greater access to global markets. Using a survey database from 232 Argentine furniture SMEs, we find that while vertical ties yield manufacturing productivity along the supply chain, horizontal ties enable the access to collective resources and joint product innovation. These collective efficiencies, in turn, serve as competitive currencies for SMEs to access global markets. We discuss implications for theory and practice.

"Inter organizational relationships" has become an important topic in the fields of strategy and entrepreneurship. Aldrich and Zimmer (1986) capture the attraction of the field to this topic by avowing the important role that social relationships play in determining who is likely to succeed in entrepreneurial ventures. Entrepreneurship research, at large, has addressed not only how social structures differ across contexts (e.g., Rosenkopf and Schilling 2008), but also how such differences matter for firm advantages such as venture development (e.g., Stuart and Sorenson 2008), access to information (Gulati et al. 2000), opportunity recognition (McMullen and Shepherd 2006), endorsement for entrepreneurial initiatives (Cooper 2001), as well

L.F. Mesquita (✉)
Arizona State University, W. P. Carey School of Business, 4701 West Thunderbird Rd., FAB N130., 85306-4908, Glendale, AZ
e-mail: mesquita@asu.edu

S.G. Lazzarini
Insper Institute of Education & Research, Rua Quata, 300, 04546-042 São Paulo, SP, Brazil

[1] A previous version of this research was published as "Mesquita LF, Lazzarini SG (2008) Horizontal and vertical relationships in developing economies: implications for SMEs' access to global markets. Acad Manage J 51(2):359–380".

D.B. Audretsch et al. (eds.), *New Frontiers in Entrepreneurship: Recognizing, Seizing, and Executing, Opportunities*, International Studies in Enterprepreneurship,
DOI 10.1007/978-1-4419-0058-6_3,

as resources (Rothaermel 2001) and capabilities (Calabrese et al. 2000) that are necessary to thrive in dynamic and volatile markets. Although entrepreneurship research does acknowledge the importance of inter firm ties, most of the field has looked at the matter from a network perspective, whereby the structure and the combined pattern of ties may differ across industries. In this chapter, we expand on the entrepreneurship literature outlined above, by looking at how small firms can attain particular forms of competitive advantages as they strategically craft a unique set of relationships.

We are particularly concerned with small firms in developing economies. Within this context, firms are urged to become internationally competitive to boost exports and decrease country-risk exposure; at the same time, however, they tend to be deprived of superior technology and the supporting infrastructure often found in developed countries – e.g., government support, efficient ports, shared scale-efficient resources – to reach such global markets (Porter 1998). Small and medium enterprises (SMEs) in these contexts are also plagued with severe scale constraints to invest in productive assets and to develop international channels. A possible way to circumvent such scale and infrastructure limitations is to promote joint action among SMEs through interfirm agreements (Markusen 1999; Storper 1997; Tallman et al. 2004). By forging extensive collaborative ties, SMEs can exploit complementary competencies and solve common production problems (Amin and Thrift 1992; Pouder and St. John 1996), share knowledge, technologies, and inputs (Storper 1997), develop greater responsiveness to global demands (Canina et al. 2005; Tallman et al. 2004; Tendler and Amorim 1996), and attain greater export levels as a result (Schmitz 1995: 537).

Ironically, while forging inter organizational collaborative arrangements appears to be critical for SMEs within weak infrastructure settings, it is precisely in those countries that firms also suffer from a host of institutional failures – e.g., poor legal systems, discretionary governmental policies, and inefficient regulation – that hinder the pursuit of such joint action and impose high investment uncertainties and exchange hazards (Mesquita 2003; North 1990). Suppose, for instance, that SMEs wish to articulate complementary competencies to overcome infrastructure shortcomings. As they invest in resources specific to their joint project and form expectations of outcomes which are difficult to meter ex ante, they may suffer severe contractual hazards. For example, some firms may renege on collective agreements and free ride on investments of others, as contracts are difficult to enforce.

These weak infrastructure and poor institutional setting dilemmas seem to be common across emerging markets (Hoskisson et al. 2000), where the combination of small scale and lack of country-level support poses formidable challenges for SMEs. As such, we ask *how can SMEs' joint actions enable them to overcome weak infrastructure and institutional settings and become internationally competitive?* To address this question, we draw on three complementary theoretical lenses: the resource based view, transaction cost economics, and institutional theory. In a nutshell, we employ resource-based logic (Barney 1991) to model how coordinated efforts to articulate distinct sets of interfirm resources and competencies allow SMEs to attain *collective efficiencies* – i.e., efficiencies that are unavailable to firms operating alone (Schmitz and Nadvi 1999) – and overcome infrastructure limitations.[2] Such efficiencies in turn enhance SMEs' access to global markets. As these environments also present institutional challenges, we further employ transaction cost logic (Williamson 1985) and institutional theory (North 1990); these perspectives are particularly useful to demonstrate how SMEs can overcome institutional failures and avoid contractual hazards by forging relational governance mechanisms, i.e., sets of commitments, informal rules, and unwritten codes of conduct that affect the behavior of partners (Baker et al. 2002; Macneil 1980). In sum, our model states that relational governance helps SMEs supplant weak institutions, and make possible their attaining *collective efficiencies* necessary to overcome the infrastructure constraints in emerging markets; such efficiencies then enable the firms to access global markets. We find empirical support for this model with tests on a sample of 232 furniture SMEs located in the province of Buenos Aires, Argentina.

Our study brings at least three important literature contributions. First, we highlight, as previously suggested by Hoskisson et al. (2000), how the integration of distinct theories may help bring to light the important aspects overlooked by individual frames. As we explore events falling in the interstices of the theories mentioned above, we are able to enrich our understanding of more complex phenomena. Second, unlike studies focusing on a particular type of inter organizational tie – e.g., vertical relationships (Dyer 1997; Helper 1991) or horizontal ones (Doz and Hamel 1998; Gulati 1999; Kogut 1988) – we analyze how SMEs can attain export-enhancing collective efficiencies through the management of a complex web of *both* vertical and horizontal relationships. As such, our work helps expand a growing line of inquiry demonstrating the virtues of a more integrated picture (e.g., Brandenburger and Nalebuff 1997; Choi et al. 2002; Lazzarini et al. 2001; Storper 1997) as we explicit the impact of collaborative processes on the creation of export-enhancing collective efficiencies. Finally, our model also helps highlight important contributions to the international management and cluster-development literatures, not only as it fine tunes the theoretical aspects but also through the application of novel empirical methods not used in strategy studies before.

[2] Our argument is also related to the so-called "relational view" (Dyer and Singh 1998), which establishes the value of resources in the context of inter organizational relationships. Specifically, we examine how firms develop collective efficiencies by employing resources that "extend beyond firm boundaries" (Dyer and Singh 1998: 660).

3.1 Inter Organizational Relationships, Collective Efficiencies, and SMEs' Access to Global Markets

3.1.1 Promoting Collective Efficiencies Through Interfirm Coordination

The resource-based view of the firm (RBV) states that the possession of distinctive resources is critical if one wishes to attain a competitive advantage (Barney 1991; Miller and Shamsie 1996; Peteraf 1993). Smaller scale firms may be particularly pressed to reach beyond their own boundaries to find and control such key resources (Dyer and Singh 1998; Stinchcombe 1965). For instance, SMEs may work together to integrate the complementary assets, or even jointly promote investments in common resources (e.g., logistic infrastructure) which would otherwise be prohibitively costly. Essentially, this possibility of joint efforts results from various forms of interfirm interdependencies that make the performance of a firm dependent on the performance of other firms in the same industry or market domain. To more didactically develop our theoretical model, we rely on Thomson's (1967) categorization of interdependencies which, though not central to our model, helps illustrate the multiple ways in which interfirm coordination can lead to distinct types of collective efficiencies (Gulati and Singh 1998; Lazzarini et al. 2001).

First, the activities of firms may be related to each other in a *pooled* way. In this case, although firms are loosely coupled, they may wish nonetheless to be interdependent so as to benefit from resources which any firm alone would be unable to acquire due to scale constraints. Here, firms pool their common needs to *collectively source* the provision of a broad set of scale-efficient resources, such as export infrastructure (e.g., roads and ports), aggregate market information, and other types of governmental support (e.g., the promotion of products in foreign markets). Second, firms' activities may be related to each other in a *sequential* fashion, where one's input is another's output. This type of interdependence typically occurs among firms in a supply chain, where the performance of a particular activity (e.g., assembly) will be heavily dependent on the performance of upstream stages of production (e.g., the supply of components). Thus, firms may attain *manufacturing productivity* (e.g., inventory and delivery efficiencies) if they coordinate their sequential activities and jointly develop the competencies to manage their supply chain. Finally, activities may be related to each other in a *reciprocal* way, whereby each agent's input is dependent on the others' output and vice versa. For instance, SMEs interested in jointly developing new products can mutually deploy resources and cospecialize their knowledge through simultaneous, recurring interactions (Gulati and Singh 1998). By combining distinct and complementary resources, SMEs can, for example, collectively achieve rates of *product innovation* that would be unattainable individually. We, therefore, focus our analysis on three major types of collective efficiencies that SMEs can achieve through the coordination of their efforts: sourcing of collective resources, manufacturing productivity, and product innovation.

3.1.2 Relational Governance as a Mechanism of Interfirm Coordination

As parties integrate the above resource interdependencies to attain collective efficiencies, they must align expectations and mitigate associated trade hazards. Given the relationship-specific nature of these efforts, transaction cost logic suggests that parties will need to employ safeguarding mechanisms, such as formal contracts, to avoid opportunistic expropriation (Williamson 1985). Contracts, however, require the existence of solid institutions to guarantee their good functioning. For example, scholars point out that the existence of strong courts offers a context that help curb opportunism; parties behave as contracted within these institutional settings, aware of the dire consequences arising otherwise (North 1990; Stone et al. 1996). In most emerging economies, however, firms are plagued with weak institutions, making the enforcement of such safeguards ineffectively and costly. In these settings, firms are likely to resort to informal, *relational* mechanisms of governance to support their joint action and supplant the absence of adequate legal enforcement (e.g., Ellickson 1991; Greif 1994; Xin and Pearce 1996).

Relational governance mechanisms are interfirm cooperative arrangements based on informal rules and unwritten codes of conduct that affect the behavior of firms when dealing with others (Baker et al. 2002: 39). Partners engaged in relational governance rely on generic processes for periodic ex post negotiations (Macneil 1980), and thus overcome the difficulties involved in formally spelling out actions and responsibilities ex ante. As such, parties institutionalize the very environment surrounding their trade with elements that conform a "mini-society" (Williamson 1985: 71) within which they solve conflicts based on mutual assessment of circumstances as they unveil (e.g., Baker et al. 2002; Heide and Miner 1992). Fundamentally, relational governance mechanisms are based on recurring exchanges between firms. Theories of contractual self-enforcement posit that parties may honor unwritten agreements in order to preserve their reputation and avoid the termination of valuable, long term relationships (Axelrod 1984: 124; Heide and Miner 1992: 267). As parties continue transacting over time, social norms and trust will also tend to emerge and further support a collaborative orientation (Fichman and Levinthal 1991).

Relational governance involves a complex, multidimensional set of norms (Macneil 1980). We follow Palay (1984) and Kaufmann and Stern (1988) by focusing on particular relational norms supporting informal agreements. First, parties engaged in relational governance should share information so as to facilitate their current interaction and promote subsequent changes in product design and schedules (Palay 1984). Second, firms should maintain a high level of mutual assistance (Macneil 1980), for instance by helping each other during unanticipated crises, or recommending alternative courses of action when new contingencies emerge. Finally, firms should pay attention to distributive norms (Kaufmann and Stern 1988; Ring and Van de Ven 1992) by sharing the costs and benefits of their joint efforts; here, unilateral bargaining is supplanted by a mutual orientation to promote fair returns for the parties involved in a given project or activity.

3.1.3 Horizontal and Vertical Relationships and the Distinct Types of Collective Efficiencies

Based on the above, we next explain the link between relational governance and distinct types of collective efficiencies. Then, we address how these resulting collective efficiencies associate with improved access to global markets (Fig. 3.1).

Our discussion on the effects of relational governance distinguishes between two types of ties that may occur among SMEs: *horizontal* (involving SMEs located in the same industry segment or producing complementary products) and *vertical* (involving SMEs specialized in sequential activities of a particular supply chain). Consider first how SMEs may secure the provision of collective resources. As Schmitz (1995) explain, collective sourcing is especially relevant when firms need resources that require large-scale initiatives, such as when firms pool their efforts to more effectively lobby their government for improved financing or jointly collect the information on new opportunities in global markets (Bartlett and Ghoshal 1992). To do so, SMEs must establish common rules and patterns of interaction that guide their joint action while preserving their autonomy (Thompson 1967). For example, if SMEs would like to improve their access to global markets, they may decide to establish a common brand, and even integrate individual efforts to collectively lobby their government for financial support or investments in infrastructure. A critical decision will be how to assign responsibilities and share the costs to perform particular collective actions, given that the benefits will be equally available

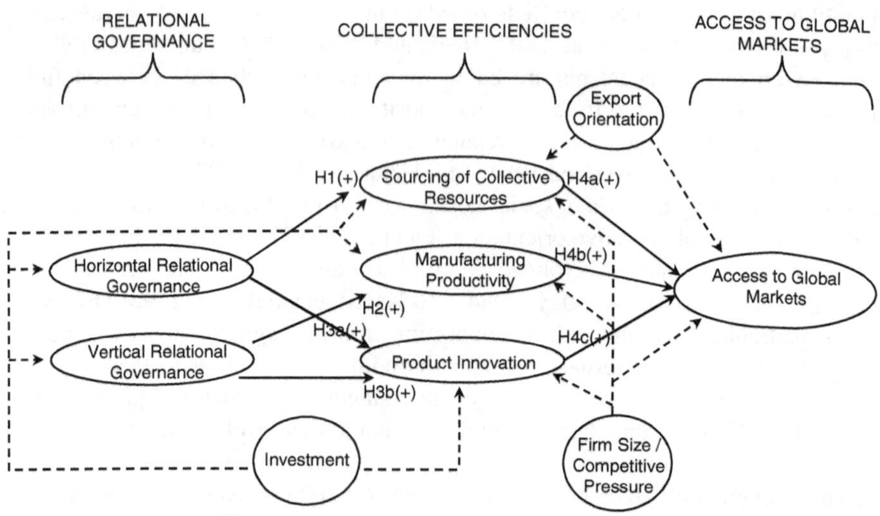

Fig. 3.1 Theoretical model: interfirm relationships among SMEs in developing economies. Obs: This is a simplified version of the actual model. It does not show error terms, exogenous factor variances, disturbance terms, the error correlations, or correlations between exogenous factors. *Full line paths* are hypothesized effects. *Dotted paths* are control paths.

to all SMEs in the same industry or market domain. Free-riding will be a possibility: some firms may bear a proportionally higher fraction of the necessary time and effort to secure collective resources while others may try to free-ride on those efforts (Nault and Tyagi 2001; Olson 1965).

Relational governance helps SMEs overcome such coordination dilemmas by enhancing their ability to align expectations and craft common strategies to secure collective resources. For example, implicit commitments to share information and mutually assist one another enable the parties to resolve pending conflicts in their process of adaptation to new standards and other types of collective strategies (Heide and Miner 1992; Helper 1991). Moreover, relational governance discourages free-riding and promotes mutual trust due to evolving social norms and procedures guiding collective action (Ostrom et al. 1992). Thus, we expect that a group of firms is likely to be more willing to invest time and effort to obtain government support for their joint export initiatives when they are confident that all the other parties are fully committed to the process.

We posit that the relational governance of *horizontal* ties will be particularly important to guarantee the provision of collective resources because it will be easier to establish a common agenda when SMEs are in the same industry or market segment. Horizontally linked SMEs face similar challenges in their competitive arenas, and hence will more likely agree on common strategies and more equally benefit from industry-specific norms. In contrast, SMEs with vertical ties will likely have more differentiated demands with respect to collective resources. For instance, while manufacturers of final goods may be more interested in governmental support to collect information on international clients, suppliers of components may be more interested in domestic financing or local investments in logistics. Even though vertically linked firms should also have a set of overlapping interests, we contend that the likelihood of effective joint action for the provision of collective resources will be higher in the case of horizontally linked, relationally governed SMEs. Thus, in weak infrastructure and institutional environments:

H1: *An SME's relational governance of horizontal ties associates positively with its sourcing of collective resources*

Relationships should also contribute to the attainment of superior manufacturing productivity along the supply chain. SMEs can coordinate their sequential activities to guarantee, for example, higher inventory turnover and timely delivery (Boyer et al. 1997). Such coordination also involves severe challenges, as parties need to jointly plan their production schedules and constantly check for inconsistencies and nonconformities (Thompson 1967). Because of the sequential nature of the process, interfirm coordination to achieve manufacturing productivity largely benefits from *vertical* relationships among suppliers and their clients.

The critical role of relational governance on the coordination of vertical ties can be explained by two distinct, yet related arguments (Mesquita and Brush 2007). The first of these, based on transaction cost economics, explains that relational governance contributes to an attenuation of contractual hazards occurring in complex buyer–supplier arrangements involving the deployment of relationship-specific resources (Poppo and Zenger 2002; Williamson 1985). Because vertical exchanges are commonly subject to moral hazard (e.g., the seller delivers core inputs of lower quality, in an untimely manner, or the buyer bargains for price reductions after the seller consummates specific investments), parties can benefit from social norms and commitments that accompany such relationships as these can help mitigate those hazards, reduce transaction costs, and increase exchange efficiencies as a result (Dyer 1997). As Helper (1991) explains, the relational commitments to "voice" concerns help firms resolve their conflicts and avoid ex post negotiation hazards.

The second argument explains that relational governance mechanisms affect the efficiency with which parties mutually coordinate their interdependent assembly systems and build up competencies to manage their activities (Gulati and Singh 1998). The development of vertical relationships, in particular, can help SMEs develop competencies to coordinate their production activities in a flexible way. For instance, commitments for information exchange, especially on market demand conditions, enable the parties to more accurately track the expectations of one another and adjust production processes accordingly (Van de Ven and Walker 1984). Likewise, commitments for mutual assistance, especially during emergency production line breakdowns, can help the parties either prevent unwanted supply interruptions or even react quicker to avert major losses when disruptions inadvertently occur; thus, such commitments help firms enhance the reliability of processes in the supply system (Boyer et al. 1997) . Therefore, in weak infrastructure and institutional environments:

H2: *An SME's relational governance of vertical ties associates positively with its manufacturing productivity.*

Relational governance also allows SMEs to leverage their rates of product innovation. We propose, in particular, that *both* vertical and horizontal relationships will help SMEs achieve this type of collective efficiency. Thus, buyer and supplier may jointly develop a new product or adjust the attributes of existing products (the architecture of components, the functionality of the overall design, and so on). To do so, they will likely have to cospecialize their resources and competencies: the seller will have to develop knowledge and production processes that are specific to the manufacturer, and the manufacturer will have to develop operations and marketing efforts that rely on the specific attributes of the product (Teece 1992: 9). Cospecialization will be greater if parties are willing to fully exchange the proprietary information, mutually assist one another, and guarantee that there will be a fair division of the net value arising from such investments in innovation. Relational norms will therefore promote greater support for cospecialization efforts (Dyer and Singh 1998; Poppo and Zenger 2002), which leads us to propose that vertical relational mechanisms are likely to induce higher rates of product innovation.

The same is true in the case of horizontal ties. Firms that are part of the same industry or segment may want to share complementary knowledge to improve their existing product portfolio, create new products, or jointly develop product bundles (Audretsch and Feldman 1996). Because horizontally linked firms tend to operate in the same industry or segment, knowledge sharing may lead to imitation or expropriation of proprietary technology (Dussauge et al. 2000; Zhao et al. 2004).

For instance, a firm may learn the design processes of one of its peers, and then apply this knowledge in the development of competing products. This behavior may not occur, however, if peers form horizontal links whereby norms and social attachments become prevalent (Granovetter 1985; Uzzi 1997). Therefore, in weak infrastructure and institutional environments:

H3: *An SME's relational governance of (H3a) horizontal and (H3b) vertical ties associate positively with its product innovation.*

3.1.4 Collective Efficiencies and the Improved Access to Global Markets

In the second part of our model, we posit that the benefits resulting from collective efficiencies enable SMEs to improve their access to global markets. Our argument derives from propositions established in the earlier international management literature (Buckley and Casson 1976; Dunning 1981). Dunning (1981), for example, posits that firms will have a better chance to access global markets if they have the necessary resources and capabilities to scan the international clients and meet their expectations in terms of quality, timely delivery, etc. (see also Bartlett and Ghoshal 1992:10). Specifically, as more and more industries have exhibited increasing scale economies, and faster rates of product innovation induced by skyrocketing R&D investments, firms are increasingly required to muster superior knowledge and capabilities to seek, find, and flexibly serve the needs of global customers. Firms can position themselves as high-scale, low-cost providers, and even, in some cases, attempt to out innovate competitors (Buckley and Casson 1976; Caves 1982).

Because SMEs often lack individual resources and capabilities to address such scale-based and innovation challenges in global markets, we theorize that collective efficiencies resulting from the proper coordination of joint action among SMEs allows these firms to overcome such difficulties and strengthen their ability to compete globally. Thus, manufacturing productivity emanating from the relational coordination of sequential activities is likely to bring cost-based competitive advantages for SMEs in global markets. Moreover, increased product innovation resulting from the relational coordination of knowledge-based resources is likely to improve SMEs' ability to satisfy the needs of diverse international customers. Finally, improved sourcing of collective resources is likely to enable SMEs to leverage their presence in global markets if, for instance, they influence local governments to invest in export infrastructure or collectively gather information about potential foreign clients. Such collective sourcing provides firms with capabilities to seek, find, and supply international clients – capabilities that each SME, alone, would be unable to gather. In sum, consistent with the resource-based view of the firm, we posit that these collective efficiencies borne by the articulation and creation of distinctive interfirm resources and competencies will allow firms to develop competitive advantage and better access global markets. Thus, within weak infrastructure and institutional environments:

H4: *An SME's improved (H4a) sourcing of collective resources, (H4b) manufacturing productivity, and (H4c) product innovation associate positively with its access to global markets.*

3.2 Data and Methods

3.2.1 Industry Setting

We tested the proposed model with a survey data set from SMEs producing furniture in the province of Buenos Aires, Argentina. These firms make finished goods such as tables, chairs, cabinets and other pieces which are sold as single units or as sets, and also preassembled whole parts, such as machined table structures, bed frames and other complex compositions of separate parts. To ensure consistency, we excluded makers of smaller parts, such as laminated wood, tubes, connections, wheels and nuts-and-bolts.

We believe that the country in question and the industrial setting are appropriate given our objectives. First, Argentina is known to suffer from a lack of strong export-enhancing infrastructure as well as solid institutions as those found in more developed countries. Such conditions create barriers for local companies that need to expand globally or even simply coordinate joint actions (Mesquita 2003). Moreover, recent studies demonstrate that exports have become an important means to gage success of firms in Argentina, as it represents a source of hard currency for firms competing in a shrinking local market as well as a form of diversification against country level risk (Carrera et al. 2003). Thus our study setting provides an invaluable opportunity to model how SMEs can overcome common environmental difficulties by coordinating their joint action so as to attain collective efficiencies and successfully access global markets.

The Argentine furniture sector is also adequate for testing our model given the profile of its firms. Most firms are small family businesses (CSIL Research 2003); as such they lack the necessary scale to compete on costs and search for global opportunities. Further, responding to a request of the local trade association, the Foreign Ministry of Argentina developed an exports sponsorship program coordinated by its agency *Fundación ExportAR*. Such program provided furniture makers with the necessary support in foreign relations, market information and even partial financial support aimed at facilitating their involvement in export activities. We consider this governmental service to be a collective resource that a group of firms can access through interfirm coordination.

3.2.2 Data Collection

In collecting our data set, we mostly followed prescriptions by Dillman (2000). We initially developed a questionnaire by identifying construct items from previous studies. We then interviewed entrepreneurs and managers to develop and adapt items, to refine survey wording and check the overall validity of questions vis-à-vis their industry environment. With the help of the local trade association, we assembled a list of 521 firms. Based on information from the Argentine Ministry of Economy, we believe the population of furniture-makers is as large as 2,000 firms. Thus, we believe that our initial sample is fairly representative of the population. Based on this initial sample, our response rate was roughly 45% (232 responses). We also assessed whether nonrespondents could have produced any significant biases, by comparing early to late respondents through *t* tests (see Armstrong and Overton 1977 for similar treatment). We found no significant differences.

In the survey, respondents assessed their vertical and horizontal ties and performance. They were asked to consider the past 3 years of their relationships to avoid capturing biased responses due to peak performance at given occasions or even one-time negative relationship experiences. Likert-scale measures ranged from 1 (not at all) to 5 (to a high extent).

3.2.3 Measures

Relational governance of vertical and horizontal ties. We asked entrepreneurs[3] to indicate on a 5-point Likert scale the degree to which they were committed to establishing a set of behavioral norms in the partnerships they held. Vertical and horizontal partnerships were referred to in separate questions. As such, we measure the degree to which respondents rely on social commitments of collaboration as gaged by their efforts to (a) share information, (b) assist each other and (c) promote fair sharing of cost savings and benefits arising out of joint efforts. The two first survey items were adapted from Heide and John (1992) and Artz and Brush (2000). The third was adapted from Ring and Van de Ven (1992).

Sourcing of collective resources. To measure the degree to which firms share resources, we were careful to select a form of resource sharing that was meaningful to the particular population studied. As mentioned above, a particular type of collective resource provided to this group of firms involved the efforts by *fundación ExportAR* in assigning a foreign ministry counselor to assist the furniture makers in matters related to (a) contacting potential foreign customers through their web of consulates in other countries, (b) coordinating and financing their showing products in international fairs, and (c) promoting their collective "country image" (i.e., "made in Argentina"). As such, we inquired firms as to the degree to which the respondent's firm pooled demand with other peer firms for specialized services such as these.

Manufacturing productivity. To gage productivity we refer to past research using metrics associated with performance of production systems (Boyer et al. 1997; De Meyer and Ferdows 1985; Ward et al. 1995). These scholars suggest the use of

[3] To the extent the owner-CEO is invariably the person who has the authority for all major decisions taken by the small organization, we take interfirm relationship effects of the "owner-manager to be tantamount to those of the organization". See McEvily and Zaheer (1999) – footnote, p. 1,137 for similar treatment.

inventory turns and timely deliveries. The first directly gages productivity, i.e., the amount of input tied to production output, whereas the second gages efficiencies in the handling of production processes as goods move from up to downstream stations in the value chain. Thus, we asked respondents to indicate the (a) number of inventory turns necessary to support 12 month sales as well as (b) the percentage of goods delivered as timely as promised. An analysis of those measures indicated that timely delivery was highly skewed; because our analysis requires normally distributed data, we dropped this measure from our study.

Product innovation. Product innovation has become one of the most important aspects of competition in the world market for furniture (CSIL Research 2004). A measure of product innovation that is often used in the industry (CSIL Research 2004) is the rate of "catalog turn over" defined in our survey as both (a) the percentage of revenue arising out from new products, and (b) the percentage of new products in a firm's catalog.

Access to global markets. To gage the degree to which SMEs have successfully accessed global markets, entrepreneurs suggested that we should use some indicator related to the percentage of revenues coming from foreign clients. Thus, we measure SMEs' access to global markets as the percentage from a firm's total sales that go to foreign markets.

Control variables. Although we are interested in developing a parsimonious model, other alternative factors may also influence the relationships stated in Fig. 3.1. Therefore, we include control variables to that the ensure results are not unjustifiably influenced by these factors. First, we control for firm size. Because larger firms may possess a larger pool of resources, such as capital and managerial talent to go international alone, it may be the case that their international success results from higher scale instead of collective efficiencies developed through interfirm relationships. Firm size is a composite measure of log of (a) 3-year average yearly revenues and (b) number of employees. Second, we control for "competitive pressure" in the marketplace. If a firm suffers from stiff competition in its domestic market segment, it is more motivated to pursue foreign markets. Competitive pressure is measured as the log of number of competitors, that is, firms selling similar products in the same domestic market.

We also adopt a set of variables to control for spurious causality involving relationships, collective efficiencies, and export performance. For instance, a firm with greater strategic orientation to export would be both more likely to access global markets and also more interested to participate in collective sourcing of specialized government support for going abroad. Therefore, we add the control variable "export orientation", measured in Likert-scale form as the degree to which respondents believe that firms that export their goods (a) are more competitive than those which do not, and (b) can better weather home market recessions. If a significant effect is found on both constructs, it could mean that the association between collective sourcing and access to global markets is spurious. Finally, we control for "investments" in (a) just in time (JIT), (b) total quality management (TQM), and (c) new information technology equipment and processes (IT). Our worry here is the possible spurious causality of the effects of horizontal and vertical relational governance on collective efficiencies, particularly manufacturing productivity and innovation.

Firms that are in the process of implementing JIT and TQM related practices may *search* for closer partnerships because these are seen as part of the overall scheme of implementing leaner forms of manufacturing (Boyer et al. 1997). Failing to control for "investments" may therefore yield spurious associations. In this case, if 'investments' associate with both relational governance and collective efficiencies, our theorized effects of relational governance on collective efficiencies could be either spurious or even causally reversed.

3.2.4 Structural Equation Method

We performed a structural equation analysis, which, by definition, is a hybrid of factor and path analysis. To implement the model, we followed recommendations by Anderson and Gerbing (1988). Specifically, in the first stage we used confirmatory factor analysis to test whether the variables selected to measure each construct show convergent validity (i.e., whether items are fairly correlated with one another) and discriminant validity (i.e., whether variables across constructs clearly measure different constructs). In the second stage, we compute the structural model, based on the measurement model found in the first stage. Here, inter factor correlations are estimated for all factors, making this an oblique, rather than an orthogonal analysis. Anderson and Gerbing (1988) recommend that, when moving to the second stage, one should compare two other models to the theoretical model: the next-best constrained and the next-best unconstrained models. The former is based on the theoretical model but is subtracted one or another previously specified path representing important alternative theoretical arguments. The latter contains all paths included in the theoretical model plus one or more previously unspecified paths representing important alternative theoretical arguments. Thus, for the next-best unconstrained model, we added nonhypothesized paths between horizontal governance and manufacturing productivity, as well as vertical governance and collective sourcing to assess whether our parsimonious model is appropriate. For the next-best constrained model, we dropped the path between horizontal relational governance and innovation. Previous studies argue that firms are more likely to cooperate with suppliers, whom they see as partners, as opposed to collaborating with peer firms, whom they see as competitors (Choi et al. 2002; Nalebuff and Brandenburger 1997).

Because our analysis of alternative models involves interactions, a note on how we model interaction terms is in order. Analyzes of latent variable interactions are not common in strategy studies and only recently have they been adopted in marketing and psychology (see Bollen and Curran 2005 for a review). Here, we use Ping's (1995, 1996) techniques for interaction terms with a single indicant. The single indicant for two factors X and Y, with respective indicants as x_1, x_2 and y_1, y_2, is computed as $X{:}Y=(x_1+x_2)(y_1+y_2)$. In such case, Ping proposes that the loadings and errors for $X{:}Y$ be given respectively by $\lambda x{:}y=(\lambda_{x1}+\lambda_{x2})(\lambda_{y1}+\lambda_{y2})$ and $\theta_{\varepsilon x:y}=(\lambda_{x1}+\lambda_{x2})^2 \mathrm{Var}(X)(\theta_{\varepsilon y1}+\theta_{\varepsilon y2})+(\lambda_{z1}+\lambda_{z2})^2 \mathrm{Var}(Y)(\theta_{\varepsilon x1}+\theta_{\varepsilon x2})+(\theta_{\varepsilon x1}+\theta_{\varepsilon x2})(\theta_{\varepsilon y1}+\theta_{\varepsilon y2})$. As far as specification of the measurement model is concerned, based on Anderson and Gerbing (1988: 418), Ping (1995: 339) indicates that the unidimensionality of X and Y

enables the omission of the nonlinear latent variables from the linear-terms-only measurement model. Because *X* and *Y* are each unidimensional, their indicants are unaffected by the presence or absence of other latent variables in a measurement or structural model. Stated differently, this provides similar measurement parameter estimates between measurement and structural models.

3.3 Results and Discussion

3.3.1 Measurement Model

Table 3.1 reports basic statistics and correlations. Tables 3.2, 3.3, 3.4 and 3.5 report results of our SEM analysis, based on the two stage procedure recommended by Anderson and Gerbing (1988). A brief analysis of the correlation matrix shows initial evidence of good convergent and discriminant validity: all 14 values greater than 0.58 involve intra factor correlations, while inter factor correlations do not surpass the 0.36 level. We also followed Anderson and Gerbing's (1988) formal analysis for convergent validity by computing *t*-tests for factor loadings. We kept indicators for which factor loadings were greater than twice their standard errors (Table 3.2). Lastly, we assessed discriminant validity. Here, we used chi-square difference tests for constrained and unconstrained models. The constrained model sets the covariance between two constructs equal to one; a significantly lower chi-square value for the unconstrained model supports the discriminant validity criterion. As Table 3.3 indicates, all multiitem constructs exhibit satisfactory discriminant validity.

Table 3.4 present summary statistics for all models estimated in both stages as well as difference statistics for all tests of one model against another. As far as our test of the initial measurement model (model 1) is concerned, we look at chi-square and five other goodness-of-fit statistics: the goodness of fit index (GFI), the normed and the nonnormed fit indices (NFI and NNFI), the comparative fit index (CFI), and the root mean square error of approximation (RMSEA). A commonly accepted rule of thumb is that the first four fit indices should be greater than 0.90 (Anderson and Gerbing 1988)[4]. RMSEAs of 0.05 or less indicate good models. Probability

[4]GFI indicates the relative amount of variance and covariance jointly explained by the model. The NNFI (Bentler and Bonnett 1980) is defined as "the percentage of observed-measure covariation explained by a given measurement or structural model … that solely accounts for the observed measure variances" (Anderson and Gerbing 1988: 421). NNFI is often viewed as a superior variation of the Bentler and Bonnett's (1980) normed fit index (NFI) since it has been shown to be more robust in reflecting model fit regardless of sample size (Anderson and Gerbing 1988; Bentler 1989). Bentler's (1989) CFI, is similar to the NNFI in that it provides an accurate assessment of fit regardless of sample size. The CFI tends to be more precise than the NNIF however in describing comparative model fit as it corrects for small sample size by subtracting the degrees of freedom from their corresponding χ^2 values (Bentler 1989). RMSEA (root-mean-square error of approximation) incorporates both model complexity (expressed in the degrees of freedom) and sample size in the analysis, and is thus suggested for analyses relying on maximum likelihood (Browne and Cudeck 1993) with smaller sample sizes.

Table 3.1 Basic statistics and Pearson matrix

			Basic statistics & Pearson matrix																						
			Mean	S.D.	Kurtsis	1	2	3	4	5	6	7	8	9	10	11	12	13	14	15	16	17	18	19	20
HG1	1	Horizontal norms of information exchange	2.35	1.28	–0.90	1																			
HG2	2	Horizontal norms of assistance	2.38	1.24	–0.79	.80(**)	1																		
HG3	3	Horizontal norms of fair sharing	2.38	1.27	–1.02	.80(**)	.83(**)	1																	
VG1	4	Vertical norms of information exchange	2.75	1.09	–0.72	.35(**)	.37(**)	.35(**)	1																
VG2	5	Vertical norms of assistance	2.77	1.09	–0.68	.3 6(**)	.35(**)	.34(**)	.73(**)	1															
VG3	6	Vertical norms of fair sharing	2.72	1.07	–0.81	.35(**)	.33(**)	.32(**)	.75(**)	.72(**)	1														
INV1	7	Manufacturing productivity	13.98	7.94	–0.67	0.1	0.11	0.1	.28(**)	.21(**)	.26 (**)	1													
INN1	8	% Revenues from new products	15.67	8.11	–0.25	.20(**)	.22(**)	.26(**)	0.04	.16(*)	0.06	.15(*)	1												
INN2	9	% New products in catalog	15.72	8.07	–0.30	.19(**)	.19(**)	.24(**)	0.04	.15(*)	0.08	0.13	97(**)	1											
CS1	10	Collective sourcing for contacting international customers	2.33	1	–0.73	.15(*)	.17(*)	.20(**)	0.05	0.12	.17(*)	0.09	0.05	0.04	1										

(continued)

Table 3.1 (continued)

			Basic statistics & Pearson matrix																						
			Mean	S.D.	Kurtsis	1	2	3	4	5	6	7	8	9	10	11	12	13	14	15	16	17	18	19	20
CS2	11	Collective sourcing for coordinating international fairs	2.32	1.02	–0.60	0.09	0.13	.16(*)	–0.03	0.09	0.08	0.09	0.01	0	.72(**)	1									
CS3	12	Collective sourcing for promotion of "country brand"	2.32	1.02	–0.58	0.12	.14(*)	.17(**)	0.03	0.08	0.05	.131(*)	0.02	0	.67(**)	.68(**)	1								
AG1	13	% Products that are exported	18.63	11.3	0.99	.19(**)	.18(**)	0.13	.16(*)	.19(**)	.14(*)	.28(**)	.14(*)	0.11	.22(**)	.21(**)	.24(**)	1							
SIZ1	14	Firm size – log sales in US$	5.49	0.52	–0.77	0.01	0.07	0.05	0.12	.15(*)	.15(*)	0.07	–0.01	–0.03	.13(*)	0.09	0.12	.17 (**)	1						
SIZ2	15	Firm size – log employees	1.16	0.23	–0.64	–0.02	0.02	0	0.07	0.1	0.06	0.05	–0.05	–0.06	0.08	0.07	0.07	.17(**)	.89(**)	1					
COMP1	16	Market pressure – log competitors	2.36	1.68	–1.26	0.11	0.05	0.04	–0.05	–0.02	–0.01	–0.03	–0.01	0	0	–0.04	0.02	.18(**)	–0.11	–.13(*)	1				
EO1	17	Exporters are more competitive	2.42	1.45	–1.15	0.04	0.01	0.01	0.07	0.03	–0.04	0.03	–0.01	0	–0.02	0.03	0.08	.28(**)	–0.12	–0.11	.27(**)	1			
EO2	18	Exporters are more protected from recession	2.44	1.52	–1.05	0.03	–0.01	0	0.04	0	–0.06	0.01	–0.03	–0.01	0.02	0.04	0.08	.16(*)	–.14(*)	–.13(*)	.27(**)	.86(**)	1		
INV1	19	Investments in JIT	2.29	1.29	–0.09	–0.01	–0.10	–0.03	–0.03	0.02	–0.01	.33(**)	.27(**)	.26(**)	–0.10	–0.11	–0.05	.15(*)	0.02	0.05	0.06	0	–0.02	1	
INV2	20	Investments in IT equipment & processes	2.39	1.24	–0.79	0	–0.07	–0.03	–0.01	0.01	–0.01	.28(**)	.20(**)	.20(**)	–.13(*)	–.135(*)	–0.04	0.11	–0.04	0.01	–0.03	–0.01	–0.02	.776(**)	1.00
INV3	21	Investments in TQM	2.37	1.31	–1.02	–0.02	–0.11	–0.03	–0.03	0.01	–0.03	.20(**)	.21(**)	.20(**)	–0.09	–.13(*)	–0.12	0	–0.04	0.01	–0.03	–0.06	–0.05	.745(**)	585(**)

†$p<0.1$; *$p<0.05$; **$p<0.01$; ***$p<0.001$

Table 3.2 Comparison of measurement model to best model

Observed variable	Latent factor		Loading	C.R.		Loading	C.R
HG1	Horizontal norms of information exchange	F1	Horizontal relational governance	1.002		0.958	
HG2	Horizontal norms of assistance	F1	Horizontal relational governance	1	21.064	1	20.973
HG3	Horizontal norms of fair sharing	F1	Horizontal relational governance	0.958	19.755	1.001	19.695
VG1	Vertical norms of information exchange	F2	Vertical relational governance	1		1	
VG2	Vertical norms of assistance	F2	Vertical relational governance	0.962	14.93	0.96	14.847
VG3	Vertical norms of fair sharing	F2	Vertical relational governance	1.026	15.862	1.025	15.662
CS1	Contacting international customers	F3	Sourcing of collective resources	1		1	
CS2	Coordinating international fairs	F3	Sourcing of collective resources	1.025	14.038	1.024	14.006
CS3	Promotion of "country brand"	F3	Sourcing of collective resources	0.961	13.282	0.961	13.297
INV1	Manufacturing productivity						
INN1	% Revenues from new products	F4	Product innovation	1		1	
INN2	% New products in catalog	F4	Product innovation	0.982	12.597	0.971	12.551
AG1	Access to global markets						
SIZ1	Log sales in US$	F5	Firm size	1		1	
SIZ2	Log employees	F5	Firm size	0.983	13.643	0.924	12.851
COMP1	Market pressure						
EO1	Exporters are more competitive	F6	Export orientation	1		1	
EO2	Exporters are more protected from recession	F6	Export orientation	0.977	11.145	0.974	11.112
INV1	Investments in JIT	F7	Investment	1		1	
INV2	Investments in IT equipment & processes	F7	Investment	1.094	12.588	1.095	12.631
INV3	Investments in TQM	F7	Investment	1.067	13.969	1.059	13.989

Table 3.3 Chi square difference test

X2 difference test among following factors and variables				χ^2 statistics		Chi-sq > 3.85 (d.f.1)
F1	Horizontal relational governance			(d.f. = 149)	(d.f. = 148)	
F1	Horizontal relational governance	F2	Vertical relational governance	199	155.4	43.6
F1	Horizontal relational governance	F3	Sourcing of collective resources	231.7	155.4	76.3
F1	Horizontal relational governance	INV1	Manufacturing productivity	236.5	155.4	81.1
F1	Horizontal relational governance	F4	Innovation	215	155.4	59.6
F1	Horizontal relational governance	AG1	Access global markets	221.3	155.4	65.9
F1	Horizontal relational governance	F5	Firm size	283.4	155.4	128
F1	Horizontal relational governance	COMP1	Competitive pressure	207.8	155.4	52.4
F1	Horizontal relational governance	F6	Export orientation	215.7	155.4	60.3
F2	Vertical relational governance	F7	Investments	267.5	155.4	112.1
F2	Vertical relational governance	F3	Sourcing of collective resources	248.4	155.4	93
F2	Vertical relational governance	INV1	Manufacturing productivity	212.4	155.4	57
F2	Vertical relational governance	F4	Innovation	241.3	155.4	85.9
F2	Vertical relational governance	AG1	Access global markets	222.7	155.4	67.3
F2	Vertical relational governance	F5	Firm size	264.8	155.4	109.4
F2	Vertical relational governance	COMP1	Competitive pressure	226.5	155.4	71.1
F2	Vertical relational governance	F6	Export orientation	219	155.4	63.6
F3	Sourcing of collective resources	F7	Investments	160.7	155.4	5.3
F3	Sourcing of collective resources	INV1	Manufacturing productivity	164	155.4	8.6
F3	Sourcing of collective resources	F4	Innovation	255.5	155.4	100.1
F3	Sourcing of collective resources	AG1	Access global markets	215.3	155.4	59.9
F3	Sourcing of collective resources	F5	Firm size	276.2	155.4	120.8

(continued)

Table 3.3 (continued)

X2 difference test among following factors and variables				χ^2 statistics		Chi-sq>3.85 (d.f.1)
F3	Sourcing of collective resources	COMP1	Competitive pressure	225.2	155.4	69.8
F3	Sourcing of collective resources	F6	Export orientation	217.4	155.4	62
INV1	Manufacturing productivity	F7	Investments	284.9	155.4	129.5
INV1	Manufacturing productivity	F4	Innovation	227.7	155.4	72.3
INV1	Manufacturing productivity	AG1	Access global markets	203.3	155.4	47.9
INV1	Manufacturing productivity	F5	Firm size	278.7	155.4	123.3
INV1	Manufacturing productivity	COMP1	Competitive pressure	222.4	155.4	67
INV1	Manufacturing productivity	F6	Export orientation	213	155.4	57.6
F4	Innovation	F7	Investments	204.3	155.4	48.9
F4	Innovation	AG1	Access global markets	224.5	155.4	69.1
F4	Innovation	F5	Firm size	294.9	155.4	139.5
F4	Innovation	COMP1	Competitive pressure	218.1	155.4	62.7
F4	Innovation	F6	Export orientation	217.4	155.4	62
AG1	Access global markets	F7	Investments	211.1	155.4	55.7
AG1	Access global markets	F5	Firm size	255.6	155.4	100.2
AG1	Access global markets	COMP1	Competitive pressure	189.6	155.4	34.2
AG1	Access global markets	F6	Export orientation	182.8	155.4	27.4
F5	Firm size	F7	Investments	229.3	155.4	73.9
F5	Firm size	COMP1	Competitive pressure	254.4	155.4	99
F5	Firm size	F6	Export orientation	269.1	155.4	113.7
F6	Export orientation	F7	Investments	285.1	155.4	129.7
		F7	Investments	291.8	155.4	136.4

Table 3.4 Model statistics and testing sequence across models

Model	Model name	Chi-sq	df	Probability	GFI	NFI	NNFI	CFI	RMSEA	AIC	BCC	BIC
	Null	155.41	193	> .5								
1	Measurement	155.41	147	0.364	0.94	0.95	0.97	0.998	0.01	317.3	334.35	596.49
2	Theoretical	231.51	167	>0.01	0.91	0.93	0.94	0.981	0.04	353.39	366.23	563.64
3	Next-best constrained	246.3	168	>0.01	0.91	0.93	0.94	0.976	0.04	366.21	378.84	573.01
4	Next-best unconstrained	231.35	165	>0.05	0.91	0.93	0.94	0.98	0.04	357.28	370.54	574.42
5	Best model	162.4	160	0.5	0.94	0.95	0.96	0.997	0.01	298.35	312.67	532.73
6	Alternative model 1	160.23	157	0.5	0.94	0.95	0.95	0.998	0	300.23	314.97	541.5
7	Alternative model 2	1,503.93	222	0.001	0.74	0.68	0.68	0.71	0.16	1,653.93	1,672.13	1,912.43
8	Alternative model 3	192.23	177	0.25	0.93	0.94	0.94	0.98	0.02	338.26	354.4	589.87

Testing sequence and difference tests

Comparison	AX^2	Probability	*A df*	A AIC	A BCC	A BIC	Model preference
Model 2 vs. 3	14.79	<0.001	1	12.82	12.61	9.37	2
Model 2 vs. 4	–0.16	>0.1	–2	3.89	4.31	10.78	2
Model 2 vs. 5	–69.11	<0.001	–7	–55.04	–53.56	–30.91	5
Model 2 vs. 6	–2.17	>0.1	–3	1.88	2.3	8.77	5
Model 2 vs. 7	1,341.53	<0.001	62	1,355.58	1,359.46	1,379.70	5
Model 2 vs. 8	29.83	<0.001	17	39.91	41.73	57.14	5

Note1: The variance-covariance matrix of the best model (model 5) is based on 231 moments (21 observed variables). These moments are used to estimate the following 71 parameters: 11 factor loading paths, 21 causal paths, 18 variances of measurement errors, four variances of exogenous factors, siz variances for estimation errors of endogenous factors, and 11 covariance paths among exogenous latent factors. For the more avid reader wishing to replicate our results, we indicate these covariance paths (along with covariance paths of model 2) in Table 3.5. *Note2*: results above are based on maximum likelihood (ML) estimation, which tends to produce unbiased estimators under assumptions of normality (Browne and Cudeck 1993). Critics argue, however, that ML-estimators rely heavily on the assumption of normal distribution, and propose that small sample analysis (such as this one) should rely instead on the generalized least squares (GLS) method. As a comparison, GLS estimates for model 5 are as follows: GFI=0.93; NFI=0.94; NNFI=0.95; CFI=0.98; RMSEA=0.02. We are thus confident our data set does not severely depart from normality.

Table 3.5 Results: path coefficients and covariance paths from theoretical and best models

Path name		Path description	Theoretical model (model 2)	Best-model	(model 5)
			Path	Path	Critical ratio
Hypothesis 1	PF1F3	Horizontal relational governance –>sourcing of collective resources	0.18**	0.18**	2.72
Hypothesis 2	PF2INV1	Vertical relational governance –>manufacturing productivity	0.34***	0.34***	4.7
Hypothesis 3a	PF1F4	Horizontal relational governance –>product innovation	0.30***	0.29***	4.2
Hypothesis 3b	PF2F4	Vertical relational governance –>product innovation	–0.01		
Hypothesis 4a	PF3AG1	Sourcing of collective resources –>access to global markets	0.27***	0.27***	3.32
Hypothesis 4b	PINV1AG1	Manufacturing productivity –>access to global markets	0.25***	0.25***	3.96
Hypothesis 4c	PF4AG1	Product innovation –>access to global markets	O.llt	O.llt	1.69
Control	PF5AG1	Firm size –>access to global markets	0.14*	0.13*	2.04
Control	PF5F3	Firm size –>sourcing of collective resources	0.09	0.09	1.51
Control	PF5INV1	Firm size –>manufacturing productivity	0.01	0.01	0.22
Control	PF5F4	Firm size –>product innovation	–0.07	–0.07	–1.09
Control	PCOMP1AG1	Competitive pressure –>access to global markets	o.iot	o.iot	2.35
Control	PCOMP1F3	Competitive pressure –>sourcing of collective resources	–0.01	–0.01	–0.25
Control	PCOMP1INV1	Competitive pressure –>manufacturing productivity	–0.03	–0.03	–0.63
Control	PCOMP1F4	Competitive pressure –>product innovation	–0.04	–0.07	–1.12
Control	PF7F3	Investments –>sourcing of collective resources	o. lot	–0.09	–1.49
Control	PF7INV1	Investments –>manufacturing productivity	0.37***	0.37***	5.26
Control	PF7F4	Investments –>product innovation	0.32***	0.32***	4.52
Control	PF7F1	Investments –>horizontal relational governance	–0.06	–0.06	–0.89
Control	PF7F2	Investments –>vertical relational governance	–0.01	–0.01	–0.12
Control	PF6AG1	Exports orientation –>access to global markets	0.13**	0.13*	2.77
Control	PF6AF3	Exports orientation –>sourcing of collective resources	0.03	0.03	0.67
Covariance	D(F1)×D(F2)	Residual of horizontal relational governance<–>residual of vertical relational governance		0.35***	5.51

(continued)

Table 3.5 (continued)

Path name		Path description	Theoretical model (model 2)	Best-model	(model 5)
			Path	Path	Critical ratio
Covariance	D(F1) × D (COMP1)	Residual of horizontal relational governance <-> error term of competitive pressure		0.09	1.08
Covariance	D(F2) × E (COMP1)	Residual of vertical relational governance <-> error term of competitive pressure		–0.03	–0.39
Covariance	D(F3) × E(INV1)	Residual of sourcing of collective resources <-> error term of manufacturing productivity		0.10*	2.00
Covariance	D(F3) × D(F4)	Residual of sourcing of collective resources <-> residual of product innovation		0.01	0.20
Covariance	E(INV1) × D(F4)	Error term of manufacturing productivity <-> residual of product innovation		0.03	0.47
Covariance	E(COMP1) × F5	Error term of competitive pressure <-> firm size		–0.20*	–2.03
Covariance	E(COMP1) × F6	Error term of competitive pressure <-> export orientation		0.61***	4.15
Covariance	F6 × F5	Export orientation <-> firm size	–0.20*	–0.20*	–1.99
Covariance	F7 × F6	Investments <-> export orientation	–0.04	–0.04	–0.46
Covariance	F7 × F5	Investments <-> firm size	0.05	0.05	0.76

†$p<0.1$; *$p<0.05$; **$p<0.01$; ***$p<0.001$

levels on chi-square of 0.10 or higher are generally considered evidence of ideal models (Bentler 1989). Because the chi-square statistic of model 1 is insignificant ($p < 0.364$), and because all goodness-of-fit indices are within the expected range, we conclude that this is a strong measurement model.

3.3.2 *Structural Model*

We therefore proceeded to stage 2, which involves path analyzes with the latent and observed variables resulting from the measurement model obtained in the first stage. Our theoretical model (model 2), represented in Table 3.4, has a significant chi-square, which could be cause for concern. In such cases, Anderson and Gerbing (1988) argue that the chi-square test is frequently not valid in applied settings, and recommend that this statistic be treated as a general goodness of fit index, but not as a statistical test in the strict sense. Many researchers use the informal criterion that the model may be acceptable if the chi-square value is less than twice the size of the degrees of freedom (Bentler 1989). The fact that our model 2 chi-square of 231.5 is less than twice the degrees of freedom of 167 together with the fact that all other goodness of fit indices are within expected ranges (i.e., above 0.9, while RMSEA is below 0.05) indicates ours is a strong and acceptable theoretical model.

From here, the second step in the path analysis is to compare the next-best constrained model (model 3) with our theoretical model (model 2). Model 3 gains one degree of freedom (Table 3.4), but that comes at a cost of a significant increase in chi-square ($\Delta\chi^2 = 14.79$; $p < 0.001$). Thus, we still prefer our original model 2. We next test model 2 against the next-best unconstrained model (model 4). Here we lose degrees of freedom ($\Delta df = -2$), while there is no significant improvement in chi-square ($\Delta\chi^2 = 0.16$; $p > 0.1$). We therefore discard the next-best unconstrained model, and following Anderson and Gerbing, retain model 2. As a follow up step, we examined modification indices resulting from Lagrangian multiplier tests (Bentler 1989) to see if any unspecified paths could be added to improve model fit. Here, we find it necessary to add a covariance path between the error terms of *horizontal* and *vertical relational governance*. Additionally, we find that several elements in our model are correlated, and that adding covariance paths among them would help ensure our findings are robust. We thus also add covariance paths between the error terms of the three *collective efficiencies*, as well as between three exogenous factors (i.e., *investments, firm size, and export orientation*) and the error terms of *competitive pressure, horizontal* and *vertical relational governance.* Lastly, we trim off insignificant parameters estimates to obtain a most constrained version of the theoretical model; based on the marginal significance cutoff of $p < 0.10$, and z-statistic of 1.645, we dropped the path between vertical relational governance and product innovation. We however retain paths involving control variables and covariances between the items mentioned above, even if their coefficients were insignificant.

As a result of the above mentioned changes, we specified our "best model" (model 5), shown in Fig. 3.2. The chi-square statistic for model 5 is not significant ($\chi^2 = 162.4$; $p \sim 0.5$), and represents a significant reduction from the chi-square of model 2 ($\Delta\chi^2 = -69.11$; $p < 0.001$). Though a statistically noninsignificant chi-square often indicates a good fit to the model, we are only cautiously optimistic. Critics often argue that statistically nonsignificant chi-squares can also represent unstable chi-square statistics when one uses small samples (e.g., less than 300 observations, as is our case). In these circumstances, adding covariance paths to control for correlation (as we did from model 2 to model 5) can result in a model that is *over fitted* (e.g., Byrne 2001: 92; Wheaton 1987: 123). To ensure this is not the case, we also contrast other fit indices, as shown in Table 3.4. There, not only do we look at GFI, NFI, NNFI, CFI, and RMSEA, but also at the Akaike's Information Criteria (AIC), the Browne-Cudeck Criteria (BCC) and the Bayes Information Criteria (BIC)[5]. The last three measures are used to compare models, where one accepts the model with the lowest values. As results in Table 3.4 demonstrate, model 5 is superior to model 2 across all of these indices. Therefore, we are confident that model 5 is indeed our "best model".

Table 3.2 compares the measurement structure of model 5 to that of model 1. The loadings are highly consistent across the two models. Table 3.5 presents results for our best (model 5) and theoretical models (model 2). Here, we can see that parameters from model 5 and model 2 are highly similar, a fact which indicates parameters are robust. In Table 3.5, the first seven rows summarize path coefficients, Z-statistics, and significance tests of our best model. The next 15 rows summarize the control paths, and the following 11 rows, covariances.

3.3.3 Relational Governance and Collective Efficiency Hypotheses

Based on our analysis of model 5, six of the seven hypotheses receive support. Primarily, all hypotheses related to the impact of *horizontal governance* on *collective efficiencies* specified in our theory are supported. The path coefficient associated with H1 (i.e., *relational governance of horizontal ties associates positively with sourcing of collective resources*) is positive (0.18) and statistically significant ($Z = 2.72$; $p < 0.001$). H3a (i.e., *relational governance of horizontal ties associates positively with product innovation*) is supported as well. The associated path coefficient

[5] The AIC can be said to represent an operational way of trading off the complexity of an estimated model against how well the model fits the data (Akaike 1987). Another measure with a similar intent, the BCC is known to impose a slightly greater penalty for model complexity than does the AIC (Browne and Cudeck 1993). In comparison to AIC and BCC, the BIC assigns a greater penalty to model complexity, and so has a greater tendency to pick parsimonious models (see Raftery 1995; Schwartz 1978 for reviews).

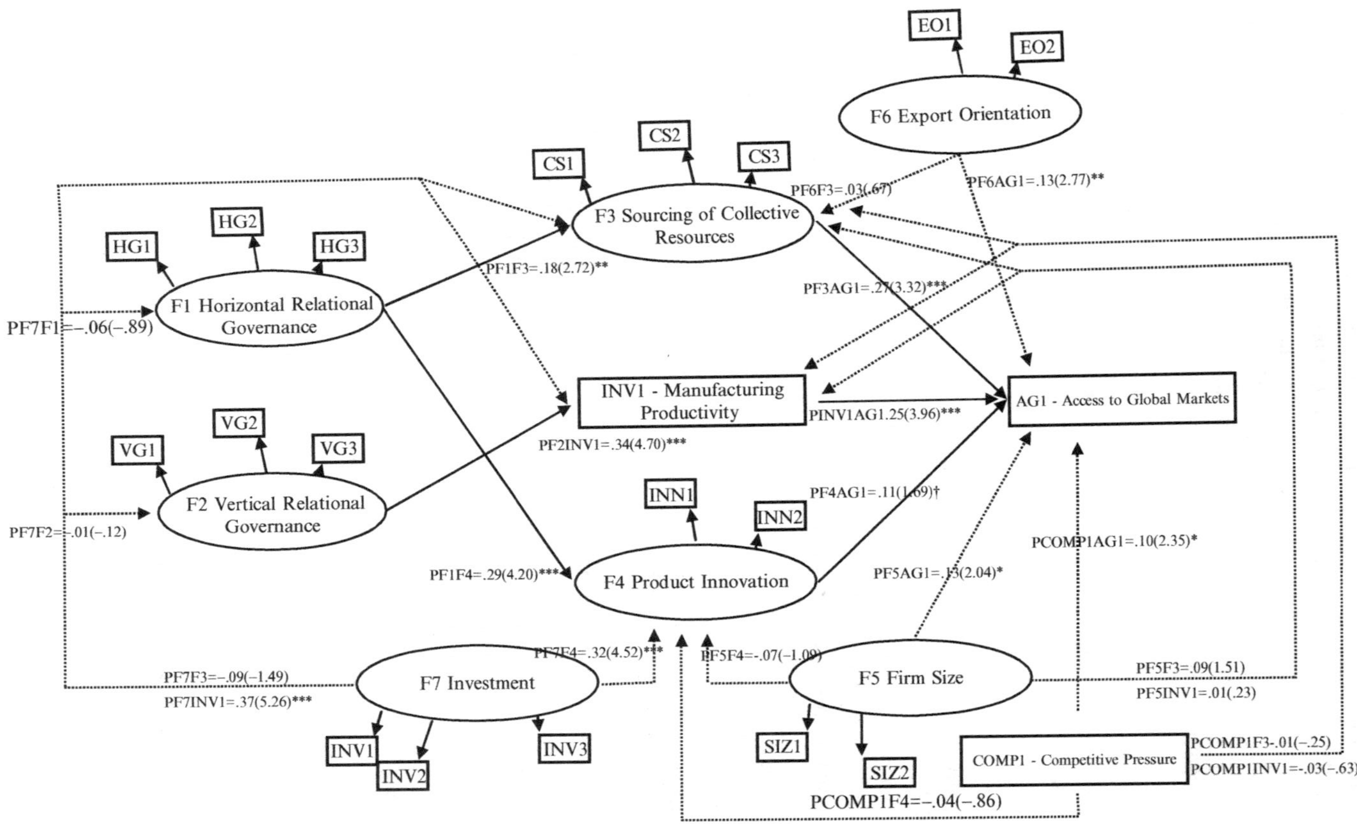

Fig. 3.2 Best model. *Note*. We follow the Bentler's (1989) EQS convention of identification: "F"=Factor, "P"=Path (e.g., PF1F3=path from factor F1 to factor F3). Ellipses are latent factors, whereas rectangulars are observed variables. *Full line arrows* are paths, *dotted-line arrows* are controls. This simplified version of the actual best model does not show error terms, exogenous factor variances, endogenous variable disturbance terms, covariance paths, and error correlations. For the more avid reader wishing to replicate our results, covariance paths are included in Table 3.5

is positive (0.29) and statistically significant ($Z=4.20$; $p<0.001$). Not all hypotheses related to the impact of vertical ties on collective efficiencies, however, receive support. On the one hand, H2, asserting that *relational governance of vertical ties positively associates with production efficiencies*, is strongly supported. The path coefficient is positive (0.34) and statistically significant ($Z=4.70$; $p<0.001$). There is no evidence, however, that relational governance of vertical relationships improve product innovation. Thus, H3b is not supported.

3.3.4 Collective Efficiencies and Access to Global Market Hypotheses

All hypotheses tracing the successful access to global markets to the particular collective efficiencies that associate with horizontal and vertical governance are supported. Particularly, hypotheses 4a, 4b and 4c respectively establish that *access to global markets positively associates with collective sourcing, manufacturing productivity and product innovation*. The path coefficients are positive and statistically significant (respectively, path=0.27; $Z=3.32$; $p<0.001$ for hypothesis 4a; path=0.25; $Z=3.96$; $p<0.001$ for hypothesis 4b; and path=0.11; $Z=1.69$; $p<0.1$ for hypothesis 4c).

3.3.5 Testing Alternative Models

Because SEM provides information regarding the fit of a proposed model but cannot determine if that model is the "correct" one, we examine three theoretically plausible alternative models. The first alternative model (model 6) theorizes that horizontal governance and vertical governance *directly* affect SMEs abilities to access global markets in addition to the mediated collective efficiencies effects. Direct effects are plausible in that firms may simply coordinate export efforts without engaging in deliberate actions to achieve the particular forms of collective efficiencies discussed here. The second alternative model (model 7) includes interaction terms between collective efficiencies and access to global markets. These interactions identify ways in which distinct types of collective efficiencies may complement one another in the achievement of superior export performance. For instance, manufacturing productivity may create cost advantages and hence increase the degree to which SMEs with innovative products can access global markets. The third alternative (model 8) differs from the best model (model 5) in that it suggests an interaction between horizontal and vertical relationships onto collective efficiencies. Our expectation arises from previous theorizing that firms do integrate such forms of partnerships to attain not only innovation, but also manufacturing productivity (e.g., Choi et al. 2002; Lazzarini et al. 2001; Teece 1992: 9) – e.g., in our case, if horizontal ties provide scale and coordination to the group, vertical partners may have improved channels to export their supplies.

We rely on an analysis of AIC, BCC, and BIC goodness of fit indices to contrast the best model with the alternative models. [6]As it can be seen in Table 3.4, none of the alternative models result in improvements from our best model. Specifically, ΔAIC, ΔBCC, and ΔBIC are all positive, indicating an increase in these goodness of fit indices. We therefore conclude that model 5 is indeed the best model of how SMEs attain superior export performance.

3.3.6 *Interpretation of Results*

Our findings indicate that by coordinating their joint actions through horizontal and vertical relational governance, SMEs can attain a set of collective efficiencies that contribute to superior access to global markets. Specifically, we find that particular types of relationships (i.e., horizontal or vertical) yield different types of collective efficiencies. While horizontal relational governance promotes the provision of collective inputs and product innovation, vertical relational governance yields manufacturing productivity gains along the supply chain. Our finding that product innovation is mostly restricted to horizontal relationships in our context is interesting because it is somewhat inconsistent with received theory that knowledge exchange among horizontal competitors tends to be more difficult than in transactions involving vertically related partners, who are not in direct competition (Choi et al. 2002; Brandenburger and Nalebuff 1997). We believe this interesting result reflects the nature of our export context, where cooperation is less likely to be hindered by competition between SMEs. Specifically, in general, firms find it difficult to cooperate with competitors when they are sharing the same limited market opportunity. To the extent that export-oriented cooperation improves both the focal firm and the competitor, then there is no change in the relative advantage of one firm vis-à-vis another. In this circumstance, the concerns about cooperating with competitors are less relevant, since the "size of the pie" effect overwhelms any concerns about sustaining the "share of the pie".

Our results also indicate that superior export performance associates with a host of collective efficiencies – sourcing of collective resources, manufacturing productivity, and product innovation – which require complex links among local partners. Our test of the best-unconstrained model indicates, however, that there are no synergistic effects among those collective efficiencies. Put another way, it appears that the collective efficiencies outlined in our model work independently of one another.

Moreover, from our alternative models, it seems the direct effects of horizontal and vertical relational governance on access to global markets are insignificant in light of the mediator effects of collective efficiencies (model 6). These results suggest

[6] Here, we avoid comparisons through chi-square statistics since some of our alternative models are *non nested*. The *non nested* nature of our models arises from our implementing Ping's interaction term procedure (1995, 1996), which, as explained above, creates a new single-indicant variable from two other factors.

that the engine behind SME's global competitiveness is the set of collective efficiencies firms attain from their horizontal and vertical ties. In other words, collective efficiencies appear to mediate the impact of vertical and horizontal relationships on SMEs' abilities to access global markets. Additionally, we did not find synergistic effects among the different types of collective efficiencies (model 7), nor interaction effects among horizontal and vertical partnerships (model 8) that could explain gains beyond those they would get by simply adding those partnerships to their portfolio of ties. Horizontal and vertical relationships appear, in our context, to have independent effects triggering different types of collective efficiencies.

Control effects. As it can be seen from Table 3.5, the factors "firm size" and "competitive pressure" help partially explain why some firms are more active in accessing global markets than others. However, these factors do not appear to concomitantly explain any of our three forms of collective efficiencies. We thus remain confident that collective efficiencies are powerful mediating factors behind the success of Argentine small and medium furniture makers in competitively accessing global markets. Second, our control for the degree of investments in JIT, TQM and IT also indicates that relational governance between peer firms and buyers and suppliers do not result from such investments. This indicates that firms investing in these production and innovation capabilities do not become more likely or more attractive to form stronger partnerships with other firms. According to entrepreneurs interviewed, this happens because a firm's investments in JIT relates more to limited internal changes to manufacturing layout and inventory control than to the implementation of seamless JIT systems linking all partners in a supply chain. We are therefore more confident that the association between relational governance and collective efficiencies are in the direction proposed, and do not appear to be subject to spurious effects. Lastly, our control of "export orientation" does seem to indicate that firms with stronger beliefs about exports seem to enjoy greater levels of exports, although it does not indicate that firms with such beliefs are more likely to jointly pursue governmental support for their efforts. We thus believe that the association between collective sourcing and access to global markets is indeed robust.

3.4 Implications and Conclusion

In this study, we model how SMEs can overcome their weak infrastructure and poor institutions environment, so as to garner export-enhancing collective efficiencies. Specifically, we submit that the relational governance of horizontal ties (i.e., relationships with local peer firms) promotes collective sourcing of resources and superior innovation rates. Likewise, the relational governance of vertical ties (i.e., relationships with local suppliers) enables higher manufacturing productivity. Such efficiencies, in turn, associate with SMEs' improved access to global markets. Our empirical results, using data from a group of Argentine furniture manufacturers generally supports our model.

Our research brings significant implications for the management literature. Primarily, our model integrates three theoretical perspectives – the resource-based view, transaction cost economics, and institutional theory – and in the process, highlights important aspects of their interactions. For example, previous research hinted that institutional constraints found in emerging economies limits possibilities for resource access (e.g., Hoskisson et al. 2000; Peng and Heath 1996), and call for further research to examine the interstices of these two theoretical perspectives. Hoskisson et al. (2000: 256–257) indicates that little research using a resource-based view has examined strategy differences in social contexts of emerging economies, or even the value of intangible relationship-based resources (as opposed to product-market-based ones). Here, our theoretical and empirical analyzes illustrate how SMEs overcome institutional shortages by *institutionalizing* behavioral commitments and norms within particular partnerships. Network ties therefore help substitute for the lack of a stronger institutional settings, and enable the combination of interfirm complementary resource endowments that associate with export-enhancing collective efficiencies.

Our study also highlights important institutional factors leading to choices of relationship governance under threats of exchange hazards. Particularly, many criticisms towards the transaction cost literature mention that this theory has been primarily applied to developed market contexts, which are often characterized by strong legal regimes and binding social norms; less is known about governance structures devised to govern transactions in emerging economies (Hoskisson et al. 2000: 254). In contexts where official discretion as opposed to the rule of law describes property rights, the enforcement of contracts is unlikely to occur (la Porta et al. 1997). In these circumstances, the coordination of either resource complementarities or joint resource-acquisition efforts by local SMEs (in search of collective efficiencies) could be threatened by the impossibility of their forming contractual safeguards to reduce the opportunistic behavior and transaction costs. Indeed, in our survey we found that only four firms had formal contracts with partners; interviews indicated entrepreneurs mistrust their country's legal system and thus deem such *formalities* useless. In a way, our findings support Peng and Heath's (1996) suggestions that in emerging economies, owing to the lack of property rights and unstable institutional environments, firms may strengthen informal ties to reduce transactional hazards and pool resources to achieve scale and scope economies that are unavailable otherwise.

In addition to helping better integrate the above discussed theoretical perspectives, our study also reconciles several models of interfirm alliances. Although the received alliance literature has advanced our knowledge on the sources of inter organizational value creation, studies have often focused on particular types of interfirm ties (i.e., horizontal or vertical – see for example Doz and Hamel 1998; Dyer 1997; Gulati 1999; Helper 1991; Kogut 1988). The challenges posed by weak infrastructure and institutional difficulties in emerging economies, however, are likely to require the integration of both vertical and horizontal ties. Consider for example the following illustration, taken from an interview with a prominent small wood furniture maker in Argentina. She revealed that her focus as a CEO had always been on excelling at the coordination of vertical partnerships along the supply chain. Through such efforts, she managed to obtain competitive production costs vis-à-vis her local competitors. However, given her small scale, she felt that it would be difficult to leverage such competencies in foreign markets; finding and engaging international customers proved too costly for her to "do it alone." Her scale liabilities, she argued, could even prove to be fatal, given the fast-shrinking Argentine market of the early twenty first century. To circumvent these limitations, the entrepreneur had to interact with local peers to accrue other equally important joint activities – for example, the collective lobbying of the foreign ministry of Argentina to support the search for international clients and the sharing of costs to advertise products in international fairs. In sum, besides developing competencies in supply chain management resulting from her vertical partnerships, she also managed to craft horizontal ties with competitors to overcome her small scale and poor export infrastructure of her country. By integrating distinct types of ties and exploring how they enable firms to create competitive advantages, our model is better able to accommodate the more complex patterns of partnering that occur among SMEs. Therefore, our model contributes to recent research on interfirm relations integrating different forms of relationships found among firms (e.g., Brandenburger and Nalebuff's "value net", 1997; Choi et al.'s "vertical and horizontal relationships" model, 2002; Lazzarini's et al. "netchains", 2001). In particular, our model submits that horizontal and vertical ties create value in very specific ways, i.e., they yield very particular forms of collective efficiencies which mediate the access of SMEs to global markets.

Our study also contributes to an important and growing stream of the literature dealing with international management. This literature has often focused on international alliances as a means of enabling firms to globally source commodities (Murray et al. 1995), knowledge (Simonin 1999; Zhao et al. 2004) or cutting edge technologies (Nordberg et al. 1996). Our research focuses instead on the role of *local* alliances in fostering firms' ability to compete globally through collective sourcing of resources, manufacturing productivity, and product innovation. Specifically, our focus is on the economies enabled by local partnerships and how they matter for SMEs' access to global markets. This shift in focus (international alliances versus local alliances to go global) integrates the strategic alliances and entrepreneurship research streams, as pointed by Hitt et al. (2001), and turns out to be considerably more useful for entrepreneurial ventures which may yet lack the resources to go abroad to begin with or even establish international alliances.

Lastly, our study adds to a growing stream of the literature in strategy and entrepreneurship dealing with the emergence and competitiveness of clusters (i.e., sectoral and geographical concentrations of firms, Schmitz and Nadvi (1999: 1503)). While early cluster literature accentuated the benefits that passively resulted to firms from their geographically agglomerating into larger markets (for example, bigger and more specialized pools of labor and supply – Schmitz and Nadvi 1999), recent treatments of the concept have tended to move away from this emphasis on passive agglomeration economies towards that of active networking among clustered firms. Given the complex interfirm interdependencies occurring in clusters, firms can consciously build cooperative governance structures so as to improve cluster-wide competitiveness (see also Christopherson and Storper 1986; Markusen 1999; Mesquita 2007; Storper 1997; Tallman et al. 2004). Our study contributes to this latter trend of the cluster literature by outlining specific mechanisms through which firms that properly coordinate their actions with other firms perform better than those firms that do not. Further, though literature to date has relied excessively on anecdotal accounts instead of rigorous theorizing, and case studies, instead of meticulous statistical validation (see the criticisms in Gordon and McCann 2000: 17; Martin and Sunley 2003: 16), our study integrates three important theoretical streams to model clustered SMEs' interfirm relationships to collective efficiencies and access to global markets and applies modern quantitative techniques – including the interaction terms of structural models.

Admittedly our research is limited in some ways, which suggest several opportunities for future research. First, our study is limited in scope, as it suits a particular context – that of firms sharing environments with limited infrastructure and weak institutions, such as emerging economies. We do not evaluate whether our argument holds in other settings. A possible extension of our study would contrast our model in developed vis-à-vis emerging countries. Arguably, developed countries in general exhibit stronger legal institutions that increase the viability of alternative forms of contracting (e.g., formal contracts, equity-based partnerships, and joint ventures). Further, governments tend to be more effective in the provision of public goods. Thus, we can suppose that SMEs in emerging markets resort to inter organizational relationships supported by informal, relational means of governance to a greater degree than SMEs in developed economies (e.g., Peng and Heath 1996). Future research should therefore try to examine relationships among SMEs in a diverse set of countries in a way that the costs and likelihood of contractual enforcement vary.

Although we expect that the role of relational governance in creating collective efficiencies will decrease when formal institutions become more efficient, we believe that, even in countries with stronger institutions, interfirm relationships will still have a role in creating collective efficiencies jointly with formal means of governance. Recent research has discussed complementarities among formal and informal means of governance (e.g., Poppo and Zenger 2002). For instance, relational governance can help enforce exchange dimensions that are difficult to specify in formal contracts (Lazzarini et al. 2004), while formal contracts can align expectations and provide guidance for the development of long term relationships (Mayer and Argyres 2004).

Additionally, our paper also observes only the benefits of relational governance and disregards its costs – for instance, the "overembeddedness" that may result when long-term partners avoid transacting with new actors and hence fail to benefit from novel information and opportunities (e.g., Uzzi 1997). We are interested, however, in environments subject to weak institutions, where establishing relational governance is often the only way to govern inter organizational arrangements that are critical for the creation of collective efficiencies. It is possible that in settings involving stronger institutions SMEs will be able to use contracts and other formal means of governance to support relationships with shorter duration and hence avoid the risk of "overembeddedness". Therefore, another important issue that future research should observe is whether SMEs maintain partners for longer periods of time or adopt a more arm's length approach by switching partners from time to time.

Lastly, our methods can be improved. Future research may tackle similar phenomena through the use of panel datasets that observe SMEs through time. In this case, one could examine how past efforts to develop relational ties create collective efficiencies in future periods. One could also model how vertical and horizontal relationships appear and evolve over time – an issue we do not tackle in the present study, but that is critical to advise SME managers about how to leverage local partnerships to better access global markets.

Despite the limitations mentioned above, our hope is that our study will encourage further work to examine the global competitiveness of SMEs established within emerging economy contexts. A lot of strategy research has discussed the significance of emerging economy environmental traits; we believe it is time for us to examine these through more varied theoretical perspective combinations, as well as deeper empirical analyzes.

Acknowledgements We thank Jay Anand, Oana Branzei, Patricia Friedrich, Robert Hoskisson, Werner Hoffman, Laura Poppo, Harbir Singh, Fred Walumbwa, Libby Weber, and seminar participants at Arizona State University, the University of Illinois in Chicago, and the University of Connecticut for comments and suggestions on earlier drafts. We also thankfully acknowledge Maria Belen Lopez Aleman for her research assistance with data-collection. This research received funds from the Inter American Development Bank and Brazil's National Council for Scientific and Technological Development (CNPq), as well as institutional support from the IAE School of Management & Business, Universidad Austral, Argentina. An earlier draft of this research appeared in the Academy of Management Journal.

References

Aldrich Howard E, Zimmer C (1986) Entrepreneurship through social networks. In Sexton, DL & Smilor, RW (editors). The art and science of entrepreneurship. Cambridge, MA Ballinger. Pages 3–23

Amin A, Thrift N (1992) Neo-Marshallian nodes in global networks. Int J Urban Reg Res 16(4):571–587

Anderson JC, Gerbing DW (1988) Structural equation modeling in practice: a review and recommended two-step approach. Psychol Bull 103:411–423

Armstrong JS, Overton TS (1977) Estimating nonresponse bias in mail surveys. Journal of marketing research, 14(3):396–403

Artz K, Brush TH (2000) Asset specificity, uncertainty and relational norms: an examination of coordination costs in collaborative strategic alliances. J Econ Behav Organ 41(4):337–362

Audretsch DB, Feldman MP (1996) R & D spillovers and the geography of innovation and production. Am Econ Rev 86(3):630–640

Axelrod R (1984) The evolution of cooperation. Basic Books, New York, NY

Baker G, Gibbons R, Murphy KJ (2002) Relational contracts and the theory of the firm. Quart J Econ 117(1):39–84

Barney JB (1991) Firm resources and sustained competitive advantage. J Manage 17(1):99–120

Bartlett CA, Ghoshal S (1992) Transnational management, 2nd ed. Irwin, London

Bentler PM (1989) Comparative fit indexes in structural models. Psychol Bull 107(March):238–246
Bentler PM, Bonnett DG (1980) Significance tests and goodness of fit in the analysis of covariance structures. Psychol Bull 88:588–606
Bollen KA, Curran PJ (2005) Latent curve models: a structural equation perspective. Wiley, New York
Boyer KK, Leong GK, Ward PT, Krajewski LJ (1997) Unlocking the potential of advanced manufacturing technologies. J Oper Manage 15:331–347
Brandenburger AM, Nalebuff BJ (1997) Co-opetition: a revolution mindset that combines competition and business. Doubleday, New York, NY
Browne MW, Cudeck R (1989) Single sample cross-validation indices for covariance structures. Multivariate Behav Res 24:445–455
Browne MW, Cudeck R (1993) Alternative ways of assessing model fit. In: Bollen KA, Long JS (eds) Testing structural equation models. Sage, Newbury Park, CA, pp 136–162
Buckley PJ, Casson M (1976) The future of the multinational enterprise. MacMillan, London
Byrne BM (2001) Structural modeling with AMOS. Lawrence Erlbaum Associates, Mahwah, NJ
Calabrese T, Baum JAC, Silverman B (2000) Canadian biotechnology start ups, 1991–1997: the role of incumbents' patents and strategic alliances in controlling competition. Soc. Sci. Res. 29 4, pp 503–534
Canina L, Enz CA, Harrison JS (2005) Agglomeration effects and strategic orientations: evidence from the US lodging industry. Acad Manage J 48(4):565
Carrera A, Mesquita L, Perkins G, Vassolo R (2003) Business groups and their corporate strategies in the Argentine roller coaster of competitive and anti-competitive shocks. Acad Manage Exec 17(3):32–44
Caves RE (1982) Multinational enterprise and economic analysis. Cambridge, England. Cambridge University Press
Choi TY, Wu Z, Ellram L, Koka BR (2002) Supplier-supplier relationships and their implications for buyer–supplier relationships. IEEE Trans Eng Manage 49(2):119
Christopherson S, Storper M (1986) The city as studio, the world as back lot: the impact of vertical disintegration on the location of the motion picture industry. Environ Plann Soc Space 4:305–320
Cooper, AC (2007). Behavioral characteristics of entrepreneurial activity. Strategic Entrepreneurship Journal, 1(1):145–146
De Meyer A, Ferdows K (1985) Integration of information systems in manufacturing. Int J Oper Prod Manage 5(2):5–12
Dillman DA (2000) Mail and internet surveys: the tailored design method. Wiley, New York, NY
Doz YL, Hamel G (1998) Alliance advantage: the art of creating value through partnering. Harvard University Press, Cambridge, MA
Dunning JH (1981) International production and the multinational enterprise. Allen & Unwin, Winchester, MA
Dussauge P, Garrette B, Mitchell W (2000) Learning from competing partners: outcomes and durations of scale and link alliances in Europe, North America and Asia. Strateg Manage J 21:99–126
Dyer JH (1997) Effective interfirm collaboration: how firms minimize transaction costs and maximize transaction value. Strateg Manage J 18:553–556
Dyer JH, Singh H (1998) The relational view: cooperative strategy and sources of interorganizational competitive advantage. Acad Manag Rev 23(4):660–680
Ellickson RC (1991) Order without law: how neighbors settle disputes. Harvard University Press, Cambridge, MA
Fichman M, Levinthal DA (1991) History dependence and professional relationships: ties that bind. Res Sociol Organ 8:119–153
Gordon IR, McCann P (2000) Industrial clusters: complexes, agglomeration, and / or social networks? Urban Stud 37(3):513–535
Granovetter MS (1985) Economic action and social structure. Am J Soc 91(3):481–510
Greif A (1994) Cultural beliefs and the organization of society: a historical and theoretical reflection on collectivist and individualistic societies. J Polit Econ 102(4):912–950
Gulati R (1999) Network location and learning: the influence of network resources and firm capabilities on alliance formation. Strateg Manage J 20(5):397–420

Gulati R, Singh H (1998) The architecture of cooperation: managing coordination costs and appropriation concerns in strategic alliances. Adm Sci Q 43(4):781–814
Gulati, Ranjay "Network Location and Learning: The Influence of Network Resources and Firm Capabilities on Alliance Formation." Strategic Management Journal 20, no. 5 (May 1999): 397–420
Heide JB, John G (1992) Do norms matter in marketing reltionships? J Mark 56(2):32–44
Heide JB, Miner AS (1992) The shadow of the future: effects of anticipated interaction and frequency of contact on buyer–seller cooperation. Acad Manage J 35(2):265–291
Helper S (1991) Strategy and irreversibility in supplier relations: the case of the US automobile industry. Bus Hist Rev 65(4):781–824
Hitt MA, Ireland RD, Camp SM, Sexton DL (2001) Strategic entrepreneurship: integrating entrepreneurial and strategic management perspectives. Strateg Manage J 22(special issue):479–491
Hoskisson RE, Eden L, Lau CM, Wright M (2000) Strategy in emerging economies. Acad Manage J 43(3):249–267
Kaufmann PJ, Stern LW (1988) Relational exchange norms, perceptions of unfairness and retained hostility in commercial litigation. J Conflict Resolut 32(September):534–552
Kogut B (1988) Joint ventures: theoretical and empirical perspectives. Strateg Manage J 9(4):319–332
la Porta R, Lopez de Silanes F, Schleifer A, Vishny A (1997) Legal determinants of external finance. J Finance 52:1131–1150
Lazzarini SG, Chaddad FR, Cook M (2001) Integrating supply chain and network analyses: the study of netchains. J Chain Netw Sci 1(1):7–22
Lazzarini SG, Miller GJ, Zenger T (2004) Order with some law: complementarity vs substitution of formal and informal agreements. J Law Econ Organ 20(2):261–298
Macneil IR (1980) The new social contract. Yale University Press, New Haven, CT
Markusen A (1999) Sticky places in slippery space. In: Gertler MS (ed) New industrial geography: regions, regulations and institutions. Routledge, Florence, KY, pp 98–124
Martin R, Sunley P (2003) Deconstructing clusters: chaotic concept or policy panace? J Econ Geogr 3:5–35
Mayer KJ, Argyres NS (2004) Learning to contract: evidence from the personal computer industry. Organ Sci 15(4):394–410
McEvily W, Zaheer A (1999) Bridging ties: a source of firm heterogeneity in competitive capabilities. Strateg Manage J 20(12):1133–1156
McMullen JS, Shepherd DA (2006) Entrepreneurial action and the role of uncertainty in the theory of the entrepreneur. Academy of Management Journal 31(1): 132–152
Mesquita L (2003) Rationality as the basis for a new institutional environment: Argentina's former presidential candidate Ricardo Lopez Murphy. Acad Manage Exec 17(3):44–50
Mesquita LF (2007) Starting over when the bickering never ends: rebuilding aggregate trust among clustered firms through trust facilitators. Acad Manag Rev 32(1):72–91
Mesquita LF, Brush TH (2008) Untangling safeguard and production coordination effects in long term buyer supplier relationships. Academy of Management Journal 51(4):785–807
Miller DJ, Shamsie J (1996) The resource-based view of the firm in two environments: the Hollywood film studios from 1936–1965. Acad Manage J 39(3):519–543
Murray JY, Masaaki K, Wildt AR (1995) Strategic and financial performance implications of global sourcing. J Int Bus Stud 26(1):181
Nault BR, Tyagi RK (2001) Implementable mechanisms to coordinate horizontal alliances. Manag Sci 47(6):787–799
Nordberg M, Campbell AJ, Verbeke A (1996) Can market based contracts substitute for alliances in high technology markets? J Int Bus Stud 27(5):963
North DC (1990) Institutions, institutional change, and economic performance. Cambridge University Press, New York
Olson M (1965) The logic of collective action. Harvard University Press, Cambridge
Ostrom E, Walker J, Gardner R (1992) Covenants with and without a sword: self-governance is possible. Am Polit Sci Rev 86(2):404–417

Palay T (1984) Comparative institutional economics: the governance of rail freight contracting. J Legal Stud 13(June):265–287
Peng MW, Heath PS (1996) The growth of the firm in planned economies in transition: institutions, organizations, and strategic choice. Acad Manag Rev 21:492–528
Peteraf MA (1993) The cornerstones of competitive advantage: a resource-based view. Strateg Manage J 14:179–191
Ping RAJ (1995) A parsimonious estimating technique for interaction and quadratic latent variables. J Mark Res 32(3):336–347
Ping, R. A. J. 1996***. Estimating latent variable interactions and quadratics: the state of this art. Journal of management, 22(3)
Poppo L, Zenger T (2002) Do formal contracts and relational governance function as substitutes or complements. Strateg Manage J 23(8):707–725
Porter ME (1998) Clusters and competition: new agendas for companies, governments, and institutions. In: Porter M (ed) On competitiveness. Harvard Business School Press, Cambridge, MA, pp 197–288
Pouder R, St. John CH (1996) Hot spots and blind spots: geographical clusters of firms and innovation. Acad Manage Rev 21(4):1192–1225
Raftery A (1995) Bayesian model selection in social research. In Marsden PV (ed) Sociological methodology. San Francisco, pp 111–163
Research CSIL (2003) The furniture industry in Argentina, Brazil, Chile. CSIL Milano, Milano
Research CSIL (2004) World furniture outlook. CSIL Milano, Milano
Ring P, Van de Ven A (1992) Structuring cooperative relationships between organizations. Strateg Manage J 13:483–498
Rosenkopf L, Schilling M (2007) "Comparing Alliance Network Structure Across Industries: Observations and Explanations". Strategic Entrepreneurship Journal, 1:191–209
Rothaermel FT (2001) Incumbent's advantage through exploiting complementary assets via interfirm cooperation. Strategic Management Journal, 22(9):687–699
Schmitz H (1995) Collective efficiency: growth path for small-scale industry. J Dev Stud 31(4):529–567
Schmitz H, Nadvi K (1999) Clustering and industrialization: introduction. World Dev 27(9):1503–1514
Schwartz G (1978) Estimating the dimension of a model. Ann Stat 6:461–464
Sengenberger W, Loveman GW, Piore MJ (1990) The re emergence of small enterprises: industrial restructuring in industrialized countries. ILO, Geneva
Simonin BL (1999) Ambiguity and the process of knowledge transfer in strategic alliances. Strateg Manage J 20:595–623
Stinchcombe AL (1965) Social structure and organizations. In: March JG (ed) Handbook of organizations. Rand McNally, Chicago, pp 142–193
Stone A, Levy B, Paredes R (1996) Public institutions and private transactions: a comparative analysis of the legal and regulatory environment for business transactions in Brazil and Chile. In: Alston LJ, Eggertsson T, North D (eds) Empirical studies in institutional change. Cambridge University Press, New York, NY
Storper M (1997) The regional world: territorial development in a global economy. Guilford Press, New York, NY
Stuart TE, Stuart Sorenson O (2007) Strategic networks and entrepreneurial ventures. Strategic Entrepreneurship Journal 1(1) : 211–227
Tallman S, Jenkins M, Henry N, Pinch S (2004) Knowledge, clusters, and competitive advantage. Acad Manag Rev 29(2):258
Teece D (1992) Competition, cooperation, and innovation: organizational arrangements for regimes of rapid technological progress. J Econ Behav Organ 18:1–25
Tendler J, Amorim M (1996) Small firms and their helpers: lessons on demand. World Dev 24(3):407–426
Thompson JD (1967) Organizations in action: social science bases of administration. McGraw-Hill, New York, NY

Uzzi B (1997) Social structure and competition in interfirm networks: the paradox of embeddedness. Adm Sci Q 42:35–67

Van de Ven AH, Walker G (1984) The dynamics of inter-organizational coordination. Adm Sci Q 29(4):598–622

Ward PT, Duray R, Leong GK, Sum C-C (1995) Business environment, operations strategy, and performance: an empirical study of Singapore manufacturers. J Oper Manage 13:99–115

Wheaton B (1987) Assessment of fit in overidentified models with latent variables. Sociol Methods Res 16:118–154

Williamson O (1985) The economic institutions of capitalism. Free Press, New York, NY

Xin KK, Pearce JL (1996) Guanxi: connections as substitutes for formal institutional support. Acad Manage J 39(6):1641–1659

Zhao, Z., Anand, J., & Mitchell, W. 2004. Transferring collective knowledge: teaching and learning in the Chinese auto industry. Strategic organization, 2(2)

Chapter 4
Corporate Governance Systems: Effects of Capital and Labor Market Congruency on Corporate Innovation and Global Competitiveness*

Robert E. Hoskisson, Daphne Yiu, and Hicheon Kim

Abstract Drawing on institutional economics, this article addresses how institutional congruence between capital and labor markets influences corporate governance systems, which, in turn, create differences in national corporate innovation and entrepreneurship systems and subsequently global competitiveness. We argue that such institutional congruence cultivates two ideal corporate governance systems. The first ideal type is the market-based system with transactional capital and external labor markets. This corporate governance system facilitates more explorative and revolutionary innovations. The second ideal type is the relationship-based governance system with relational capital and internal labor markets. This system facilitates more exploitative and evolutionary innovations. We wrap up by discussing how institutional adjustments are being pursued for each governance system because each type has advantages and disadvantages that require adjustments. Finally, we present implications that our congruence model suggests for global competitiveness, high-tech management, and public policy regarding national innovation systems.

Robert E. Hoskisson
George R. Brown Professor of Strategic Management, Jesse H. Jones Graduate School of Business, Rice University,
6100 Main Street, MS-531 Houston, Texas 77005
e-mail: robert.hoskisson@rice.edu

D. Yiu
Department of Management, Chinese University of Hong Kong, Hong Kong, China

H. Kim
Korea University Business School, Korea University, Seoul, 136-701, Republic of Korea

*This chapter has appeared in *Journal of High Technology Management Research*, 15 (2004) 293–315.

D.B. Audretsch et al. (eds.), *New Frontiers in Entrepreneurship: Recognizing, Seizing, and Executing, Opportunities*, International Studies in Entrepreneurship,
DOI 10.1007/978-1-4419-0058-6_4, © Springer Science+Business Media, LLC 2010

4.1 Introduction

Governance systems in a national setting may provide a source of competitive advantage in the global arena (Kim and Hoskisson 1997; Porter 1992; Roe 1994). There has been a debate regarding the relative efficiency and competitiveness of corporate governance systems in different countries. The miraculous growth of Japanese firms in the 1980s fostered criticism regarding the shortsightedness of the Anglo-Saxon market-based governance system. Accordingly, Porter (1992) suggested that US firms ought to incorporate features from the more relationship-based governance system found in Japan and other countries. Nonetheless, with Japan's economy being in a depressed state more recently, the supremacy of the Anglo-Saxon market-based system has been argued (Dvorak et al. 2001). This article addresses the debate over which system, the market- or the relationship-based, is better for global competitiveness (Yoshikawa and Phan 2001). Is one system best in all situations, or should we blend the two systems together into one that combines the near-term efficiency of the US system with the greater willingness to invest in long-term capabilities that is said to distinguish the Japanese and German systems (Porter 1997)? Underlying such debate is the assumption that there is no institutional barrier in transferring national corporate governance systems across country boundaries.

However, institutional economists (e.g., Knack and Keefer 1997) find that the institutional environment is the main obstacle for the convergence between richer and poorer countries. They conclude that countries cannot easily improve their economic fortunes because they are embedded in their own institutional context. In fact, in the past 30 years, the US has continued to have a persistent global dominance in the sectors of aircraft, drugs and medicine, biotechnology, prepackaged software, consulting, information services, banking, etc., while Japan enjoyed competitive advantage over the US in automobiles, home electronics, optoelectronics, machine tools and robotics, flexible manufacturing, etc. across all indicators of competitiveness including share of global export markets, productivity, FDI ratio, etc. (Jin 2001). This persistent disparity in the sectoral patterns of the US and Japan's competitiveness may be indicative of the institutional embeddedness effect.

There are two main characteristics of institutions that help explain the institutional embeddedness effect: complementarity and path dependence. First, as Milgrom and Roberts (1995) argue, institutions are complementary with one another and may work well only when all of them are in the same national economy. According to North (1990), institutions work in association with each other and thus function simultaneously to create a transaction environment. Furthermore, the relationship between institutions is a self-enforcing structure or framework because the institutions that evolve require a consensus among people to be willing to support and defend it (Weingast 1993). As such, a wealth-creating economy requires complementarities among institutions to build an appropriate institutional mix to achieve a desired economic outcome. For instance, a country's system of corporate governance is embedded in the idiosyncratic national institutions and ideologies of the country (Pauly and Reich 1997). An ideal governance system requires congruence among the institutions, which implies that restructuring undertaken in one institution but not in others will not achieve effective governance (Groenewegen 1997).

The privatization experiment in Russia and other Eastern European countries illustrates this point. Through a voucher system in the former Soviet Union (Filatotchev et al. 1996), privatization of over 80% of the formally state-owned enterprises was accomplished in a very short period (1992–1994). However, the implementation of radically different incentive and control mechanisms based on a Western approach has not resulted in significant success. Filatotchev et al. (2000) concluded that the giveaway nature of the privatization program could not improve firm performance due, in part, to the lack of complementary institutional changes, such as the development of capital markets to provide new capital and legal protection to potential foreign investors.

Second, as noted above, institutions are path dependent (North 1990). Institutional change requires learning, thus resulting in cognitive path dependencies and technological path dependencies. Consequently, institutions shape a development path by favoring new institutions that increase the preexisting institutions' presence and outcomes. Taken together, the characteristics of complementarity and path dependence of institutions make the transfer of corporate governance systems from one country to another rather difficult. Therefore, in response to the debate presented above, we suggest an institutional perspective to argue that corporate governance systems may not be an isolated source of global competitiveness. Instead, they are shaped by, and will shape, corresponding institutions. As such, it is the congruence among related institutions that gives rise to governance efficiency and potential global competitiveness effects. Despite some variance in governance practices across firms within a country, this article focuses on national governance systems and their consequences on corporate innovation and entrepreneurship systems and associated global competitiveness. Due to complementarities and path dependence in the development of national institutions, national governance systems tend to exhibit enduring differences and make a significant impact on firm behavior accordingly (Nelson and Rosenberg 1993).

In the following sections, we examine how the institutional congruence between the capital and labor markets of a country and the associated corporate governance system will affect corporate risk-taking behavior and innovation activities, which, in turn, affect firms' competitiveness in the global arena. We first examine the transactional versus relational capital market systems. The subsequent section describes internal versus external orientations of labor markets. Following this, two corporate governance systems based on the congruence between capital and labor markets will be presented. As an illustration, we examine specifically how the traditional US and the Japanese main-bank keiretsu systems achieve separate but optimal efficiencies, as well as how their capital and labor markets affect their national innovation systems in terms of risk-taking inducements created for managers and entrepreneurs.

Specifically, we suggest how larger, existing firms associated with relationship systems, such as the Japanese keiretsu, may be better at exploitative innovation systems, whereas firms, especially startups, in market-based systems may be better at explorative innovation systems (Benner and Tushman 2003; Madhok 1997; March 1991). However, both the market- and relationship-based systems have their downsides. We also discuss how relational properties are increasingly found in market-based systems, while relationship-based systems are incorporating market-based characteristics. Accordingly, institutional adjustments in each system are discussed. Finally, we conclude by providing implications for public policy regarding national innovation systems, high-tech entrepreneurial management, and global competitiveness.

4.2 Basic Institutions: Capital and Labor Markets

Our institutional congruence model specifically looks into two institutional factors, the capital and labor markets. There are two main reasons for choosing these two institutional aspects. First, both capital and labor markets are related to a country's ultimate competitiveness. Under a market-based system or "investor capitalism" (Useem 1992), an effective governance system is one that can achieve a more optimal allocation of capital, thereby creating benefits for the economy as a whole. In addition, the changing nature of competition and the increasing pressure of globalization make capital investment the most critical determinant of national competitive advantage (Porter 1996). As such, the relationship between a capital market and a corporate governance system is critical to the global competitiveness of an economy. Under a relationship-based system or "alliance capitalism" (Gerlach 1992), cospecialized investment in interfirm relations is essential to firm survival in the long run. Investment in cospecialized assets involves the development of human capital through which cooperation is fostered. Boards of directors, even in the US market-based system, must not only look out for shareholders interests but also hire executives from the labor market and establish a contract that facilitates the use of managerial decision making in an optimal way (Baysinger and Hoskisson 1990). Blair (1995) also argued that the failure to represent the employees' interests in governance arrangements could lead to an underinvestment in job- and firm-specific skills. Therefore, the relationship between labor market and corporate governance is an important issue regarding entrepreneurial behavior and firm competitiveness in the global context.

Second, an effective governance system must facilitate the joint operational success of the two markets as implied above. Agency theory suggests that corporate governance is a means used in firms to establish order between the firm's owners and its top-level managers whose interests may be in conflict. That is, corporate governance deals with the agency problem arising from the separation of ownership and control (Jensen and Meckling 1976). This principal-agent view of corporate governance rests on the premise that the market for capital and the market for managerial talent provide the most effective restraints on managerial discretion, and that shareholders, as the residual claimants, should ultimately commit corporate resources to value-maximizing ends (Fama and Jensen 1983). As such, an effective governance system is one that bridges the gap between the owner-principals who provide capital and the manager-agents who provide managerial skill to a firm.

4.2.1 *Transactional Versus Relational Capital Markets*

There are two general types of capital markets: transactional and relational. Both capital markets provide different incentives and disciplinary systems to align the interests of the owners and those of the managers. While transactional capital markets rely more on transactional elements in the external markets to govern firms, relational capital markets rely more on intercorporate, family, and bank relationships to monitor firms. The governance attributes of these two capital markets are listed in Table 4.1 and described below.

4.2.1.1 Ownership Structure

Transactional capital markets are characterized by diffused, low corporate shareholdings (Kaplan 1997), low concentration of ownership and insignificant commercial bank shareholdings, less interfirm shareholdings, and faster turnover of controlling blocs (Berglof 1990).

On the other hand, relational capital markets are characterized by having more concentrated ownership by families, corporations, or banks (Kaplan 1997), widespread interfirm shareholdings, and relatively slow turnover of controlling blocs (Berglof 1990; McGuire and Dow 2003). The diffused ownership structure in the transactional capital markets indicates that the role of individual shareholder voice is limited in transactional capital markets and there are virtually unrestricted, low-cost exit opportunities for shareholders due to the access to liquid stock markets (Hirschman 1970). Conversely, the less developed markets for financial instruments in relational capital markets reduce investors' incentives to exit or leave established relationships. This "lock-in" effect (Berglof 1990) induces voice behavior by making exit very costly in relational capital markets.

4.2.1.2 Executive Compensation

Executive compensation, in the forms of salaries, bonuses, and contingent compensation, is used to tie the interests of management and shareholders. From the agency theory perspective, shareholders (as the risk-bearing specialists) can diversify their

Table 4.1 Attributes of transactional and relational capital markets

Governance attributes	Transactional capital market	Relational capital market
Ownership structure	Low concentration	High concentration by families or financial institutions
Executive compensation	Managerial stock options	Seniority-based
Boards of directors	Outside directors dominate	Inside directors dominate
Market for corporate control	External groups pursue takeovers	Dominating shareholders and banks arrange reorganization or assume control when firms are under financial distress

risks in the market, while managers (as the decision-making specialists) will minimize their employment risks in making strategic decision. As such, managers are willing to take risky strategic behaviors, such as product innovations, only when their employment risks are being compensated. The more developed stock market in the transactional capital markets offers opportunities to provide high-powered incentives, for example, through managerial stock options.

Alternatively, close monitoring and well-functioning remuneration committees promote stronger relations between executive compensation (versus market incentives) and firm performance in the relational systems.

4.2.1.3 Board of Directors

Essential to corporate governance is the board of directors who are charged with directing and managing the business of the corporation on behalf of the owners. Transactional capital markets are often referred to as systems in which outside directors dominate the boards of directors, while in relational capital markets inside managers and employees are considered dominant, although other stakeholders often sit on boards. Outsider-dominated systems are better at responding to change, whereas insider-dominated systems are superior at implementing policies that require the development of relations with other related stakeholders.

4.2.1.4 Markets for Corporate Control

One of the major distinctions between transactional capital markets and relational capital markets is how the systems handle financial distress problems. In transactional capital markets, takeover by an external group of shareholders is the predominant mechanism in handling managerial failure. There are rules pertaining to commercial banks that prevent them from intervening when their client firms are in financial difficulties (Berglof 1990). In relational capital markets, markets for corporate control can be regarded as inactive or even nonexistent. They are substituted for close monitoring by the concentrated shareholders, such as banks and other financial institutions, that have significant monitoring and disciplining roles on firm behaviors through their ownership of shares, appointment of bank employees as directors, and close intercorporate relationships (Kaplan 1997). When firms are in financial distress, banks and other financial institutions, being both lenders and central risk-bearers, are willing to accept higher debt levels since they can exercise control much more freely than their counterparts in the transactional capital markets (Sheard 1994), and they normally arrange reorganization or assume control through their large shares of claims (Kester 1991). In addition, research has found that banks have a significant role in reducing the costs of financial distress in relational capital markets (Hoshi et al. 1990). However, in light of the current situations in the Japanese economy, the widely embraced efficient bank-centered corporate governance proposition seems unable to furnish satisfactory answers. Therefore, although the received literature recognizes the relational nature of bank–client relationships, the conclusion that such relationships facilitate efficient corporate governance may be premature. Bank–client relationships may facilitate monitoring as this literature suggests, but there may be other aspects of this system that reduce its economic and monitoring efficiency. As we suggest further on, it may have significant effects on competitiveness and innovation systems in regard to quick adjustments that are facilitated with a more efficient market for corporate control.

4.2.2 *External Versus Internal Labor Markets*

We classify labor markets into external labor markets and internal labor markets. We will compare the governance characteristics of these two types of labor markets along three dimensions as discussed in the following section and summarized in Table 4.2.

4.2.2.1 Selection

Selection is important to corporate governance as it directly relates to whether the manager selected will be a good agent who works for the shareholders' interests. In external labor markets, firms find managers in a well-organized market where each manager is priced according to the market assessment of his productivity and effectiveness. A well-functioning external labor market will reflect all the observable characteristics of the managers. Hence, market wages serve as good signals about managers' quality, thus mitigating the problem of adverse selection (Hoshi 1998), which occurs when a potential employee misrepresents his/her skills and abilities. In an internal labor market, managers start at the entry managerial levels of the firm hierarchy and likely get similar entry-level salaries. The firm and management monitor the managers' performance and promote them to the next rank if they meet certain performance criteria. Over time, through the hierarchy (Aoki 1988), firm executives observe managers' long-term performance. Thereby, firms obtain signals about managers' quality, which also alleviates to a large extent the problem of adverse selection (Hoshi 1998).

Table 4.2 Issues in external versus internal labor markets

Governance attributes	External labor market	Internal labor market
Selection	Market wages serve as signal of quality	Management monitors worker performance
Monitoring	External reputations affects mobility	Internal reputation is more crucial due to the lack of exit
Accumulation of skills	More general	More firm-specific and knowledge

4.2.2.2 Monitoring

A disciplinary system to facilitate corrections of managerial weakness is critical for effective corporate governance. In an effective external labor market, any misconduct by a manager to stakeholders may hurt the reputation of the manager and adversely affect the probability of getting a lucrative management position in the future. This credible threat prevents managers from abusing their informational advantage against stakeholders and monitors. In this regard, a well-functioning external labor market for managers can be a substitute for internal corporate governance (Hoshi 1998). However, external reputation is not a significant threat in an internal labor market because of the lack of exit opportunities, although internal reputation is crucial to promotion opportunities. Due to the lack of mobility, managers within an internal labor market have to fully commit to existing firms and maintain a long-term relationship with stakeholders.

4.2.2.3 Accumulation of Skills and Knowledge

The types of skills and knowledge that managers can gain from their work is effective in providing managers' incentives to operate in the interests of the firm since it affects the marketability of the managers in both the external and internal labor markets. External labor markets tend to encourage the development of general managerial skills and knowledge. Since managers are mobile across firm boundaries, they will try to accumulate skills and knowledge that are applicable in a wide range of firms so as to increase their value in the labor market. Consequently, more general managerial skills are developed in external labor markets. Furthermore, in external labor markets, the uncertainty of the firm's employment may increase the employees' incentives to keep their industry-specific skills high (Gilson and Roe 1998). Alternatively, firms may have less desire to invest in the development of human capital because individual managers may be able to appropriate that value by moving to another firm or by starting their own company (Coff 1997). Conversely, internal labor markets encourage accumulation of firm-specific human capital (Hoshi 1998). Internal labor markets facilitate long-term employment relationships. Managers have incentives to invest in firm-specific skills and knowledge, and firms are willing to invest in firm-specific training programs because they are not afraid that managers will leave the firm once they are trained. Consequently, the more firm-specific skills and knowledge accumulated, the more likely managers have the incentive to maintain a long-term relationship with their firm's stakeholders.

4.3 Institutional Congruence, Corporate Governance Systems, Corporate Innovations, and Global Competitiveness

Based on the classifications of capital markets and labor markets described above, a congruency continuum is outlined in Fig. 4.1. As mentioned above, we emphasize the importance of the institutional congruence between capital and labor markets for two reasons. The first idea regarding such a fit concerns the issue of institutional complementarity. The strength of each institution arises not just from its own productivity, but also from its ability to make other institutions more productive. In other words, there should be a correspondence across the capital and labor markets so as to produce the most efficient corporate governance system. The second concern is path dependence. Complementary institutions create path dependence that shapes new institutions that favor the consequences of the preexisting institutions. In particular, we propose that corporate governance systems are part of a set of institutions that create opportunity for corporate innovation activities, and subsequently, country global competitiveness.

The two ends of the continuum represent the two ideal cases in which the capital market is congruent with the labor market, thus giving rise to an optimal corporate governance system. The first ideal case is one that adopts a transactional capital market system and an external labor market. We will illustrate this (see Fig. 4.1) by examining the US corporate governance system. The second ideal case is one in which relational capital and internal labor markets are the predominant modes in the economy. We will illustrate this by examining the Japanese keiretsu governance system.

We suggest below that the market-based system is better at explorative innovation and that the relationship-based system is better at exploitative innovation (March 1991). Explorative innovation is focused on developing new products and capabilities using newly developed invention and is more future-oriented and opportunity seeking. Exploitative innovation is focused on extending current capabilities to new products or product line extensions. Of course, a balance of exploitation and exploration is necessary for any firm to survive (Madhok 1997). However, a congruent governance system may emphasize one system of innovation versus another, as we argue below, and this may lead to tradeoffs regarding innovation systems.

4.3.1 The Market-Based System: The Case of the United States

4.3.1.1 Institutional Congruence

To reduce agency costs associated with the separation of ownership and control (Fama and Jensen 1983), external control mechanisms, such as external managerial labor markets and markets for corporate control, are necessary because they are complementary to the market-based governance system. In the US transactional capital market system, corporate control is often exercised through a change in the management by takeovers. Such a change is easier if firms are not hindered by long-term relational contracts with their managers, as such reorganization may lead to great internal organizational conflicts. As such, the absence of a relational managerial labor market is conducive to the arm's-length transactional capital market in the US.

Furthermore, to cope with frequent management changes under arm's-length financing, an external labor market that allows labor mobility and fixed market

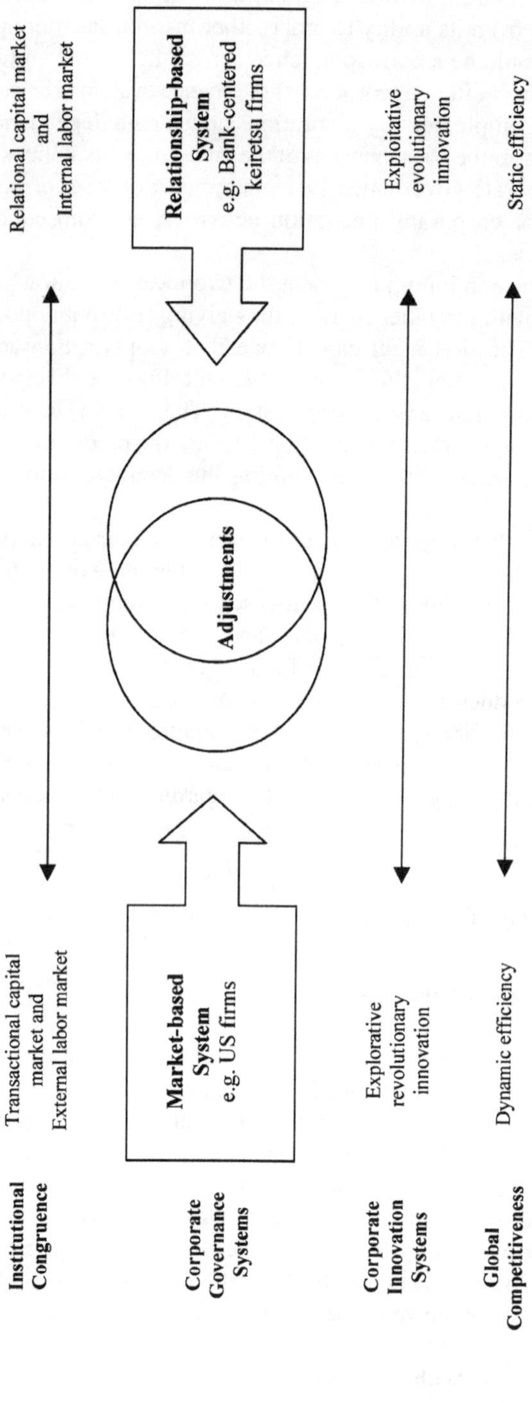

Fig. 4.1 Institutional congruence and corporate innovation

wages is necessary. Imagine how difficult it would be to introduce an internal-oriented labor market into the US market-based governance system. As Kim and Hoskisson (1997) pointed out, excessive reliance on internal labor markets in the US economy would generate unintended consequences. When outside job opportunities arise, it is likely that managers who have a high propensity for risk-taking are more likely to consider these opportunities. As a consequence, internal labor markets – when they are exposed to external labor markets – tend to retain risk-averse managers while losing risk-seeking managers. This problem is aggravated by the nature of internal labor markets. As managers move up the career ladder, they accumulate more firm-specific, nondiversifiable human assets, which make them even more risk-averse. On the whole, an internal labor market would likely retain those individuals that would be less likely to take on risky projects, which are needed to create innovation. Accordingly, internally oriented labor markets in a market-based system may adversely affect the potential for innovation.

One of the unique features in the US economy is the venture capital market, which is a demonstration of the complementarity and path dependency between the transactional capital market and the external labor market. Venture capital is defined as investment by specialized organizations in high-growth, high-risk, and often high-technology firms that need equity capital to finance product development or growth (Black and Gilson 1998). A venture capital market requires an active stock market (i.e., a transactional rather than a relational capital market) and an active stock market requires a supply of entrepreneurs and deals, which in turn create the demand for a venture capital market. A well-developed stock market permits venture capitalists to exit through an initial public offering (IPO), which then allows the venture capital provider and the entrepreneur to enter into an implicit contract over future control of the company. This distinctive mechanism is not prevalent in a relational capital market. For instance, the venture capital market in Germany lagged behind its development in the UK and other European countries in part because there was no effective IPO exit (Steinmetz 1995). Similarly, in Korea, the dominance of the chaebol and weak capital markets for midsize firms have retarded the development of its venture capital market (Economist 1998). In summary, the development of the venture capital market in the US was spawned by the preexisting congruence between its transactional capital market and external labor market. The close cooperation among stock market, venture capital market, and external supply of entrepreneurs contributes to the greater success of venture capital and fosters more innovations in countries with transactional capital markets as opposed to relational capital markets.

Proposition 1: Institutional congruence is achieved in a market-based governance system when the capital market is more transactional in nature and the labor market is external.

Up to this point, we have suggested that a market-based governance system is characterized by a high congruence between a transactional capital market and an external labor market. Now, let us examine how the congruence between a transactional capital market and external labor market facilitates innovations in the market-based system.

4.3.1.2 Emphasis on Explorative Innovations

Capital markets impose effects on corporate innovation activities in terms of their monitoring and risk-taking propensities. In regard to monitoring, transactional capital markets have been criticized as being inefficient in monitoring managers' opportunistic behavior, thus giving rise to agency problems.

Holmstrom (1989) stated that the contracting costs associated with promoting inventive activity are especially high because of the five characteristics of innovation: long-term, high-risk, unpredictable, labor-intensive, and idiosyncratic nature. Francis and Smith (1995) found that diffusely held firms, which are the most common type of ownership in transactional capital markets, are less innovative along the dimensions of patent activity, growth by acquisition versus internal development, and timing of long-term investment spending.

In addition, investors in transactional capital markets are more short-term oriented. With increasing presence of foreign investors, Japanese managers are realizing that foreign investors are far more concerned with quarterly earnings, at least when compared to Japanese investors (Dvorak et al. 2001).

Besides, professionally managed mutual funds record a high turnover rate of securities. One professional observed that "the industry's annual rate of portfolio turnover is 85 percent, suggesting an average holding period of about 1.2 years for a given security" (Bogle 1999). With large numbers of listed companies, liquidity, and anonymous markets available, investors are readily convinced, given quarterly earnings statements, to reshuffle their stock portfolio if they can increase their return on investment by doing so. This is especially true of professionally managed mutual funds because their incentives are tied to market performance (Hoskisson et al. 2002). In response, managers are under pressure to perform and look good every quarter and, as a result, may act myopically by choosing short-term projects with faster paybacks (Stein 1989).

Although transactional capital markets give rise to transient, diffused ownership that causes short-term orientation in resource allocation and underinvestment in R&D, they also offer important advantages in regard to risk-taking. In transactional capital markets where stable, close relationships with financial institutions are lacking, firms could, and should, rely on a wide range of sources for capital. Such "openness" of capital markets has considerable dynamic advantages in providing finance for firms in situations of high uncertainty and complexity (Allen 1993).

For instance, in a "closed" system such as Japan's, only a few select banks decide whether the firm will be financed. This system works relatively well in mature industries and in financing exploitative innovations which entail less uncertainty about their return and risk. However, this system is much less likely to finance emerging fields and explorative innovations. By contrast, in an "open" system, such as that of the US, a firm can be financed as far as it attracts a sufficient number of investors out of a very large number of potential investors in the capital market.

As a consequence, explorative innovations are much more likely to find investors in an open system. Indeed, the capital allocation in the open system depends on a much wider range of opinions, which is crucial to financing explorative innovations. In accordance with Schumpeter's (1934) view, it takes both a special person and a well-organized capital market to provide the opportunity and support for an entrepreneur's unconventional and often revolutionary ideas. Therefore, a transactional capital market featuring innumerable and diverse participants is a key factor in providing funding opportunities for explorative innovations (Watts 2001).

Labor market type also exerts effects on innovations in terms of knowledge creation. External labor markets are conducive to explorative innovations, radical changes, and development beyond the firm's existing knowledge base. In the presence of external labor markets, individuals tend to have weak commitment to particular employers and high incentives to continually examine their employment options elsewhere (Williamson 1985). As such, people value highly explicit, objective, and transferable quantitative knowledge. The accumulation of this type of knowledge, in turn, gives rise to a knowledge creation system that is centered on formal education, independent R&D, and systematic codification of information. This, subsequently, facilitates explorative innovations, such as scientific and technological breakthroughs. The argument above can help explain the success of the US in the sectors of aircraft, biotechnology, and pharmaceuticals, as well as in software, consulting services, information processing, and online businesses where the codification and quantification of information is key for competitive advantages (Jin 2001).

Innovation usually constitutes creative recombination of existing and new technologies (March 1991; Schumpeter 1934). Internal labor markets work relatively well when ingredients of new combinations reside in the single firm. Firm-specific knowledge and social capital among organizational members, which are nurtured and reinforced by internal labor markets, facilitate sharing and transfer of skills, capabilities, and knowledge. Thus, internal labor markets are conducive to exploitative innovations, incremental change and development from the firm's existing knowledge base. However, internal labor markets are quite limited in carrying out new combinations when ingredients reside in multiple firms and across industries in particular (Hoskisson and Busenitz 2002). Instead, interfirm mobility through external labor markets promotes transfer of skills, capabilities, and knowledge across firms and industries. While explicit knowledge can be codified and transmitted across firms through formal, systemic documentation without the involvement of knowledge holders, tacit knowledge – which refers to the understanding embedded in people's experience often existing in the form of intuition, speculation, and feeling – is difficult to communicate without the active involvement of knowledge holders. Therefore, effective transfer of tacit knowledge often requires the transfer of knowledge holders, which occurs through external labor markets and through the takeover or acquisition process.

In sum, market-based governance systems are supportive of innovations that are explorative (March 1991) and often revolutionary (Utterback 1994). As a consequence, they are better able to achieve dynamic efficiency; that is, the efficiency resulting from developing new products, processes, and capabilities that are unconstrained by existing resources, opportunities, and beliefs (Ghemawat and Costa 1993).

Proposition 2: Market-based governance systems are more likely to produce explorative innovations and dynamic efficiency in the economy.

4.3.2 The Relationship-Based System: The Case of Japan's Bank-Centered Keiretsu System

4.3.2.1 Institutional Congruence

The Japanese keiretsu corporate governance system is characterized by the complementarity between its bank-centered, relationship-oriented financial system and internal labor market practice of lifetime employment. The Japanese capital market has historically relied on neither a source of external capital nor an external source of discipline on corporate management (Gerlach 1992). Market-based influence by independent and institutional investors is replaced by a closely connected community of mutually positioned, long-term trading partners. The forging of this stable relationship-based governance system has gone hand in hand with the development of an internal labor market.

Under lifetime employment, managers of large Japanese firms are sheltered by their affiliate-firm shareholders from the pressure facing US managers for radical labor cost reductions when firm performance declines. Even when staff reductions are necessary, voluntary leaves and long-term phasing out of positions are preferred. There is also a "Japanese-style layoff system," under which employees in firms in the depressed industries are transferred to firms in the growth industries (Gerlach 1992).

Furthermore, the lack of an external labor market motivates firms to invest in firm- and relationship-specific human capital (Gilson and Roe 1998) and motivates employees to strengthen their commitment toward the firm and its trading partners. Hence, both the relational capital and internal labor markets reinforce each other and produce a congruent system of monitoring and incentives for both owners and managers.

As mentioned before, the development of institutions is nonrecursive. The practice of lifetime employment fosters the closure of external labor markets. Similarly, the development of bank-centered, relational capital markets in the Japanese economy prevents the development of robust primary and secondary capital markets found in the transactional system. Macey and Miller (1995) have criticized the powerful banks in the Japanese corporate governance scheme by suggesting that the system prevents equity claimants from undertaking socially optimal risks, thereby hindering the development of robust capital markets.

The relationship-based system of corporate governance in Japan also substitutes for the more market-oriented transactional system in the US. For instance, banks, affiliate-firm shareholders, and corporate group structures play a role that is similar to that of takeovers and proxy fights in the US (Kester 1991). Cross shareholding among Japanese keiretsu firms serves to keep the internal labor market in place; it serves the same function as poison pills, greenmail, and shark repellents do in US firms. Likewise, the main bank system serves as a substitute for the market of corporate control (Aoki et al. 1994). In sum, the Japanese bank-oriented system is said to provide better monitoring and control of the moral hazard problem (see Macey and Miller 1995, for details).

Firms that have close ties to Japanese banks have been shown to increase shareholder wealth in important investment decisions, such as acquisitions. In a study on acquisitions in Japan, Kang et al. (2000) found "announcement returns display a strong positive association with the strength of an acquirer's relationships with banks." This effect is contrary to the US evidence that shows that acquiring firms often lose value upon acquisition announcement. However, Kang et al.'s study also found that these returns were greater when the banking sector was healthy. As another study suggests, there is collateral damage to firms that have close affiliation with banks when the banking sector performs poorly as it has in recent years (Kang and Stulz 2000). In general, Japanese banks control the moral hazard of firms with which they have strong ownership and credit relationships, reducing the banks' aggregate risk, which contributes to profitability. This superiority in controlling moral hazard suggests that Japanese firms would find bank financing more attractive than capital-market financing. Although banks reduce the potential gain from investing in the stock market by limiting upside gains to residual claimants, concentrated ownership patterns reduce the need to pursue costly hostile takeovers. This, together with the substitution for external monitoring mechanisms in transactional capital markets and the superiority of banks in handling the moral hazard problem, contributes to why there is little need for a strong equity capital market in Japan. The relational capital market goes hand in hand with the internal labor market, giving rise to effective corporate governance in the Japanese keiretsu system.

> Proposition 3: Institutional congruence is achieved in a relationship-based governance system when the capital market is more relational in nature and the labor market is internal.

4.3.2.2 Emphasis on Exploitative Innovations

The relationship-based governance system mitigates incentive, information, and control problems (Aoki et al. 1994) via concentrated ownership. The greater concentration of ownership overcomes incentive or free-riding problems associated with monitoring (Gedajlovic and Shapiro 2002). With significant stakes as both shareholders and debt holders, Japanese banks have a strong incentive to monitor management action to safeguard their own interests. Relational capital markets are also characterized by dedicated capital. The dominant owners of established firms are virtually permanent owners who seek long-term appreciation. Suppliers and customers own stakes in each other, with the aim not of profiting from share ownership so much as cementing their business relationships. While being protected from pressure to maximize short-term profit that managers in contractual capital markets face, managers in relational capital markets can allocate resources in pursuit of maximizing long-term profit.

While relational capital markets give rise to dedicated, concentrated ownership that causes long-term orientation, they also have important disadvantages. In relational capital markets, firms maintain stable, close relationships with financial institutions and other firms. Thus, in raising funds, firms turn to a few banks rather than to a myriad of diffused owners as in the capital markets in the US. In Japan, unless a firm can persuade its main bank, it is unlikely to obtain funds from other banks and financial institutions, which usually respect the main bank's evaluation. This small number of potential investors does not generate underinvestment problems in mature industries and in financing exploitative innovations, which entails less uncertainty about their return and risk. However, in financing emerging fields and explorative innovation entailing higher unpredictability, the small number of potential investors easily turns into underinvestment. Indeed, the small number of potential investors in relationship-based systems does not generate a wide range of opinions, which is crucial to financing explorative innovation.

In the labor market context, there are two dimensions that bear on innovation: risk-taking propensity and knowledge creation. The lack of external labor markets makes the costs of exit exceedingly high.

While firm-specific, human capital is crucial to improving internal coordination and recognizing and utilizing the firm's idiosyncratic competencies, it increases the costs of exit because its value sharply declines outside employment within the firm. Furthermore, internal labor markets have difficulties in providing strong incentives for risk taking, due to the internal norms of equity and fairness. This is the case even in the US firms, which traditionally appreciate individual excellence. Taken together, risk taking inside the internal labor market may involve low upside returns yet high downside risks, which make managers more risk averse in pursuing innovation. As a consequence, internal labor markets are less likely to induce managers to pursue explorative and revolutionary innovations.

In regard to knowledge creation, compared to the market-based system, tacit, firm-specific, and relationship-specific knowledge is accumulated in the relationship-based system. In fact, knowledge creation and innovation are the responsibility of each of the employees in Japan (Jin 2001).

Also, firm-specific knowledge and social capital nurtured and reinforced by internal labor markets, facilitate sharing and transfer of skills, capabilities, and knowledge inside the firm. Therefore, in Japan, human capital is centered on shop floor experience, cross-functional knowledge integration, and individual capabilities in contributing to group knowledge. Thus, internal labor markets are supportive of exploitative and incremental innovations. Japanese firms have been known for their prowess in producing process innovation rather than product innovation, and in adapting and improving on existing technology rather than creating new technology (Imai and Itami 1984; Mansfield 1988). The famous practices of just-in-time delivery, quality circles, and job rotations demonstrate Japanese focus on incremental improvement in their knowledge creation systems. Such characteristics of the Japanese innovation strategy are a product of their heavy reliance on internal labor markets.

However, heavy reliance on internal labor markets constrains the firm's capabilities to recognize and mobilize skills, capabilities, knowledge, and capabilities outside the firm.

While promoting firm-specific knowledge, shared language, and social capital, internal labor markets tend to engender inward-looking myopia (Kogut and Zander 1992, 1996). Coordination is good within the firm but poor across firms, although keiretsu affiliation may facilitate sharing within the larger network. As a consequence, under internal labor markets, innovations tend to be exploitative in nature and innovations that require radical change on existing technology base or cross-pollination of technologies dispersed in multiple industries are relatively rare. In sum, firms in a national economy with a relational capital market and internal labor market are more likely to pursue innovations that are exploitative (Levinthal and March 1993; March 1991) and evolutionary (Utterback 1994; Tushman and O'Reilly 1996). Relationship-based governance systems are in agreement with static efficiency, that is, the efficiency realized from the refinement of existing products, processes, or capabilities (Ghemawat and Costa 1993). This can be supported by the global competitiveness of Japanese firms in mature, complex fabricating manufacturing sectors, such as automobile, home electronics, and optomechatronics, where exploitative innovation is the key to success (Jin 2001).

Proposition 4: Relationship-based governance systems are more likely to produce exploitative innovations and static efficiency in the economy.

4.4 Discussion

Although our model focuses on ideal innovation types facilitated by a match between capital and labor market systems, more than one type of innovation exists in each system. As discussed in the following section (see Fig. 4.1), we examine how market-based governance systems make institutional adjustments to mitigate their disadvantages by incorporating relationship-based governance elements. Likewise, we discuss similar adjustments in relationship-based governance systems. Once these institutional adjustments are discussed, we elaborate on the implications for public policies designed to encourage entrepreneurial entry, high tech entrepreneurial management, and global competitiveness.

4.4.1 Institutional Adjustments: Market-Based Systems

The market-based system has the dynamic advantage of generating explorative and revolutionary innovation. In many cases, explorative and revolutionary innovation is experimented with by entrepreneurial start-ups since established firms fail to offer strong incentives to promote risk-taking due to internal norms of equity and fairness. Established firms may also be less willing to recognize the value of emerging technologies that would render their own competencies obsolete (Christensen 1997). By contrast, start-up firms can be relatively free from the incentive and cognitive limitations of established firms (Wright et al. 2000), and market-based systems provide supportive environments for the formation of start-ups. In the presence of flexible labor markets, talented engineers are willing to take the risk of joining entrepreneurial start-ups. In turn, the arm's-length type of capital market provides risk capital to entrepreneurial start-ups and ways to liquidate the investment once start-ups become successful.

Indeed, the emergence of the "new economy" has mainly been fueled by entrepreneurial start-ups backed by venture capital. Many studies of US firms have documented the frequent fall of incumbent firms and the concomitant rise of successful start-ups in the face of discontinuous technological changes (Abernathy and Utterback 1978; Christensen 1997; Tushman and Anderson 1986).

While the market-based system is associated with the dynamism, flexibility, and fluidity necessary for experimentation and exploration, it fails to furnish strong incentives and efficient mechanisms to monitor and influence management action of established firms. As a consequence, investors look for short-term gains from their investments, which further leads to a short-term orientation in management decisions.

The resulting "myopia" has often been blamed for being one of the primary causes of underinvestment in strategic resources (e.g., R&D) and subsequent decline in the global competitiveness of US established firms (Hill et al. 1988). To this extent, some institutional adjustments might be necessary to improve the global competitiveness of established firms.

For instance, the increased concentration of institutional ownership, which currently accounts for 56% of US outstanding shares (Edwards and Hubbard 2000), might constitute such institutional adjustments (Black 1997). With sizable ownership stakes, institutions have strong incentives and power to become influential shareholders and monitors. The spread of institutional activism suggests that institutions increasingly rely on "voice" to influence management decisions instead of "exit" from equity positions (Pound 1997). Hoskisson et al. (2002) found that pension fund (versus retail mutual fund) investors were particularly aligned with established firm managers to not only overcome agency problems, but also have longer time horizons necessary to promote more strategic investments and innovation. Thus, the growth of institutional ownership can reduce agency problems stemming from diffused ownership and help overcome problems with innovation.

4.4.2 Institutional Adjustments: Relationship-Based Systems

Although promoting a long-term orientation in resource allocation and being effective in facilitating exploitative and incremental innovation, the relationship-based system has its own Achilles' heel. It fails to provide strong incentives and environments to experiment with explorative and revolutionary innovation. When Japanese firms competed mainly on the adaptation and improvement of foreign technologies, the relationship-based system worked well. As Japanese firms compete at the technological frontier, however, their inability to generate explorative and revolutionary innovation becomes a liability.

Some institutional adjustments, facilitated by globalization and deregulation, are needed in order to promote more explorative innovations for Japanese firms to remain competitive in the global market. Although all large firms in Japan have main bank relationships, some of them are independent of major keiretsu. These independent firms, unlike keiretsu firms, have a more arm's-length type of relationship with shareholders and business partners. Although independent firms cannot substitute for the vibrant venture capital market found in the US, they provide additional institutional pluralism in the Japanese economy, allowing for more explorative innovation than would otherwise be the case. Indeed, independent firms, such as Sony and Honda, tend to be more risk seeking, innovative, and flexible. According to Gerlach (1992), relative to keiretsu firms, independent firms have a far greater presence in consumer markets (vis-à-vis producer markets), which also corroborates their high risk-taking propensity, innovativeness, and flexibility. The penetration of foreign capital brought by the globalization of capital markets also helps provide more private capital for riskier explorative innovation.

As mentioned above, explorative innovations are usually developed by entrepreneurial start-ups. Recently, many measures have been taken to increase start-up rates. The supply of risky capital has been enhanced, and exit mechanisms, such as the IPO market for venture capitalists, have been improved (Imai and Kawagoe 2000). Similarly, Japanese firms have been pursuing leveraged buyouts where major players have been creating new organizational independence through management and investor-led buyouts (Wright et al. 2003). Although it remains to be seen how effective these measures will be, they certainly constitute attempts of more market-based components. As we explain next, the difficulty of these incremental adjustments is also found in making corresponding changes in public policy and the institutional environment.

4.4.3 *Implications for Public Policy*

Our institutional congruence model offers clear policy implications. Many scholars and policymakers claim that, owing to rapid globalization, the convergence of institutions and corporate governance is likely. To the extent that institutions and corporate governance systems affect corporate innovation systems and global competitiveness, firm-level competition in global markets indeed represents competition between corporate governance systems (Porter 1992). As global competition weeds out poor governance systems, "global standards" of governance systems are likely to emerge. However, past predictions of such convergence seem to be premature. During the 1980s, for instance, it was fashionable to decry the shortsightedness of the market-based governance system. In spite of repeated calls for restructuring US institutions to move toward the more relationship-based model that prevails in Japan (Porter 1992), the US system still remains market-based. Likewise, the recent Asian crisis raised concerns about inefficiencies embedded in relationship-based systems, calling for governance system reform in Japan.

However, the Japanese system still remains predominantly relationship-based (Gedajlovic and Shapiro 2002; Johnston and McAlevery 1998).

Our argument suggests that institutions shape a development path by favoring a new institution that increases dominance and productivity of the existing institutions. Therefore, institutions should be analyzed together – not just in piecemeal fashion. Imitating piecemeal aspects of the other system is seldom enough to create momentum for change. Unless other complementary supporting institutions change accordingly, initial changes often become ineffective or are reversed. Promoting entrepreneurial start-ups in Japan is one example. The infusion of additional venture capital alone would not meet the needs of such startups. The relative immobility of Japanese labor markets makes it difficult for entrepreneurs to lure engineering and management talent away from established firms. The lack of consulting and law firms that help start-up processes makes starting new independent ventures more onerous. Social value systems favoring established firms over small firms discourage talent from leaving large firms and starting their own firms in the first place. Unless increases in venture capital are supplemented by increased mobility of labor force, emergence of related service providers, and changes in social value systems, Japan is unlikely to see high rates of start-up formation compared to places like Silicon Valley in the US, where each of the associated complementary institutions stated above exist.

4.4.4 Implications for High-Tech Management

Our institutional congruence model linking governance systems and corporate innovation provides managerial implications for high-tech firms. Market-based systems facilitate explorative and revolutionary innovation rather than exploitative and incremental innovation; the reverse is true for relationship-based systems. Thus, firms in each system should recognize and act upon the strengths and weaknesses associated with the dominance and path dependence of their institutions.

For instance, advantages in nurturing entrepreneurial start-ups of market-based systems pose both threats and opportunities to established firms. On the one hand, established firms in market-based systems are often challenged and replaced by start-ups because of their relative disabilities in recognizing and pursuing radical and disruptive innovations (Chesbrough 1999; Christensen 1997; Utterback 1994). Thus, for established firms competing in a rapidly evolving industry, it becomes essential for them to think about how to improve their internal capabilities of recognizing, nurturing, and exploiting radical and disruptive innovations (Foster and Kaplan 2001). Setting aside some portions of resources for radical innovations (Wheelwright and Clark 1992), establishing internal units mimicking incentives and autonomy of start-ups (Bart 1988), and improving overall entrepreneurial orientation (Lumpkin and Dess 1996) would help in this regard.

On the other hand, the availability of a plethora of independent start-ups provides established firms with an alternative route of monitoring, experimenting, and acting upon emerging technological opportunities. Indeed, many high-tech firms in the US have set up corporate venture capital operations to tap into a wider range of ideas and expertise outside (Gompers and Lerner 1999; Watts 2001). While capital gains cannot be ignored, these corporate venture capital operations usually emphasize strategic benefits of developing new business opportunities and strengthening core businesses.

By contrast, established firms in relationship-based systems are relatively free from the competitive pressure of the entrepreneurial start-ups. Without disruption by start-ups, established firms often play a significant role in creating and leading high-tech industries. However, such continuity and stability becomes a source of liability in cases when firms compete against competitors from the market-based systems in the global market context. Although maintaining leadership in domestic markets, established firms in relationship-based systems tend to play a catch-up game in global markets, thereby foregoing monopolistic rent associated with first-mover advantages. To compete globally, established firms in relationship-based systems should also improve their capabilities to deal with radical and disruptive technologies. They can do so by changing the resource allocation pattern, organizational structure, and corporate culture. Furthermore, due to the lack of promising start-ups domestically, international diversification can help these firms to link with ideas and expertise outside. In fact, Hurry et al. (1992) report that high-tech venture investments in the US by Japanese firms embrace the strategic logic of securing implicit call options on new technologies, which are often followed by further investments to fully exploit emerging opportunities.

4.4.5 Implications for Global Competitiveness

The linkage between governance system differences and global competitiveness is clearly illustrated by the semiconductor industry (Thomas and Waring 1999). Japanese firms outperform US firms in memory chip markets (e.g., DRAMs). Although it was the US firms who took the lead from the inception of this market, their competitiveness in generating and taking advantage of exploitative innovations was surpassed by the Japanese memory chip manufacturers. A possible reason is that the long-term commitment from constituents including shareholders, debtholders, labor, and suppliers allowed Japanese firms to focus on improvements in process technology, enabling the low-cost manufacturing necessary for the success in memory chip markets (Johnson et al. 1989; Rappa 1985). However, Japanese firms are not as competitive in the logic chip markets (e.g., microprocessors) of the same semiconductor industry. Success in the logic chip markets requires excellence in product design and technology rather than in manufacturing and process technology, and the US firms outperform Japanese firms in these latter markets. The dynamism and fluidity characterizing the US markets for capital and labor greatly facilitate a focus on product innovation as well as on the formation of start-ups. Note that the continuity and commitment of the Japanese system proved to be superior in memory chip markets, while the dynamism and fluidity of the US system allowed for superiority in logic chip markets.

In a similar vein, Anchordoguy (2000) relies on governance systems for explaining why Japanese firms lag behind in the computer software industry despite their global successes in related areas, such as computer hardware, telecommunication equipment, and memory chips. Bank-centered financial systems, lifetime and seniority-based employment systems, and social value systems in favor of large firms have discouraged the formation of start-ups – the key source of dynamism, creativity, and entrepreneurship necessary for building a healthy software industry. Uncontested by start-ups, the large hardware makers were able to shape and dominate the software market (Cottrell 1996). They offered computer systems based on close, incompatible standards in which software and hardware were bundled together. Such bundling and closed standards substantially reduced competition in both hardware and software markets and made it difficult for strong, independent software houses to emerge. Furthermore, economies of scale and continuous improvements on product and process, which are the strengths of relationship-based systems, have little relevance to success in the software industry. Indeed, the very institutional arrangements that explain Japan's success of catch-up strategies in computer hardware, telecommunication equipment, and memory chips are the major source of its weakness in computer software. As Benner and Tushman (2002) suggest, systems that focus on incremental innovation may become focused on exploitation and efficiency, such that exploration and long-term product innovation are not emphasized.

Market- and relationship-based governance systems create different effects on the formation of startup firms (Chesbrough 1999). In the US, an entrepreneur with a promising idea can team up with other engineers and managers, utilizing seed money from angel investors or venture capitalists, owing to flexible labor markets and venture capital markets. The lack of such flexible markets in Japan renders the formation of start-ups much more difficult. In the US, start-ups and venture capital made significant contributions to the creation of high-tech industries, such as semiconductor, software, and hard-disk drive businesses. However, it was usually large, established firms that played significant roles in creating Japanese high-tech industries. Recent studies corroborate such a comparative pattern.

While the US software industry was pioneered by start-ups (Steinmuller 1996), it was established firms that shaped the Japanese software industry (Cottrell 1996). Christensen (1997) reported that architectural changes in hard-disk drives frequently led to pioneering US incumbents being displaced, making the hard-disk drive industry a perilous place for established US firms. In contrast, however, leading Japanese incumbents undergoing the same architectural changes were much less likely to be replaced, as reported by Chesbrough (1999).

The comparative differences suggest that the viability of established firms (or start-up firms) in producing innovations cannot be understood unless the nature of the governance systems in which they operate is more fully considered. In market-based systems, start-ups often challenge established competitors by taking advantage of the inabilities of established firms in recognizing and organizing for radical and disruptive innovation on the one hand and by taking advantage of dynamism, flexibility, and fluidity in labor and capital markets on the other hand. However, established firms in relationship-based systems are for the most part, insulated, from the competition of start-ups and compete among themselves. This might explain Nelson's (1998, p. 326) observation that "new products that were pioneered by new firms in the US, were pioneered (somewhat later) by established firms in Europe and Japan."

To conclude, a country is more likely to gain global competitiveness in markets whose innovation requirements are well supported by its governance system. US firms often lead global markets when rapid introduction of breakthrough and disruptive innovation drives competition. Due to the dynamism and fluidity of the market-based systems, capital and human resources are easily mobilized and combined to pursue breakthrough and disruptive innovation, sometimes via the formation of startups.

On the other hand, Japanese firms tend to be globally competitive in markets where incremental innovations, continuous improvements, and manufacturing excellence are more important. Continuity and commitment in relationship-based systems allow for long-term and firm-specific investments (such as in human capital), which are conducive to incremental innovations, continuous improvements, and process innovations.

4.5 Conclusions

This article provides an answer to the debate on the convergence of national corporate governance systems. Taking an institutional perspective, we argue that it is the congruence between capital and labor markets that gives rise to governance efficiency, which subsequently has impacts on corporate innovation and entrepreneurship and global competitiveness. Both market- and relationship-based systems have their own strengths and weaknesses. Dynamism, flexibility, and diversity of the market-based systems are supportive of explorative and revolutionary innovations while continuity, stability, and commitment of relationship-based systems are supportive of exploitative and incremental innovations. Such linkages between national governance systems and innovation systems indicate that a country is more likely to gain global competitiveness in markets whose innovation requirements are well supported by its national governance system. The US tends to dominate markets on the technological frontier, where technological change is rapid and unpredictable and where competitiveness is driven by exploration and invention rather than by continuous improvements and manufacturing excellence; these markets are often where Japanese firms lag behind. From an individual firm's standpoint, efforts should be made to exploit the strengths and neutralize the weaknesses of its national governance system.

We argue that it is market-based systems of short-term orientation – rather than relationship-based systems of long-term orientation – that better facilitate explorative and revolutionary innovations. Behind this apparent contraction lies an interesting trade-off associated with national governance systems. The transactional capital market featuring innumerable, diverse, atomistic investors is indeed responsible for short-term orientation, which goes against the pursuit of explorative innovations.

However, the same characteristics of the transactional capital market are also sources of dynamism, flexibility, and diversity essential in funding explorative innovation. This is the case for the external labor market, too. With a high incidence of interfirm mobility, the external labor market discourages firm-specific investment and commitment on the part of both employers and employees. However, it is also high interfirm mobility rates and dubitable commitment that help start-ups to recruit key personnel. Thus, market-based systems come with the trade-off between short-term orientation on the one hand, and dynamism, flexibility, and diversity on the other hand.

References

Abernathy W, Utterback J (1978) Patterns of industrial innovation. Tech Rev 80:40–47

Allen F (1993) Strategic management and financial markets. Strategic Manage J 14:11–22

Anchordoguy M (2000) Japan's software industry: a failure of institutions? Res Policy 29:391–408

Aoki M (1988) Information, incentives, and bargaining in the Japanese economy. Cambridge University Press, Cambridge

Aoki M, Patrick H, Sheard P (1994) The Japanese main bank systems: An introductory overview. In: Aoki M, Patrick H (eds) The Japanese main bank system: Its relevancy for developing and transforming economies. Oxford University Press, Oxford, pp 3–50

Bart CK (1988) New venture units: use them wisely to manage innovation. Sloan Manage Rev 29(4):35–43

Baysinger BD, Hoskisson RE (1990) The composition of boards of directors and strategic control. Acad Manage Rev 15:72–87

Benner MJ, Tushman ML (2002) Process management and technological innovation: a longitudinal study of the photography and paint industries. Admin Sci Quart 47:676–706

Benner MJ, Tushman ML (2003) Exploitation, exploration, and process management: the productivity dilemma revisited. Acad Manage Rev 28:238–256

Berglof E (1990) Capital structure as a mechanism of control: a comparison of financial systems. In: Aoki M, Gustafsson B, Williamson OE (eds) The firm as a nexus of treaties. Sage, London

Black BS (1997) Institutional investors and corporate governance: the case for institutional voice. In: Chew DH (ed) Studies in international corporate finance and governance systems. Oxford University Press, New York, pp 160–173

Black BS, Gilson RJ (1998) Venture capital and the structure of capital markets: banks versus stock markets. J Finan Econ 47:243–277

Blair M (1995) Ownership and control: rethinking corporate governance for the twenty-first century. Brookings Institution, Washington, DC

Bogle JC (1999) Creating shareholder value for mutual fund shareholders. Corp Board 20(114):1–6

Chesbrough HW (1999) The organizational impact of technological change: a comparative theory of national institutional factors. Ind Corp Change 8:447–485

Christensen C (1997) The innovator's dilemma: when new technologies cause great firms to fail. Harvard Business School Press, Boston, MA

Coff R (1997) Human assets and management dilemmas: coping with hazards on the road to resource-based theory. Acad Manage Rev 22:374–402

Cottrell T (1996) Standards and the arrested development of the Japanese microcomputer software industry. In: Mowery D (ed) The international computer software industry: a comparative study of industry evolution and structure (. Oxford University Press, Oxford, pp 131–164
Dvorak P, Guth RA, Singer J, Zaun T (2001) Frayed by recession, Japan's corporate ties are coming unraveled. Wall St J 1:A1
Economist (1998) Business: wild careers. Economist 14:67
Edwards FR, Hubbard G (2000) The growth of institutional stock ownership: a promise unfulfilled. J Appl Corp Fin 13(3):92–104
Fama E, Jensen M (1983) Separation of ownership and control. J Law Econ 26:301–325
Filatotchev I, Buck T, Zhukov V (2000) Downsizing in privatized firms in Russia, Ukraine, and Belarus. Acad Manage J 43(3):286–304
Filatotchev I, Hoskisson RE, Buck T, Wright M (1996) Corporate restructuring in Russian privatizations: implications for U.S. investors. Calif Manage Rev 38(2):87–105
Foster R, Kaplan S (2001) Creative destruction: why companies that are built to last underperform the market and how to successfully transform them. Currency Doubleday, New York
Francis J, Smith A (1995) Agency costs and innovation: some empirical evidence. J Acc Econ 19:383–409
Gedajlovic E, Shapiro DM (2002) Ownership structure and firm profitability in Japan. Acad Manage J 45:565–575
Gerlach ML (1992) Alliance capitalism: the social organization of Japanese business. University of California Press, Berkeley, CA
Ghemawat P, Costa RIJ (1993) The organizational tension between static and dynamic efficiency (special issue). Strategic Manage J 14:59–73
Gilson RJ, Roe MJ (1998). Lifetime employment: labor peace and the evolution of Japanese corporate governance. Paper presented at the Sloan Project on Corporate Governance at Columbia Law School, May
Gompers PA, Lerner J (1999) The venture capital cycle. MIT Press, Cambridge, MA
Groenewegen J (1997) Institutions of capitalism: American, European, and Japanese systems compared. J Econ Issues 31:333–347
Hill CWL, Hitt MA, Hoskisson RE (1988) Declining U.S. competitiveness: reflections on a crisis. Acad Manage Exec 11(1):51–60
Hirschman A (1970) Exit, voice, and loyalty. Harvard University Press, Cambridge, MA
Holmstrom B (1989) Agency costs and innovation. J Econ Behav Organ 12:305–327
Hoshi, T. (1998). Understanding Japanese corporate governance. Paper presented at the Sloan Project on Corporate Governance at Columbia Law School, May
Hoshi T, Kashyap A, Scharfstein D (1990) The role of banks in reducing the cost of financial distress in Japan. J Fin Econ 27:67–88
Hoskisson RE, Busenitz LW (2002) Market uncertainty and learning distance in corporate entrepreneurship entry mode choice. In: Hitt MA, Ireland RD, Camp SM, Sexton DL (eds) Strategic entrepreneurship: Creating a new mindset. Blackwell, Oxford, pp 151–172
Hoskisson RE, Hitt MA, Johnson RA, Grossman W (2002) Conflicting voices: the effects of ownership heterogeneity and internal governance on corporate strategy. Acad Manage J 45:697–716
Hurry D, Miller A, Bowman EH (1992) Calls on high-technology: Japanese exploration of venture capital investments in the United States. Strategic Manage J 13:85–101
Imai KI, Itami H (1984) Interpenetration of organization and market. Int J Ind Organ 2:285–310
Imai Y, Kawagoe M (2000) Business start-ups in Japan: problems and policies. Oxford Rev Econ Policy 16(2):114–123
Jensen MC, Meckling WH (1976) Theory of the firm: managerial behavior, agency costs and ownership structure. J Fin Econ 11:5–50
Jin D (2001) The dynamics of knowledge regimes: technology, culture and competitiveness in the USA and Japan. Continuum, New York
Johnson CA, Tyson LDA, Zysman J (1989) Politics and productivity: how Japan's development strategy works. HarperBusiness, New York

Johnston S, McAlevery L (1998) Stable shareholdings and Japan's bubble economy: an historical overview. Strategic Manage J 19:1101–1107

Kang JK, Shivdasani A, Yamada T (2000) The effect of bank relations on investment decisions: an investigation of Japanese takeover bids. J Fin 55:2197–2218

Kang JK, Stulz RM (2000) Do banking shocks affect borrowing firm performance? An analysis of the Japanese experience. J Bus 73:1–23

Kaplan SN (1997) Corporate governance and corporate performance: a comparison of Germany, Japan, and the U.S. In: Chew DH (ed) Studies in international corporate finance and governance systems. Oxford University Press, New York, pp 251–258

Kester WC (1991) Japanese takeovers: the global contest for corporate control. Harvard Business School Press, Boston, MA

Kim H, Hoskisson RE (1997) Market (United States) versus managed (Japanese) governance. In: Keasey K, Thompson S, Wright M (eds) Corporate governance: economic, management, and financial issue. Oxford University Press, New York, pp 174–199

Knack S, Keefer P (1997) Does social capital have an economic payoff? A cross-country investigation. Quart J Econ 112(4):1251–1288

Kogut B, Zander U (1992) Knowledge of the firm, combinative capabilities, and the replication of technology. Organ Sci 3:383–397

Kogut B, Zander U (1996) What firms do? Coordination, identity, and learning. Organ Sci 7(5):502–518

Levinthal DA, March JG (1993) The myopia of learning. Strategic Manage J 14:95–112

Lumpkin GT, Dess GG (1996) Clarifying the entrepreneurial orientation construct and linking it to performance. Acad Manage Rev 21:135–172

Macey JM, Miller GP (1995) Corporate governance and commercial banking: a comparative examination of Germany, Japan, and the United States. Standford Law Rev 48(1):73–112

Madhok A (1997) Cost, value and foreign market entry mode: the transaction and the firm. Strategic Manage J 18:39–61

Mansfield E (1988) Industrial R&D in Japan and the United States: a comparative study. Am Econ Rev 78(2):223–228

March JG (1991) Exploration and exploitation in organizational learning. Organ Sci 2:71–87

McGuire J, Dow S (2003) The persistence and implications of Japanese keiretsu organization. J Int Bus Stud 34:374–388

Milgrom P, Roberts J (1995) Complementarities and fit strategy, structure, and organizational change in manufacturing. J Acc Econ 19:179–208

Nelson RR (1998) The co-evolution of technology, industrial structure, and supporting institutions. In: Dosi G, Teece DJ, Chytry J (eds) Technology, organization, and competitiveness. Oxford University Press, New York

Nelson RR, Rosenberg N (1993) Technical innovation and national systems. In: Nelson RR (ed) National innovation systems. Oxford University Press, New York

North DC (1990) Institutions, institutional change, and economic performance. Harvard University Press, Cambridge, MA

Pauly LW, Reich S (1997) National structures and multinational corporate behavior: enduring differences in the age of globalization. Int Organ 51(1):1–30

Porter ME (1992) Capital disadvantages: America's failing capital investment system. Harvard Bus Rev 62(3):65–82

Porter ME (1996) Competitive advantage, agglomeration economies, and regional policy. Int Reg Sci Rev 19:85–90

Porter ME (1997) Capital choices: changing the way America invests in industry. In: Chew DH (ed) Studies in international corporate finance and governance systems. Oxford University Press, New York, pp 5–17

Pound J (1997) Raiders, targets, and politics: the history and future of American corporate control. In: Chew DH (ed) Studies in international corporate finance and governance systems. Oxford University Press, New York, pp 147–159

Rappa MA (1985) Capital financing strategies of the Japanese semiconductor industry. Calif Manage Rev 27(2):85–99
Roe M (1994) Strong managers weak owners: the political roots of American corporate finance. Princeton University Press, Princeton, NJ
Schumpeter JA (1934) The theory of economic development: an inquiry into profits, capital, credit, interest, and the business cycle. Harvard University Press, Cambridge, MA
Sheard P (1994) Interlocking shareholdings and corporate governance. In: Aoki M, Dore R (eds) The Japanese firm: sources of competitive strength. Oxford University Press, New York
Stein J (1989) Efficient capital market, inefficient firms: a model of myopic corporate behavior. Quart J Econ 104(4):655–669
Steinmetz G (1995) German venture capitalists see big lift from listing on Nasdaq market in U.S. Wall St J 27:C7
Steinmuller E (1996) The US software industry: an analysis and interpretive history. In: Mowery D (ed) The international computer software industry: a comparative study of industry evolution and structure. Oxford University Press, Oxford
Thomas LG, Waring G (1999) Competing capitalisms: capital investment in American, German, and Japanese firms. Strategic Manage J 20:729–748
Tushman M, Anderson P (1986) Technological discontinuities and organizational environments. Admin Sci Quart 31:439–465
Tushman ML, O'Reilly CA (1996) Ambidextrous organizations: managing evolutionary and revolutionary change. Calif Manage Rev 38(4):8–30
Useem M (1992) Investor capitalism: how money managers are changing the face of corporate America. Basic Books, New York
Utterback JM (1994) Mastering the dynamics of innovation: how companies can seize opportunities in the face of technological change. Harvard Business School Press, Boston, MA
Watts RM (2001) Commercializing discontinuous innovations. Res Technol Manage 44(6):26–31
Weingast BR (1993) Constitutions as governance structure: the political foundations for secure markets. J Inst Theor Econ 149:286–311
Wheelwright SC, Clark KB (1992) Creating project plans to focus product development. Harvard Bus Rev 70(2):70–82
Williamson OE (1985) Economic institutions of capitalism. Free Press, New York
Wright M, Hoskisson RE, Busenitz LW, Dial J (2000) Entrepreneurial growth through privatization: the upside of management buyouts. Acad Manage Rev 25:591–601
Wright M, Kitamura M, Hoskisson RE (2003) Management buyouts and restructuring Japanese corporations. Long Range Plann 36(4):355–373
Yoshikawa T, Phan PH (2001) Alternative corporate governance systems in Japanese firms: implications for a shift to stockholder-centered corporate governance. Asia Pacific J Manage 18:183–205

Chapter 5
The Entrepreneurial Society

David B. Audretsch

Abstract This chapter explains why and how entrepreneurship has emerged as a driving force for economic growht, job creation and competitiveness. A framework is provided for understanding entrepreneurship in the global economy and why entrepreneurship policy has emerged as a bonafide instrument for growth and development.

5.1 Introduction

Over the course of the past six decade, the role of entrepreneurship in society and has changed dramatically. During the economic boom subsequent to the second World War, the importance of entrepreneurship and small business seemed to be fading away.

However, beginning in the late 1970s and gaining momentum into the next decades, entrepreneurship has become the engine of economic and social development throughout the world. The purpose of this chapter is to explain the emergence of what I have elsewhere termed as *The Entrepreneurial Society* and why this is important (Audretsch 2007). In particular, this chapter traces the evolution of the engine of economic growth and development from physical capital during the post-war era, to knowledge capital, and more recently to entrepreneurship capital. The chapter concludes that public policy has, accordingly, shifted its focus towards promoting entrepreneurship as an important key to economic growth, employment creation and competitiveness in globally linked markets.

5.2 Role of Entrepreneurship in the Solow Economy

Following the second World War, the policy debate focusing on growth and employment looked to the macroeconomic instruments of fiscal and monetary policy on the one hand, and the size and scale economies yielded by the large corporation on the

D.B. Audretsch(✉)
Ameritech Chair of Economic Development, Indiana University, Bloomington, IN, USA
email: daudrets@indiana.edu

D.B. Audretsch et al. (eds.), *New Frontiers in Entrepreneurship: Recognizing, Seizing, and Executing, Opportunities*, International Studies in Enterpreneurship,
DOI 10.1007/978-1-4419-0058-6_5,

other. Writing in the post-war era, Robert Solow (1956) was awarded the Nobel Prize for his model of economic growth based on what came to be termed the neoclassical production function. In the Solow model, two key factors of production – physical capital and (unskilled) labor, were econometrically linked to explain economic growth.

The sources of economic growth depicted by the Solow Model corresponded to the sources of growth in the actual post-World War II economy. The focus on physical capital as the key factor generating economic growth certainly corresponded to the post-war abundance of physical capital in the US. Several years after World War II, Robert Payne, the renowned historian from England, reflected, "There never was a country more fabulous than America. She sits bestride the world like a Colossus; no other power at any time in the world's history has possessed so varied or so great an influence on other nations … Half of the wealth of the world, more than half of the productivity, nearly two-thirds of the world machines are concentrated in American hands; the rest of the world lies in the shadow of American industry."[1]

Growth policy, if not shaped by the Solow theoretical growth model, certainly corresponded to the view that inducing investments in physical capital, in particular, was the key to generating economic growth and advances in worker productivity. The view of the economy characterized by the Solow model, framed the policy debate focusing on economic growth. The main mechanism for inducing higher growth rates was almost universally viewed as investments in physical capital. After all, the economy characterized by the Solow model was capital-driven. Increasing labor could increase the level of economic output, but not the rate of economic growth.

The policy focus on physical capital as the driving input for economic growth during the post-world war II era, generated a concomitant concern about the organization of that capital, both at industry and at firm levels. The emerging field of industrial organization, in particular, was charged with the task of identifying how the organization of capital, or structure of an industry, influenced economic performance. A generation of scholars produced theoretical and empirical evidence, suggesting that physical capital in many, but certainly not all, industries dictated a concentration of production, resulting in an oligopolisitic market structure characterized by a concentration of ownership in relatively few producers. In the post-war era, small firms and entrepreneurship were viewed as a luxury, perhaps needed by the West to ensure a decentralization of decision making, but in any case, obtained only at a cost to efficiency. Certainly, the systematic empirical evidence, gathered from both Europe and North America, documented a sharp trend towards a decreased role of small firms during the post-war period. Public policy towards small firms generally reflected the view of economists and other scholars that they were a drag on economic efficiency and growth, generated lower quality jobs in terms of direct and indirect compensation, and were generally on the way to becoming less important to the economy, if not threatened by long-term extinction. Some countries, such as the former Soviet Union, Sweden and France, adapted the policy stance of allowing small firms to gradually disappear and

[1] Cited in Halberstam (1993: 116).

account for a smaller share of economic activity. The public policy stance of the US reflected long-term political and social valuation of small firms, that seemed to reach back to the Jeffersonian traditions of the country. After all, in the 1890 debate in Congress, Senator Sherman vowed: "If we will not endure a King as a political power we should not endure a King over the production, transportation, and sale of the necessaries of life. If we would not submit to an emperor we should not submit to an autocrat of trade with power to prevent competition and to fix the price of any commodity."[2]

Preservationist policies were clearly at work in the creation of the US Small Business Administration. In the Small Business Act of 10 July, 1953, Congress authorized the creation of the Small Business Administration, with an explicit mandate to "aid, counsel, assist and protect … the interests of small business concerns".[3] The Small Business Act was clearly an attempt by Congress to halt the continued disappearance of small businesses and to preserve their role in the US economy.

Thus, in the traditional, managed economies of the post-war era, small firms and entrepreneurship were viewed as a luxury, perhaps needed by the West to ensure a decentralization of decision making, but in any case, obtained only at a cost to efficiency. Management scholars (Chandler 1977; Chandler 1990) generally backed this view up with compelling empirical evidence.

5.3 Knowledge as the Panacea to Growth?

The fall of the Berlin Wall, fell in 1989, triggered predictions of unprecedented economic growth and prosperity for the developed countries. Without the financial, military and psychological burdens of the cold war, a "peace dividend" was highly anticipated. However, the subsequent decade ushered in exactly the opposite, at least for Europe. Economic growth was stagnant and unemployed ratcheted to higher levels.

The traditional comparative advantage in mature, technologically moderate industries such as metalworking, machine tools and automobile production had provided an engine for growth, high employment, and economic stability, throughout Western Europe for most of the post-war economic period. This traditional comparative advantage was lost for two reasons. The first has to do with globalization, or the advent of competition from not just the emerging economies in Southeast Asia but also from the transforming economies of Central and Eastern Europe. The second factor has been the computer and telecommunications revolution. The new communications technologies have triggered a virtual spatial revolution in terms of the geography of production.

[2] Quoted from Scherer (1977: 980).

[3] http://www.sba.gov/aboutsba/sbahistory.html.

Globalization has triggered a virtual spatial revolution in terms of the geography of production. The (marginal) cost of transforming information across geographic space has been rendered to virtually nothing. Confronted with low-cost competition in foreign locations, producers in the high-cost countries have three options, apart from doing nothing and losing global market share: (1) reduce wages and other production costs sufficiently to compete with the low-cost foreign producers, (2) substitute equipment and technology for labor to increase productivity, and (3) shift production out of the high-cost location into the low-cost location.

Many of the European and American firms that have successfully restructured, resorted to the last two alternatives. Substituting capital and technology for labor, along with shifting production to lower-cost locations has resulted in waves of *Corporate Downsizing* throughout Europe and North America.

At the same time, it has generally preserved the viability of many of the large corporations. As record levels of both European and American stock indexes indicate, the companies have not generally suffered. For example, the headline story 'Deutschland: Export Weltmeister (von Arbeitsplätzen)' or 'Germany: Export World Leader (of jobs)' in the most prestigious weekly German magazine, *Der Spiegel*, reports 'Bye-bye "Made in Germany"'.[4] Employment in manufacturing rose throughout the era of the managed economy, increasing from 12.5 million in 1970 to 14.1 million in 1991. Then, as globalization hit home in Germany, manufacturing jobs crashed to a low of 10.2 million jobs by 2004. Between 1991 and 2004, the number of jobs in the German textile industry fell by 65%, from 274,658 to 94,432. In the construction industry, there was a 58% decrease in employment in Germany, from 1.9 million jobs to 778,000. In the metalworking industries, employment decreased from 476,299 to 250,024, or 47.5%. And in the heart and pride of German manufacturing, the machine tool industry, the number of jobs fell from 1.6 million to 947,448 or 39.1%.

Globalization did not change the importance of physical capital but rather drastically altered the geography of its location. The post-war distribution of physical capital highly concentrated in the United States, as Payne observed, did not prove to be sustainable. Rather, as first Western Europe and Japan recovered, but subsequent to 1989 Eastern Europe, and other parts of Asia as well, the comparative advantage of production based on physical capital shifted from the high-cost OECD countries to lower cost regions. As a result, employment in traditional manufacturing industries in the most developed countries plummeted (Audretsch 2007).

Thus, globalization triggered a shift in the competitiveness of the developed countries away from unskilled manufacturing towards economic activity based on ideas and knowledge. As Romer (1986) pointed out, investments in knowledge spill-over to have a multiplicative impact on economic growth. If physical capital was at the heart of the Solow economy, knowledge capital replaced it in the Romer economy. Most significantly, while it had proven feasible to locate economic activity based on physical capital at foreign locations, outsourcing and offshoring economic

[4] Bye-Bye Made in Germany. Der Spiegel 44:94–99.

ideas based on ideas, and in particular tacit knowledge, was less feasible. This suggested that the comparative advantage of high cost locations was shifting away from physical capital and towards knowledge or economic activity based on new ideas that could not costlessly be copied. While the policy goals of economic growth remained relatively unchanged, the Romer model reflected the emergence of a new emphasis on a strikingly different policy mechanism, knowledge capital, involving very different policy instruments, such as investments in human capital, research, and a focus on intellectual property protection (Romer 1986).

Investments in knowledge, such as human capital, R&D and patents, as well as broader aspects such as creativity, did not prove to be an automatic panacea for stagnant economic growth and rising unemployment. In what became known first as the *Swedish Paradox*, which was later adapted as the *European Paradox*, described the disappointment of economic growth that did not seem to respond to high levels of investment in knowledge.

Much has been made about the so-called *European Paradox*, where high levels of investment in new knowledge exist in both private firms as well as public research institutes and universities. Countries such as Sweden rank among the highest in terms of investment in research, at least as measured by the ratio of R&D to GDP (gross domestic product). Similarly, levels of human capital and education in Sweden as well as throughout many parts of Europe, rank among the highest in the world. Yet, growth rates remained stagnant and employment creation sluggish throughout the 1990s and into the new century.

Thus, it is now recognized that investment in scientific knowledge and research alone will not automatically generate growth and prosperity. Rather, such knowledge investments must penetrate what Audretsch et al. (2006) term the knowledge filter, in order to contribute to innovation, competitiveness and ultimately economic growth. In fact, the knowledge filter impeding the commercializing of investments in research and knowledge can be formidable. As the American Senator Birch Bayh warned, "A wealth of scientific talent at American colleges and universities – talent responsible for the development of numerous innovative scientific breakthroughs each year – is going to waste as a result of bureaucratic red tape and illogical government regulations …"[5] It is the knowledge filter that stands between investment in research on the one hand, and its commercialization through innovation, leading ultimately to economic growth, on the other. Certainly seen through the eyes of Senator Bayh, the magnitude of the knowledge filter is daunting, "What sense does it make to spend billions of dollars each year on government-supported research and then prevent new developments from benefiting the American people because of dumb bureaucratic red tape?"[6]

This is just as true for Europe. According to Garching Innovation, GmbH, "Would you build a car without wheels? Presumably not. But something similar

---

[5] Introductory statement of Birch Bayh, 13 September, 1978, cited from AUTUM (2004, p. 5).

[6] Statement by Birch Bayh, April 13, 1980, on the approval of S. 414 (Bayh-Dole) by the US Senate on a 91-4 vote, cited from AUTUM (2004, p. 16).

happens every day in Germany, at least when Research and Development is involved. We are investing around 17.5 billion Euros in publicly supported science and research. About half of that investment, around nine billion Euros is in basic research, which, even though it could, of course, be improved, is still at the cutting edge by global standards. However, we lack the three to four percent of this investment, required to transform these investments into new and innovative products. It is as if you would invest a huge sum of money to develop a new automobile, but in the end, realize there are not sufficient funds to purchase tires."[7]

In both of these European and American examples, there will be no, or at least only restricted knowledge spillovers. Investments were made in creating new knowledge, both privately from the firm, but also publicly, if generation of the new knowledge utilized any type of public knowledge emanating from research at universities or publicly provided investments in human capital. However, in the absence of knowledge spillover, such investments will not be appropriated either by the firm or by society. It must not be forgotten that the social investments of education and research are also expected to generate a return, in terms of growth and employment.

Thus, the spillover of knowledge that exists by assumption in the growth models, in fact, may not be so automatic, but may be impeded by a knowledge filter (Audretsch et al. 2006). The knowledge filter serves to impede, if not preempt, the spillover and commercialization of knowledge.

5.4 The Entrepreneurial Society

Entrepreneurship and small firms seemed, at least, as incompatible with the Romer knowledge-based economy, as they were in the capital-based Solow economy. The most prevalent theory of innovation in economics, the model of the knowledge production function, suggested that knowledge-generating inputs, such as research and development (R&D) were a prerequisite to generating innovative output. With their limited and meager investments in R&D, at least, in absolute terms, new and small firms did not seem to possess sufficient knowledge capabilities to be competitive in a knowledge-based economy.

Knowledge regarding both the determinants and the impact of innovative has been largely shaped by measurement. Measures of technological change have typically involved one of the three major aspects of the innovative process: (1) a measure of inputs into the process, such as R&D expenditures, or the share of the labor force accounted for by employees involved in R&D activities; (2) an intermediate output, such as the number of inventions that have been patented; or (3) a direct measure of innovative output.

[7] Konzeption eines Innovationsfonds der Deutschen Forschung (IFDF) zur Stärkung des Technologietransfers, *Garching Information*, 1/06.

The earliest sources of data R&D measured, indicated that virtually all of the innovative activity was undertaken by large corporations. As patent measures became available, the general qualitative conclusions did not change, although, it became clear that small firms were more involved with patent activity than with R&D. The development of direct measures of innovative activity, such as data bases measuring new product and process introductions in the market, indicated something quite different. In a series of studies, Acs and Audretsch (1988, 1990) found that while large firms in manufacturing introduced a slightly greater number of significant new innovations than entrepreneurial small firms, small-firm employment was only about half as great as large-firm employment, yielding an average small-firm innovation rate in manufacturing of 0.309, compared to a large-firm innovation rate of 0.202. The relative innovative advantage of small and large firms was found to vary considerably across industries. In some industries, such as computers and process control instruments, entrepreneurial small firms provide the engine of innovative activity. In other industries, such as pharmaceutical products and aircraft, large firms generate most of the innovative activity. Knowledge regarding both the determinants and the impact of technological change has been largely shaped by measurement.

Acs and Audretsch (1988, 1990) concluded that some industries are more conducive to small-firm entrepreneurial innovation, while others foster the innovative activity of large corporations, corresponding to the notion of distinct technological regimes – the routinized and entrepreneurial technological regimes.

The starting point for most theories of innovation had been the firm. In such theories, the firms are exogenous and their performance in generating technological change is endogenous. For example, in the most prevalent model found in the literature of technological change, the model of the *knowledge production function*, formalized by Griliches (1979), firms exist exogenously and then engage in the pursuit of new economic knowledge as an input into the process of generating innovative activity.

The knowledge production function has been found to hold most strongly at broader levels of aggregation. Where the relationship becomes less compelling, is at the disaggregated microeconomic level of the enterprise, establishment, or even line of business. For example, while Acs and Audretsch (1990) found that the simple correlation between R&D inputs and innovative output was 0.84 for four-digit standard industrial classification (SIC) manufacturing industries in the United States, it was only about half, 0.40 among the largest US corporations.

The model of the knowledge production function becomes even less compelling in view of the evidence by Acs and Audretsch, that entrepreneurial small firms are the engine of innovative activity in some industries, which raises the question, "Where do new and small firms get the innovation producing inputs, that is the knowledge?"

One answer, proposed by Audretsch (1995a b), is that, although the model of the knowledge production function may still be valid, the implicitly assumed unit of observation – at the level of the firm – may be less valid. The reason why the knowledge production function holds more closely for more aggregated degrees of observation, may be, that investment in R&D and other sources of new knowledge spills over for economic exploitation by third-party firms.

A large literature has emerged focusing on what has become known as the *appropriability problem.*[8] The underlying issue revolves around how firms which invest in the creation of new economic knowledge can best appropriate the economic returns from that knowledge (Arrow 1962). Audretsch (1995a, b) proposed shifting the unit of observation away from exogenously assumed firms to individuals – agents with endowments of new economic knowledge. But when the lens is shifted away from focusing upon the firm as the relevant unit of observation to individuals, the relevant question becomes, *How can economic agents with a given endowment of new knowledge best appropriate the returns from that knowledge?*

The appropriability problem confronting the individual may converge with that confronting the firm. Economic agents can and do work for firms, and even if they do not, they can potentially be employed by an incumbent firm. In fact, in a model of perfect information with no agency costs, any positive economies of scale or scope will ensure that the appropriability problems of the firm and individual converge. If an agent has an idea for doing something different than is currently being practiced by the incumbent enterprises – both in terms of a new product or process and in terms of organization – the idea, which can be termed as an innovation, will be presented to the incumbent enterprise. Because of the assumption of perfect knowledge, both the firm and the agent would agree upon the expected value of the innovation. But to the degree that any economies of scale or scope exist, the expected value of implementing the innovation within the incumbent enterprise will exceed that of taking the innovation outside of the incumbent firm to start a new enterprise. Thus, the incumbent firm and the inventor of the idea would be expected to reach a bargain, splitting the value added to the firm contributed by the innovation. The payment to the inventor – either in terms of a higher wage or some other means of remuneration – would be bounded between the expected value of the innovation, if it is implemented by the incumbent enterprise on the upper end, and by the return that the agent could expect to earn, if he used it to launch a new enterprise on the lower end.

The model proposed by Audretsch (1995a, b) refocused the unit of observation away from firms deciding whether to increase their output from a level of zero to some positive amount in a new industry, to individual agents in possession of new knowledge that, due to uncertainty, may or may not have some positive economic value. It is the uncertainty inherent in new economic knowledge, combined with asymmetries between the agent possessing that knowledge and the decision making vertical hierarchy of the incumbent organization, with respect to its expected value that potentially leads to a gap between the valuation of that knowledge.

Audretsch (1995a, b) suggested that divergences in the expected value regarding new knowledge will, under certain conditions, lead an agent to exercise what

[8]See Cohen and Levin (1989) and Baldwin and Scott (1987).

Albert O. Hirschman (1970) has termed as *exit* rather than *voice*, and depart from an incumbent enterprise to launch a new firm. But who is right, the departing agents or those agents remaining in the organizational decision making hierarchy who, by assigning the new idea a relatively low value, have effectively driven the agent with the potential innovation away? Ex post the answer may not be too difficult. But given the uncertainty inherent in new knowledge, the answer is anything but trivial a priori.

If all of the existing, status quo organizations could effectively move society into the future, there would be no particularly interesting or important role for entrepreneurship, at least, the version that is restricted to the creation of a new organization. That would mean that sufficient innovation was being generated by the status quo. If there were a deficiency of new, viable ideas, the problem area would lie in terms of people. However, the last decade or so has seen an explosion in concern about the investment society makes in what enables people to think up new ideas – education at all levels, R&D and universities. In some places, there is indeed a severe deficiency in human capital and education. In other places, the constraint may be less in terms of the formal education and more, in terms of creativity.

But in many contexts, the problem may lie less in the education, human capital, experience, or creativity of people, and be more attributable to the knowledge filter. People have ideas, aspirations, insights and visions about how to do things differently or better. That is, how to lead into a future that is better, and better equipped to compete globally. But in the actual doing of it, putting the idea into action, the implementation gets hung up in the knowledge filter.

By endogenously facilitating the spillover of knowledge created in a different organization, and perhaps for a different application, entrepreneurship may provide what Audretsch et al. (2006) describe as the missing link in economic growth (Audretsch and Keilbach 2007, 2008). Confronted with a formidable knowledge filter, public policy instruments emerging from new growth theory, such as investments in human capital, R&D, and university research may not result in adequate economic growth. One interpretation of the European Paradox, where such investments in new knowledge have certainly been vigorous and sustained, is that the presence of such an imposing knowledge filter chokes off the commercialization of those new investments, resulting in diminished innovative activity and, ultimately, stagnant growth.

By serving as a conduit for knowledge spillovers, entrepreneurship is the missing link between investments in new knowledge and economic growth. Thus, the spillover theory of knowledge entrepreneurship provides not just an explanation of why entrepreneurship has become more prevalent, as the factor of knowledge has emerged as a crucial source for comparative advantage, but also why entrepreneurship plays a vital role in generating economic growth. Entrepreneurship is an important mechanism permeating the knowledge filter to facilitate the spill over of knowledge, and ultimately generate economic growth.

Entrepreneurship policy to ignite economic growth is spreading throughout the developed countries. For example, in the Lisbon Accord of 2000, the EC made a formal commitment to becoming the entrepreneurship and knowledge leader in the world by 2020, in order to foster economic growth and prosperity on the continent. As Bresnahan and Gambardella (2004: 1) observe:

Clusters of high-tech industry, such as Silicon Valley, have received a great deal of attention from scholars and in the public policy arena. National economic growth can be fueled by development of such clusters. In the United States, the long boom of the 1980s and 1990s was largely driven by growth in the information technology industries in a few regional clusters. Innovation and entrepreneurship can be supported by a number of mechanisms operating within a cluster, such as easy access to capital, knowledge about technology and markets, and collaborators.

Entrepreneurship can contribute to economic growth by serving as a mechanism that permeates the knowledge filter. There is a virtual consensus that entrepreneurship revolves around the recognition of opportunities combined with the cognitive decision, to commercialize those opportunities by starting a new firm. If investments in new knowledge create opportunities that are asymmetric, in that they are more apparent or valued more highly by economic agents (potential entrepreneurs) than by the incumbent firms themselves, the only organizational context for commercializing that new idea will be a new firm. Thus, by serving as a conduit for knowledge spillovers that might otherwise not exist, entrepreneurship permeates the knowledge filter and provides the missing link to economic growth. Audretsch et al. (2006) show that those regions in Germany with the greatest amount of entrepreneurial activity also exhibit the highest growth rates.

5.5 Conclusions

A generation ago, scholars and public policy makers looked to large corporations engaged in manufacturing activities based on capital intensive production as the engine of economic growth, job creation and international competitiveness. More recently, ideas and knowledge became the focus of the public policy debate. The purpose of this paper has been to suggest that entrepreneurship has emerged as the new focal point for generating growth, jobs and competitiveness.

The role of entrepreneurship and small business has evolved considerably since the Second World War. What was once considered to be, perhaps, a necessary drain on Western economies, has become a central strategic instrument for competitiveness in global markets. Just as it has been important to understand how to manage entrepreneurial firms, it has now become, at least, as important to understand how to achieve an entrepreneurial society. While this emphasis on small entrepreneurial firms as engines of dynamic efficiency may seem startling after decades at looking to the corporate giants as engines of growth and development, may not be so new. Before the country was even half a century old, Alexis de Tocqueville, in 1835, reported, “What astonishes me in the United States is not so much the marvelous grandeur of some undertakings as the innumerable multitude of small ones.”

References

Acs ZJ, Audretsch DB (1990) Innovation and small firms. MIT Press, Cambridge
Acs ZJ, Audretsch DB (1988) Innovation in large and small firms: an empirical analysis. Am Econ Rev 78(4):678–690
Arrow KJ (1962) Economic welfare and the allocation of resources for invention. In: Nelson RR (ed) The rate and direction of inventive activity. Princeton University Press, Princeton
Audretsch DB (1995a) Innovation and industry evolution. MIT Press, Cambridge
Audretsch DB (1995b) Innovation and industry evolution. MIT Press, Cambridge
Audretsch DB (2007) The entrepreneurial society. Oxford University Press, New York
Audretsch DB, Keilbach M (2007) The theory of knowledge spillover entrepreneurship. J Manage Stud 44(7):1242–1254
Audretsch DB, Keilbach M (2008) Resolving the knowledge paradox: knowledge-spillover entrepreneurship and economic growth. Res Policy 37(10):1697–1705
Audretsch DB, Keilbach M, Lehmann E (2006) Entrepreneurship and economic growth. Oxford University Press, New York
Breshsnahan T, Gambardella A (2004) Building high tech clusters: silicon valley and beyond. Cambridge University Press, Cambridge
Chandler A (1977) The visible hand: the managerial revolution in American business. Belknap, Cambridge
Chandler A (1990) Scale and scope: the dynamics of industrial capitalism. Harvard University Press, Cambridge
Griliches Z (1979) Issues in assessing the contribution of R&D to productivity growth. Bell J Econ 10(Spring):92–116
Halberstam D (1993) The fifties. Villard Books, New York
Hirschman AO (1970) Exit, voice, and loyalty. Harvard University Press, Cambridge
Romer P (1986) increasing returns and long-run growth. J Polit Econ 94:1002–1037
Solow R (1956) A contribution to theory of economic growth. Quart J Econ 70:65–94

Part II
Mobilizing Capital for Fostering Entrepreneurship

Chapter 6
Mobilizing Capital for Fostering the Early Growth of Firms: The Role of Business Angels in Nascent European Entrepreneurship

Giovanni Battista Dagnino, Rosario Faraci, and Mario Sorrentino

Abstract Despite the important role recognized to outside equity in financing and fostering innovative entrepreneurial firms (i.e., entrepreneurial start-ups), relatively little is known about the key characteristics of the different fund-providers involved either in a temporal perspective (diverse stage of the early firm's life) or in an industry perspective (specialized equity investors). While business angels and venture capitalists are relatively common and welcome companions of entrepreneurs, various kinds of circumstances need to be accomplished and coordinated in order to establish and govern these relationships in a way that is really beneficial to all the parties. This chapter aims to discuss various aspects of the multifaceted relation between entrepreneurs seeking for finance to their early stage projects and business angels providing equity. In particular, we underscore the rationale for the emergence of the business angel networks in order to optimize search costs and the good match between supply and demand for funds. While business angel networks have found the way for their admittance in many European countries, in the USA, angel groups (or spontaneous investor associations) are far more developed. On the ground of a 5-year panel data extracted from the European Business Angel Network (EBAN), we explore in depth the intricacies and inefficiencies related to the action of the business angels networks in Europe and briefly juxtapose them to the Anglo-Saxon experience.

6.1 Introduction: Entrepreneurship as the Capability of Recognizing, Seizing and Executing Opportunities

The essence of entrepreneurship is recognizing, seizing and exploiting new and nascent opportunities (Zahra et al. 2006). In order to recognize, seize and exploit opportunities, we point to the fundamental of entrepreneurial capabilities intended

G.B. Dagnino (✉) and R. Faraci
University of Catania, Catania, Italy
e-mail: dagnino@unict.it

M. Sorrentino
Second University of Naples, Naples, Italy

D.B. Audretsch et al. (eds.), *New Frontiers in Entrepreneurship: Recognizing, Seizing, and Executing, Opportunities*, International Studies in Enterpreneurship,
DOI 10.1007/978-1-4419-0058-6_6,

as capabilities for growth and of wealth creation for the firm and thereby for the broad institutional environment.

Based on ideas presented by Venkataraman (1997), Shane (2003) defines entrepreneurship as "an activity that involves the discovery, evaluation and exploitation of opportunities to introduce new goods and services, ways of organizing, markets, processes, and raw materials through organizing efforts that previously had not existed" (pp. 4–5). As a central premise of his reflection, he contends that "entrepreneurship can be explained by considering the nexus of enterprising individuals and valuable opportunities... and by using that nexus to understand the processes of discovery and exploitation of opportunities; the acquisition of resources; entrepreneurial strategy; and the organizing process" (p. 9). This perspective on entrepreneurship, which has roots in Austrian economics, presents some interesting features as it focuses interest on the problem of emergence, an element that is missing in most established theories in management. While pointing out that entrepreneurship research is one-legged without considering the characteristics of the opportunity or the venture idea (Davidsson 2003), we pinpoint the need for the basic rationale for the economic process of opportunity perception, discovery and seizing (Denrell et al. 2003).

As concerns opportunity investigation, studies in the Schumpeterian tradition (Schumpeter 1934), the Penrosian view of firm growth (Penrose 1959), and the Austrian approach (Kirzner 1979; Shane 2003) have emphasized that opportunity for profit is the most important incentive for a firm to undertake an action. In this perspective, Miller (2003:971) represents a noteworthy discussion of an entrepreneurial mindframe explicitly applied to Citibank's redesign of its administrative structure (i.e., capability configuration) by using empowered key account teams and specialized information and planning systems with the purpose of homing in new business opportunities.

In this perspective, Kirznerian (Kirzner 1973:35) notion of "*alertness*" to information, and not the possession of *superior* information, is the one that enables the entrepreneur to see previously unrecognized opportunities, or to evaluate known opportunities differently. Although greater knowledge and insight about the relevant aspects of the task in question may be useful, the ability or "alertness" to link this information to some overall entrepreneurial vision or imagination of what might be possible is paramount (Hamel and Prahalad 1994). A burgeoning countervailing view about where opportunities come from suggests instead that opportunities are created endogenously by those seeking to generate economic profits who act expressly to create them (Aldrich and Ruef 2006; Alvarez and Barney 2007). According to this view, creating opportunities is characterized by serendipity since "opportunities may also arise from the entrepreneur's own activity without this activity being direct towards entrepreneurial purposes" (Buenstorf 2007:328).

This state of affairs apply to entrepreneurship in broad terms, while new venture creation (and the rationale for new venture escalation) appears an underdeveloped issue. In this chapter, we contend that the early stage entrepreneurs are generally able to either discover or create potentially profitable opportunities, but they do need some external support (in terms of both strategy and finance) to actually seize and execute them so as to turn a profit potential into profit for real; i.e., we specifically emphasize the role of business angels and business angels networks as *catalyst* figures for developing entrepreneurial capabilities and provide requisite funding for growth thereby fostering new entrepreneurship.

Despite the important role recognized to outside equity in financing and fostering innovative entrepreneurial firms (i.e., entrepreneurial start-ups), relatively little is known about the key characteristics of the different fund-providers involved either in a temporal perspective (diverse stage of the early firm's life) or in an industry perspective (specialized equity investors). While business angels and venture capitalists are relatively common and welcome companions of entrepreneurs, various kinds of circumstances need to be accomplished and coordinated in order to establish and govern these relationships in a way that is really beneficial to all the parties. This chapter aims to discuss various aspects of the multifaceted relation between entrepreneurs seeking for finance to their early stage projects and business angels providing equity. In particular, we underscore the rationale for the emergence of the business angel networks in order to optimize search costs and the good match between supply and demand for funds. While business angel networks have found the way for their admittance in many European countries, in the USA angel groups (or spontaneous investor associations) are far more developed. On the ground of a 5-year panel data extracted from the European Business Angel Network (EBAN), we explore in depth the intricacies and inefficiencies related to the action of the business angels networks in Europe and briefly juxtapose them to the Anglo-Saxon experience.

6.2 Entrepreneurial Capability as a Driver of Wealth Creation and Diffusion

According to the resource-based view of the firm (Barney 1991), entrepreneurial capability, that is the ability in recognizing, seizing and executing opportunities, is a source of firms' competitive advantage (Alvarez and Barney 2000). Indeed, entrepreneurship is an intricate part of the resource-based framework (Conner 1991; Rumelt 1987). Since entrepreneurial opportunities exist primarily because different entrepreneurs have different beliefs about the relative value of resources when they are converted from inputs into outputs (Shane and Venkataraman 2000), heterogeneity is a common attribute of both resource-based and entrepreneurship theory, although while RBV logic has tended to focus on heterogeneity of resources entrepreneurship theory has tended to focus on heterogeneity in beliefs about the value of resources (Alvarez and Busenitz 2001).

Due to these theoretical premises, to be as a source of the firm's competitive advantage, the entrepreneurial capability in recognizing, seizing and executing opportunities is not sufficient per se, but it must be turned into value and wealth creation. However, entrepreneurial opportunities are important cornerstones to assess in order to predict how the business will evolve and how the entrepreneur may raise more profits. Entrepreneurial opportunities exist when different entrepreneurs have insight into the value of resources that the other entrepreneurs do not, and the entrepreneurs with the insight act upon these un-exploited opportunities (Casson 1982).

Entrepreneurial capability consists primarily in recognizing, seizing and executing opportunities. First, recognizing opportunities is of prominent importance. Alvarez and Busenitz (2001) define the "entrepreneurial recognition" as the recognition of opportunities and opportunity seeking behavior as a resource. Entrepreneurial recognition is about cognition, discovery, pursuing market opportunities, and coordinate knowledge that lead to heterogeneous results. Second, seizing opportunities is equally important. Teece (2007) pointed out that seizing opportunities requires (multiple) investments in development and commercialization activity. In addition, the entrepreneur must select a particular "business model" (Morris et al. 2005) that defines its commercialization strategy and investment priorities, even if they will be embedded into a new venture. Third, executing opportunities is the last dimension of the entrepreneurial capability. It implies that the entrepreneurial opportunities must be turned into an "entrepreneurial action" consisting of the development of new ventures, that is equivalent to generate new economic activities. More precisely, the modes of action used to exploit opportunities entail not only the creation of new independent ventures but also the development of new entrepreneurial units within the established firms – that is, internal venturing. The assessment of a business opportunity is crucial. It influences not only the phase of creating the new venture, but also the post-entry process that, by nature, is largely affected by the risk of a death valley or high post-entry mortality rates (Cefis and Marsili 2005).[1]

As we pointed out before, the entrepreneurial capability must be turned into value (for the stakeholders) and wealth creation (for the entrepreneur and society at large). The bridge between the entrepreneurial capability and the outcomes – value and wealth – is filled by the existence of an appropriate firm's strategy and financial support to execute it. Strategic choices can be exploited along several dimensions: entering new geographical or product markets, accessing new technologies and knowledge, or reconfiguring the firm's value chain through strategic alliances and partnerships. In the instance of nascent entrepreneurship, this double crucial role of providing "good strategy and funding" to new or potential entrepreneurs can be frequently provided by business angels and business angels networks. They are the ones that are able to support entrepreneurs in filling their early stage dual gap: the "strategy gap" and the "equity gap." In fact, business angels and business angel networks are the ones who usually take the responsibility of being the catalyst figures for developing entrepreneurial capabilities and for raising the cash needed to expand

[1] Current research issues include the measurement of value creation as a result of entrepreneurship, the effect of entrepreneurs' values on the pursuit of entrepreneurship activities, the effective organizational designs for entrepreneurship, and the current state of research on entrepreneurship as well as future research opportunities (Zahra et al. 1999).

their business so that they can be a promise of success to the nascent entrepreneurs. In this chapter we explicitly deal with the equity gap leaving the treatment of the strategy gap to future studies.

6.3 Risk, Uncertainty and New Entrepreneurship: Filling the Equity Gap

The lack of financial resources is one of the most recurrent obstacles for turning good business ideas into real business projects and, consequently, creating new ventures. As for many other economic activities, the process of creating new entrepreneurship ventures is shaped by high uncertainty in addition to a natural risk-taking. The uncertainty is nurtured by several elements: the absence of the firm's track record (Wright et al. 2002), the expected high risk of new ventures (Brockhaus 1980), and the presence of information asymmetries between the business promoters and the potential financial stakeholders (Gompers and Lerner 2001). Given high uncertainty, new venture performance is extremely erratic. As Cooper said, "one of the central questions in entrepreneurship is why some new firms succeed and other fail" (Cooper 1995:109).

How to reduce the high uncertainty in the new ventures depends primarily on the entrepreneurs' capabilities of attracting and deploying cognitive and critical resources. Among such resources the most important are networking capability (Hite and Hesterly 2001), social capital (Baron and Markman 2003), entrepreneurial experience (Dyer 1992), specific knowledge (Minniti and Bygrave 2001).

Despite such resources, due to the existence of high uncertainty start ups generally incur in a lack of funding situation so that it is difficult for them to turn new business ideas, even if previously appropriately incubated, into profitable business project. This condition is representative of the so called "equity gap" (Bannock 1991; Mason and Harrison 1995).

Filling the "equity gap" is extremely important for a new entrepreneurial project to survive and thrive. This is a fertile area that has been explored by venture capital (Amit et al. 1998). However, due to the complex financial mechanisms that link the risk of a new venture with the expected internal rate of returns, venture capitalists have usually more incentives to allocate their financial resources into business projects that are placed in an expansion phase.

Consequently, to new ventures the "equity gap" largely remains an open issue. As a surrogate to venture capital financing, an important channel for much-required fresh cash is that of the well-known three Fs: friends, family and fools (Ennico 2002). While it may be very helpful to new entrepreneurial initiatives since it aims to support new ventures thereby filling the "equity gap," this channel remains largely unexplored since it is comparatively limited to the pre-seed and seed phases. Business angels and business angles networks financing largely fall into this channel as they are the ones who are able to provide seed and start up equity capital. In the next section, we will focus our analysis on the specific role of business angels in fostering new entrepreneurship.

6.4 The Role of Business Angels in Fostering New Entrepreneurship

Flanking the various long-established external investors for new entrepreneurial ventures, business angels are reported in various countries as an effective source of seed and start up equity capital. Business angels are informal, non-institutional investors making up the informal venture capital market. By means of direct search processes, business angels invest their own financial resources by acquiring equity in high-potential new and young non listed companies in which there is no family connection (Mason and Harrison 1994). Like any financial shareholder, angel investors aim to achieve capital gain from the divesture of their stake. It has been widely recognized that business angels are wealthy individuals, have a background as entrepreneurs, managers and/or consultants and, in the vast majority of cases, are males between the age of 40 and 65.

Informal venture capital market plays a major role in seeding new entrepreneurial ventures in both USA and Europe. Recent panel data suggest that in the US, angel investments raised approximately US$ 26 billion per year involving 57,120 ventures joined by over 258,000 active business angels (CVR 2009). As Europe is concerned, current appraisal suggests that the total number of active angel investors participating in networks or acting on independent basis revolves roughly around 75,000 individuals, investing approximately Euros 3 billion per year (EBAN 2008:2). As regards UK business angels, Mason and Harrison (2000) provide ball-park figure that they make eight times as many investments in start-up companies vis-à-vis venture capital funds.

Together with equity, business angels provide new companies with knowledge and valuable networking relationships, which are often able to significantly increase the success rate of new ventures. Playing a more active role than venture capitalists, the business angels assist the venture-backed firm, occasionally assuming the role of a veritable partner engaged in managing the business. Besides their own personal skills, business angels provide the firm's with their network of contacts as well as their commercial and financial connections in the new venture's local area of operation.

It is noteworthy that, unlike formal venture capitalists, business angels invest their own finance. The personal derivation of financial resources that business angels use has considerable upshot on their investment activity: since they have no obligation to guarantee externally constrained elevated thresholds of return on the capital they invested, business angels are only accountable to themselves. This state of affairs is uncovered by their greater propensity to invest in risky entrepreneurial ventures, with high variability and uncertainty, which formal venture capitalists tend increasingly to avoid. Consequently, the business angel is generally disposed to invest in seed and start-up financing or to fund small entrepreneurial companies with high growth potential and a general high level of investment risk (Gerard and Margulis 2001; Harmon 2000). At the same time, the personal origin and hence the limited figure of the capital invested in a single deal induces the business angel to focus on small or micro investments, which are also not targeted by the formal venture capitalists.

Considerable empirical evidence from Europe and the US shows that the major part of investments falls in the range of Euros 100,000–250,000. Accordingly, business angels customarily supply financial resources under the threshold below which is not profitable for the venture capitalists to invest because of the fixed nature of costs involved in assessing, monitoring and providing post-investment support to venture backed firms (Mason and Harrison 1999; Mason and Harrison 2000). In this perspective, business angels try to fill the gap that micro and early stage risky investments bear into in the financial market.

Unlike its regulated formal counterpart, the informal venture capital market operates in quasi complete darkness. The investments made are neither disclosed in a regulated market nor there is obligation to track the records since there are no institutional regulatory agencies through which the market can be monitored. As stated above, the matching between the capital supplied and emerging business opportunities mainly occurs via direct search by the counterparts and deals are essentially based on personal mutual trust. Business angels are thus low profile individuals, a feature which is further reinforced by the desire of such early stage investors to be unidentified (Wetzel 1981; Benjamin and Margulis 1996). Business angels' market informality and transparency lack affect their geographical scope: substantial evidence drew from both US and UK shows that the majority of angels seeks opportunities and makes investments on a local basis (usually within the range of km 150–200 from their home base).

On the ground of this analysis, it is important to clarify why business angels can be an effective source of equity capital to new entrepreneurial ventures despite the presence of information asymmetries and high uncertainty problems (which were analyzed in the previous sections). Given their inner nature, business angels seem to be able to reduce information asymmetries and the uncertainty of the new venture survival. This occurs in both the ex ante assessment of investment proposals and in the post-funding phase. With regard to the ex ante investment assessment phase, we need to recall that business angels are specialized investors who usually develop specific skills in evaluating investment proposals (that often are referred to industries in which they had previous entrepreneurial or management experience). Therefore, in order to reduce uncertainty vis-à-vis formal venture capitalists, angel investors are better equipped to perform an effective due diligence, reduce information asymmetries and assess risk levels (Lerner 1988). Regards post-funding issues, business angels reduce uncertainty because they are frequently involved in the firm's management (since, as we previously maintained, they are hands-on-investors). Taking charge of the firms' management means exerting some form of direct control over the venture-backed entrepreneur. Other things being equal, this contributes to reduce the moral hazard problem (Arrow 1991; Gompers 1995) and to lower risk. Consequently, the specialized and professional nature of angel investors allows them to effectively deal with high uncertainty underlying new entrepreneurial ventures.

Using a different interpretive lens, angel investors play an effective role because they accept to intimately share high levels of uncertainty with venture-backed entrepreneurs. This perspective does not take into account angels' professional ability as a relevant explanation to reduce information asymmetries and uncertainty.

At least two aspects of the informal venture capital market support this alternative perspective. First, although mainstream literature suggests that business angels contribute with personal entrepreneurial and managerial skills, a handful of empirical study has lately shown that these investors are not always knowledgeable in the industries in which they invest their fresh cash (Kelly and Hay 1996; van Osnabrugge 1998; Trotta 2001). This state of affairs reduces the professional level of the due diligence operated by angel investors, who pretty often tend to give greater importance to entrepreneurial features (e.g., motivation for success, competences, reciprocal trust) when compared with technical or market assessment of the investment proposals. It is possible that business angels invest in a specific firm mainly because they feel that the "chemical spark" established with the founder is sufficient to lead to the venture success. Second, various studies (Mason and Harrison 1996; Trotta 2001) have shown that business angels actions are also affected by non financial motivations that are related to the psychological and attitudinal profile of each investor. In fact, the business angel is often led to invest in new entrepreneurial firms by emotional and psychological factors such as the possibility of revealing that he/she has a specific entrepreneurial skill, the propensity towards investments in uncertain and challenging projects, the opportunity to develop new product ideas in agreement with the new firm's management, the possibility of creating trust-based relationships with the founder (Robinson 1987; Reitan and Sorheim 2000; Mason and Harrison 1996), or eventually the desire for personal enjoyment and fulfillment (Benjamin and Margulis 1996; Sullivan 1994).[2] The relevance of non financial incentives allows us to assume that business angels do not necessarily give sufficient amount of importance to the specialized professional assessment of the investment proposals they receive. Investing in new industries and being also motivated by non financial motivations, business angels can therefore be considered investors who act on a basis of uncertainty sharing together with the venture-backed entrepreneur.

6.5 The Contribution of the Business Angel Networks

Despite its importance and adequacy to fund high risk new entrepreneurial ventures, the informal venture capital market in both US and UK is far from be fully efficient. Various studies suggest that this market has notable undeveloped potential as most business angels do have funds available to invest (Coveney and Moore 1998) but are unable to invest as frequently or as much they would like to (Mason and Harrison 2002; Paul et al. 2003). As a result, substantial capital remains largely uncommitted.

[2] Since business angels are not moved by mere financial motivations, they do not tend to create diversified portfolios, especially given the smaller sums of capital in their range compared with formal venture capitalists. The not-only financial nature of their motivations and the smaller number of investments made also explain the greater involvement of business angels in firms funded on ad hoc basis vis-à-vis the case of the formal venture capitalist.

Potential investors; i.e., individuals who wish to become business angels but have never invested, have been estimated in the number of 850,000 in Europe and 1,75 million in US (San Josè et al. 2005).

We identified a couple of main factors that contribute to these informal venture capital market inefficiencies. First, market inefficiencies reflect the existence of market failure in the supply of early stage venture capital (Harding 2000; Sohl 2003; Mason and Harrison 2004). The assumptions of efficient capital markets with perfect information between the buyers and sellers and low transaction costs do not apply to new entrepreneurial ventures. In fact, information regularly flows pretty inefficiently especially in the early stage of the equity market. As we suggested in the previous sections, seed investing is characterized by relevant information asymmetries (Leland and Pile 1977; Binks et al. 1992) between risk capital providers and early stage entrepreneurs. The lack of track record for a new company and the absence of fully fledged developed products increase information asymmetries and create perception of higher risk for seed, start up and early growth stage businesses (Sohl 2003; Sorrentino 2009).

These inefficiencies in turn influence shortage of "small sized" early stage equity capital especially from venture capital funds. The "capital gap" is a primary source of market inefficiency since many promising high growth entrepreneurial ventures do not receive early stage capital. In the previous section, we showed that business angels try to fill this gap. However, while they provide capital to entrepreneurs beyond their ability to raise funds from their own connections (including family and friends) and below the minimum size of venture capital funds (what is usually termed as "equity gap") (Mason and Harrison 1994), business angels do not sufficiently satisfy the equity capital needs of early stage ventures. In addition, market inefficiencies are powered by the fact that both US and European formal venture capitalist have improved, especially in the last decade, their tendency to focus on later stage investments as they continue to raise the average investment size (Sohl 2003; EVCA 2007). Given that individual angels have not increased their average investment size, a new "secondary capital gap" has unexpectedly emerged; the second gap is roughly estimated to be in the \$2 million to \$5 million range in the USA (Sohl 2003; Mason 2006).

Another reason often used to explain the inefficiencies stressing the informal venture capital market is related to the high search costs borne by both demand and supply (Wetzel 1986, 1987; Mason and Harrison 1994; Sohl 1999; Mustilli 1999). According to this perspective, high search costs result from the difficulties business angels experience in receiving the investment proposals and the entrepreneurs undergo in reaching business angels. In turn, these difficulties are due to two main factors which have been noted in the previous section. First, the intricacy which both parties face in actually having the opportunity to get together originates from the investors' desire for discretion and anonymity. Second, the difficulty in matching demand and supply stems from the informal nature of the market, in which there are no public directories of business angels and is therefore hard for the entrepreneurs to identify potential investors. The informal nature of the market is also due to the fact that angel investors generally prefer to rely on their local network of informants made of trusted friends and business associates (Fiet 1995). Both the low profile of investors and the informality of channels for gathering information make the investment opportunity search process inefficient. As a consequence, few interesting proposals come to light. Thus, unlike the formal venture capital market, in which the presence of organized, visible structures facilitates the matching of risk capital demand and supply, the informal venture capital market is characterized by high search costs. On one side, business angels do not have any adequate sources of information and receive business proposals which are often inconsistent with their investment profile. On the other side, small firms seeking risk capital are not able to obtain visibility with potentially interested investors, many of whom remain anonymous and unknown. Thus, discretion, informality and substantial invisibility of the participants (Mason and Harrison 1994) generate in the informal venture capital market an information problem generally defined as an "information gap" (Sohl 1999). This gap generates market inefficiencies: high search costs, inability for business angels to invest as frequently as they would wish or as much as they would like to, entrepreneurs renouncing angel funding because of the difficulties in finding investors (Kotler et al. 2004:68).

While the "capital gap" is a consequence of a structural market inefficiency which can be hardly removed in the short term, policy makers in Europe have sponsored the birth and development of various types of matching organizations with the specific aim to reduce this "information gap" (Aernoudt 1999; San Josè et al. 2005). These organizations, referred to alternatively as matching organizations, matchmaking services or business angel networks (BANs) (Sohl 2007), have grown significantly in the past 10 years in various European countries. The role of business angel networks is to create a channel connecting the business angels and entrepreneurs, which is able to reduce mutual search costs and ensure a sufficient flow of proposals for angels. The main proponents of BANs in Europe include: Business Innovation Centres, regional and local authorities, regional development agencies, science parks, universities.

Data indicate that in the last 10 years the number of European BANs boomed from 66 to 301 in Mid-2008 (EBAN 2008). In more recent years, the number of angel networks has actually decreased in the more mature markets: UK (except Scotland), Sweden, Germany, Belgium, Italy, and the Netherlands. In these countries, the less performing networks ceased to operate after the first few years. However, this trend is balanced by the creation of new networks in countries in which the activity of business angels is increasingly disseminated. In the last 3 years, the number of networks has significantly increased in France, Spain, Portugal and new networks have been created in Eastern Europe (Bulgaria, Ukraine and Croatia) (EBAN 2008:21–22).

The considerable increase in the number of business angel networks has contributed to raise the visibility of participants on the informal venture capital market. The use of communication tools on the Web by these organizations helps overcome the problem of connecting the entrepreneurs and investors. The formers have a better ability to "shop around" for their deals because a growing number of projects can be found on multiple BANs at the same time (Lange et al. 2003). On the supply

Table 6.1 The activity of European BANs in 2007

Number of BANs	301[a]
Number of angels	15.578
Number of women investors	394
Numberof deals	1.130
Average amount of the deal	163.011£

Source: EBAN (2008)
[a]Data refer to Mid-2008

side, most matching mechanisms combine visibility of the organization and anonymity of the angel, facilitating access to a large number of proposals without eliminating the benefits of substantial investors' discretion. Accordingly, we can maintain that, for the part of the market that uses BANs, information problems can be reduced (Mason and Harrison 2002).

However, despite being potentially able to reduce information problems, the growth in the number of BANs does not have significantly affected the efficiency of the European informal venture capital market. The relative success of BANs is a matter for debate (Mason and Harrison 2002) and there exists no harmony regarding the effectiveness of such intermediate structures (Blatt and Riding 1996). Table 6.1 reports information coming out from a recent survey on 170 European BANs (which account for 56% of the 301 networks identified in Europe in Mid-2008). In 2007, more than 15,000 angel members of European BANs have concluded 1,130 deals. The average amount of the deals is appreciatively 160,000 £, and women angels account for only 2.5%. If one looks at the evolution of the activity of European BANs (Table 6.2), a positive trend in the number of angels and deals appears. However, the growth of the number of angels and deals is followed by a substantial decrease in the number of deals per angel (from 0.22 in 1999 to 0.07 in 2007). In addition, the average amount of the deals decreased from 200,178 £ in 2005 to 163,011 £ in 2008.[3]

The sharp decrease in both the number of deals per angel and the average size of the deals indicates that the European BANs are not really playing a decisive role in developing informal venture capital investments. While the increasing number of European BANs is actually reducing search costs borne by demand and supply, at the same time it does not seem to be able to increase informal venture capital market efficiency; i.e., the number of the deals and the average size of investments. Kelly and Hay (2000) argue that, as compared to investors outside BANs, angels who become members of BANs are less experienced investors who can leverage less

[3]It is interesting to note that the absolute figures in Tables 6.1 and 6.2 do not reflect the total number of business angels members of European BANs and the actual number of deals concluded by them. In the same vein, it is important to recall that the absolute figures reported in Tables 6.1 and 6.2 do not compute the larger angel activity which takes place in Europe *outside* of business angel networks.

Table 6.2 Evolution of European BANs activity

	1999	2000	2001	2002	2003	2004	2005	2006	2007	2008
Number of BANs	66	132	155	177	197	231[a]	228[a]	211[a]	236[a]	301[a]
Number of angels	1.487	2.333	3.129	4.347	13.218	12.773	8.227	10.331	15.578	
Number of deals	320	416	454	573	600	580	653	843	1.130	
Deals/angel	0,22	0,18	0,15	0,13	0,05	0,05	0,08	0,08	0,07	
Average amount of the deals	n/a	n/a	n/a	n/a	n/a	n/a	200.178£	177.311£	163.011£	

Source: Elaborations on EBAN (2005, 2008)
[a]Data refer to Mid-Year

structured commercial and financial networks. This means that angels active within networks are much more likely to be potential angels, which, in turn, might explain the relative performance of BANs; i.e., the decline in the number of deals per angel and in the average size of investments.

An increase in market efficiency where BANs predominate may arise from a substantial change in the role played by the same BANs. From being simple "neutral intermediation structures" between demand and supply, BANs are expected to play an active role to "educate the market" (Mason and Harrison 2002; Lange et al. 2003; San Josè et al. 2005). First, this means offering support to entrepreneurs in developing a high level of investment readiness (Mason and Harrison 2002). This in turn entails sustaining the entrepreneurs in setting up and presenting projects, educating them to understand investor expectations and requirements and to draw up attractive business plans for the latter. Second, BANs are also called to target market supply and train business angels in the more delicate aspects of investment techniques so as to compensate any lack of familiarity with such techniques and thus make them *ready to invest* (Mason and Harrison 2002). In this intriguing context, we actually consider the recent experience of some European angel academies (Aernoudt 2005; San Josè et al. 2005). The new generation of BANs is therefore required to be able not only to improve the quality of deal flow and matching processes, but also to exploit market potential, converting would-be angels into active informal investors.

6.6 Conclusions

This chapter has addressed the significance of business angels, a class of informal venture capitalists, in fostering new entrepreneurship among young and new ventures. Existing conceptual literature and empirical evidence both in entrepreneurship and finance have largely shown the relative importance of entrepreneurial capability, possessed by the entrepreneurs in recognizing, seizing and executing entrepreneurial opportunities.

The essay in fact locates itself in that relevant gray area which lies at the intersection between entrepreneurship and finance that is called "entrepreneurial finance."

However, it still remains an "equity gap" in financing and funding new initiatives. Such "equity gap" is increasingly filled by business angels and business angels networks that are growing in importance throughout the world, moving from the Anglo-Saxon capitalistic systems where they have initially raised great popularity and expanding to other areas and Continental Europe in particular. These circumstances occur since, as previously purported, business angels networks are expected to play an active role to "educate the market."

Due to their characteristics, business angels fuel new business projects with money, managerial resources, network capabilities and additional services that normally both venture capital and private equity firms neglect to bring into backed ventures. Even when they are able to perceive viable opportunities, considerable effort and money are necessary to new entrepreneurs to exploit and execute them properly and, not seldom, also to integrate them within their own complex mindframes. Still, a key advantage of external informal financial supports is widening the search for organizational novelty and strategic variety, making engaging the new initiatives a first priority.

For the reasons reported above, it is expected that the role of business angels and business angels supporting networks will increase over the next years in potentially the entire world's regions. A related explanation is connected to the current global economic downturn that, starting in the second semester of the year 2008, has generally shown the weaknesses of the formal financial ties among venture capital firms (or, alternatively, private equity firms) and the other people's money provided by institutional investors.

References

Aernoudt R (1999) Business angels: should they fly on their wings? Venture Cap 1(2):187–195

Aernoudt R (2005) Executive forum: seven ways to stimulate business angels' investments. Venture Cap 7:359–371

Aldrich HE, Ruef M (2006) Organizations evolving, 2nd edn. Sage, Thousand Oaks, CA

Alvarez SA, Barney JB (2007) Discovery and creation: alternative theories of entrepreneurial action. Strateg Entrepreneurship J 1(1–2):11–26

Alvarez SA, Barney JB (2000) Entrepreneurial capabilities: a resource-based view. In: Meyer GD, Heppard KA (eds) Entrepreneurship as strategy: competing on the entrepreneurial edge. Sage Publications, Thousand Oaks, pp 63–82

Alvarez SA, Busenitz LW (2001) The entrepreneurship of resource-based theory. J Manage 27:755–775

Amit R, Brander J, Zott C (1998) Why do venture capital firms exist? Theory and Canadian evidence. J Bus Venturing 13:441–466

Arrow KJ (1991) The economics of agency. In: Pratt JW, Zeckhauser RJ (eds) Principal and agents: the structure of the business. Harvard Business School Press, Boston

Bannock G (1991) Venture capital and the equity gap. National Westminster Bank plc, London

Barney JB (1991) Firm resources and sustained competitive advantage. J Manage 17:99–120

Baron RA, Markman GD (2003) Beyond social capital: the role of entrepreneurs' social competence in their financial success. J Bus Venturing 18(1):41–60
Benjamin GA, Margulis J (1996) Finding your wings: how to locate private investors to fund your business. Wiley, New York
Binks M, Ennew C, Reed C (1992) Information asymmetries and the provision of finance to small firms. Int Small Bus J 11(1):35–46
Blatt R, Riding A (1996) Where angels fear to tread? Some lessons from the Canada Opportunities Investment Network. In: Harrison RT, Mason CM (eds) Informal venture capital: evaluating the impact of business introduction services. Prentice Hall, Hemel Hempstead, pp 75–88
Brockhaus RH (1980) Risk taking propensity of entrepreneurs. Acad Manage J 23(3):509–520
Buenstorf G (2007) Creation and pursuit of entrepreneurial opportunities: an evolutionary perspective. Small Bus Econ 28(4):323–337
Casson MC (1982) The Entrepreneur: An Economic Theory. Martin Robertson: Oxford, UK.
Cefis E, Marsili O (2005) A matter of life and death: Innovation and firm survival. Ind Corp Change 14(6):1167–1192
Conner KR (1991) A historical comparison of resource-based theory and five schools of thought within industrial organization: do we have a new theory of the firm? J Manage 17:121–154
Cooper AC (1995) Challenges in Predicting New Firm Performance In.: Bull I, Thomas H, Willard G (eds) Entrepreneurship. Perespective on Theory Building. Pergamon, Elsevier, pp 109–124
Coveney P, Moore K (1998) Business angels: securing start-up finance. Wiley, Chichester
CVR (2009) Full Year 2007 Angel Market Analysis Report. Center for Venture Research, available on http://www.wsbe.unh.edu/files/2007
Davidsson P (2003) The domain of entrepreneurship research: some suggestions. In: Katz J, Shepherd S (eds) Advances in entrepreneurship, firm emergence and growth, vol 6. Elsevier, Amsterdam, pp 315–372
Denrell J, Fang C, Winter SD (2003) The economics of strategic opportunity. Strateg Manage J 24:977–990
Dyer WG (1992) The entrepreneurial experience. Jossey-Bass, San Francisco
EBAN (2005) Statistic Compendium, November, European Business Angel Network, In: www.eban.com
EBAN (2008) Statistic Compendium, European Business Angel Network, Version 1, July 4th
Ennico, C. (2002). Accepting money from family and friends. Entrepreneur, http://www.entrepreneur.com/money/financing/loansfromfriendsandfamily/article51542.html
EVCA (2007) European Venture Capital Association, EVCA Barometer, issue 53
Fiet J (1995) Reliance upon informants in the venture capital industry. J Bus Venturing 10:195–223
Gerard AB, Margulis J (2001) The angel investor's handbook: how to profit from early stage investing. Bloomerang Press, Princeton
Gompers PA (1995) Optimal investment, monitoring, and the staging of venture capital. J Finance L 50(5):1461–1489
Gompers PA, Lerner J (2001) The venture capital revolution. J Econ Perspect 15(2):145–168
Hamel G, Prahalad CK (1994) Competing for the future. Harvard Business School Press, Boston
Harding R (2000) Venture capital and regional development: towards a venture capital 'system'. Venture Cap: An Int J Entrepreneurial Finance 2(3):223–242
Harmon S (2000) Zero gravity: il venture capital per investire in internet. Egea, Milano
Hite JM, Hesterly WS (2001) The evolution of firm networks: from emergency to early growth of the firm. Strateg Manage J 22(3):275–286
Kelly P, Hay M (1996) Serial investors and early stage finance. J Entrepreneurial Small Bus Finance 5(2):59–174
Kelly P, Hay M (2000) Deal makers: a reputation that attracts quality. Venture Cap: An Int J Entrepreneurial Finance 2(3):183–202
Kirzner IM (1973) Competition and entrepreneurship. University of Chicago Press, Chicago
Kirzner IM (1979) Perception, opportunity, and profit. Chicago, University of Chicago Press
Kotler P, Kartajaya H, Young SD (2004) Attracting investors. A marketing approach to finding funds for your business. Wiley, New Jersey

Lange J, Leleux B, Surlemont B (2003) Angel networks for the 21st century: an examination of practices of leading networks in Europe and the US. J Priv Equity, Spring, pp 18–28
Leland HE, Pile DH (1977) Informational asymmetries, financial structure and financial intermediation. J Finance 32(2):371–387
Lerner J (1988) Angel financing and public policy: an overview. J Bank Finance 22:773–783
Mason CM (2006) Informal sources of venture finance. In: Parker S (ed) The life cycle of entrepreneurial ventures. Kluwer, pp 259–300
Mason CM, Harrison RT (1994) Informal venture capital market in the UK. In: Hughes A, Storey DJ (eds) Finance and the small firm. London, Routledge, pp 64–111
Mason CM, Harrison RT (1995) Closing the regional equity capital gap: the role of informal venture capital. Small Bus Econ 7:153–172
Mason CM, Harrison RT (1996) Why business angels say no: a case study of opportunities rejected by an informal investor syndicate. Int Small Bus J 14:2
Mason CM, Harrison RT (1999) Public policy and the development of the informal venture capital market. In: Cowling K (ed) Industrial policy in Europe: theoretical perspectives and practical proposition. Routledge, London
Mason CM, Harrison RT (2000) The size of informal venture capital market in the United Kingdom. Small Bus Econ 15(2):137–148
Mason CM, Harrison RT (2002) Barriers to investment in the informal venture capital sector. Entrepreneurship Reg Dev 14:271–287
Mason CM, Harrison RT (2004) Improving access to early stage venture capital in regional economies: a new approach to investment readiness. Local Economy 19(2):159–173
Miller D (2003) An asymmetry-based view of advantage: towards an attainable sustainability. Strateg Manage J 24:961–976
Minniti M, Bygrave W (2001) A dynamic model of entrepreneurial learning. Entrepreneurship: Theory Pract 25(3):5–16
Morris M, Schindehutte M, Allen J (2005) The entrepreneur's business model: toward a unified perspective. J Bus Res 58:726–735
Mustilli M (1999) L'evoluzione del venture capital nello sviluppo delle piccole e medie imprese. Cedam, Padova
Paul S, Whittam G, Johnston JB (2003) The operation of the informal venture capital market in Scotland. Venture Cap: Int J Entrepreneurial Finance 5:313–335
Penrose ET (1959) The theory of the growth of the firm. John Wiley, New York
Reitan B, Sorheim R (2000) The informal venture capital market in Norway: investor characteristics, behaviour and investment preferences. Taylor & Francis, London
Robinson R (1987). Emerging strategies in the venture capital industry. J Bus Venturing 2(1):53–77
Rumelt RP (1987) Theory, strategy, and entrepreneurship. In: Teece D (ed) The competitive challenge. Cambridge, Ballinger, pp 137–158
San Josè A, Roure J, Aernoudt R (2005) Business angel academies: unleashing the potential for business angel investment. Venture Cap 7:149–165
Schumpeter JA (1934) The theory of economic development. Harvard University Press, Cambridge (MA)
Shane S, Venkataraman S (2000) The promise of entrepreneurship as a field of research. Acad Manage Rev 25(1):271–226
Shane S (2003) A general theory of entrepreneurship. The individual-opportunity nexus. Edward Elgar, Northampton, MA
Sohl J (1999) The early-stage equity market in the USA. Venture Cap: Int J Entrepreneurial Finance 1(2):101–120
Sohl J (2003) The private equity market in the USA: lessons from volatility. Venture Cap: Int J Entrepreneurial Finance 5(1):29–46
Sohl J (2007) The organization of the informal venture capital market. In: Landström H (ed) Handbook of research on venture capital. Edward Elgar Publishing
Sorrentino M (2009) Entrepreneurial issues in competitive strategy research. In: Dagnino GB (ed) Handbook of research on competitive strategy. Elgar, Cheltenham, UK

Sullivan MK (1994) Altruism and entrepreneurship. In: Bygrave WD, Birley S, Churchill NC, Gatewood E, Hoy F, Keeley RH, Wetzel WE Jr (eds) Frontiers of entrepreneurship research 1994. Babson College, Wellesley, MA

Teece DJ (2007) Explicating dynamic capabilities: the nature and microfoundations of (sustainable) enterprise performance. Strateg Manage J 28:1319–1350

Trotta A (2001) Finanza innovativa per le piccole imprese. Le prospettive di sviluppo dell'informal venture capital market in Italia. Cedam, Padova

van Osnabrugge M (1998) Comparisons of business angels and venture capitalist: financiers of entrepreneurial firms. Venture Capital Report Ltd, Oxford

Venkataraman S (1997) The distinctive domain of entrepreneurship research: an editor's perspective. In: Katz J, Brockhaus R (eds) Advances in entrepreneurship, firm emergence, and growth, vol 3. JAI Press, Greenwich, CT, pp 119–138

Wetzel WE (1981) Informal risk capital in New England. In: Vesper KH (ed) Frontiers of entrepreneurship research. Babson College, Wellesley, MA

Wetzel WE (1986) Entrepreneurs, angels, and economic renaissance. In: Hisrich RD (ed) Entrepreneurship, intrapreneurship and venture capital. Lexington Books, Lexington, MA, pp 119–139

Wetzel WE (1987) The informal risk capital market: aspects of scale and efficiency. J Bus Venturing 2:299–313

Wright M, Lockett A, Pruthi S (2002) Internationalization of western venture capitalists into emerging markets, risk assessment and information in India. Small Bus Econ 19(1):13–29

Zahra SA, Kuratko DF, Jennings DF (1999) Guest editorial: corporate entrepreneurship and wealth creation contemporary and emerging perspectives. Entrepreneurship: Theory Pract, 24(2):7–8

Zahra SA, Sapienza HJ, Davidsson P (2006) Entrepreneurship and dynamic capabilities: a review, model and research agenda. J Manage Stud 43(4):917–955

Chapter 7
Venture Capital Financing and the Growth of New Technology-Based Firms: Correcting for Sample Self-Selection

Fabio Bertoni, Massimo G. Colombo, Diego D'Adda, and Luca Grilli

Abstract The financial literature claims that venture capital (VC) financing spurs the growth of new technology-based firms (NTBFs). First, VC investors allegedly have superior scouting capabilities, so they provide great hidden value firms with the financing they would otherwise be unable to obtain. Second, they also provide monitoring and coaching services to portfolio companies. Third, VC financing has a "certification" effect, making easier for portfolio firms obtaining support from third parties. The aim of the paper is to test whether VC financing has a positive effect on the subsequent growth of sales and employment of portfolio companies by taking into account the actual willingness of the NTBF to receive equity financing. We consider a 10 year long longitudinal dataset composed of 215 Italian NTBFs, most of which are privately held. The sample includes both VC-backed and non VC-backed firms. In order to capture the effects of VC financing on the subsequent growth of firms, we estimate an augmented Gibrat-law type dynamic panel data model. We resort to GMM-system estimation to control for the potentially endogenous nature of VC financing. The results strongly support the view that VC financing spurs firm growth. Moreover once controlled for self-selection, the effect of VC on firm growth is even larger.

7.1 Introduction

Since the seminal work by Jaffee and Russell (1976) and Stiglitz and Weiss (1981), the argument that there are frictions in capital markets that make it difficult for firms to obtain external financing and constrain their investment decisions has increasingly been gaining ground in the economic and financial literature (see Fazzari et al. 1988 and the studies mentioned by Hubbard 1998). New technology-based firms (NTBFs) are those most likely to suffer from these capital market imperfections.

F. Bertoni, M.G. Colombo (✉), D. D'Adda, and L. Grilli
Department of Management, Economics and Industrial Engineering
Politecnico di Milano, Piazza Leonardo da Vinci, 32, 20133, Milan, Italy
e-mail: massimo.colombo@polimi.it

D.B. Audretsch et al. (eds.), *New Frontiers in Entrepreneurship: Recognizing, Seizing, and Executing, Opportunities*, International Studies in Enterpreneurship,
DOI 10.1007/978-1-4419-0058-6_7,

In turn, the fact that poor access to external financing may limit the growth and even threaten the survival of NTBFs is worrisome because of the key role these firms play in assuring dynamic efficiency and employment growth in the economic system (Audretsch 1995; Acs 2004).

The above arguments especially apply to bank loans (Carpenter and Petersen 2002). In fact, banks generally do not possess the competencies required to evaluate ex ante and monitor ex post the investment projects proposed by young high-tech firms that lack a track record. In principle, the above mentioned adverse selection and moral hazard problems can be alleviated through the recourse to collateralized loans (Berger and Udell 1998). Nonetheless, most of high-tech investments is in intangible and/or firm-specific assets that provide little collateral value.

Venture capital (VC) financing is generally considered by both academics and practitioners as a more suitable financing mode for NTBFs than bank loans. In fact, it is contended in the financial literature that this financing mode offers a fundamental contribution to the success of high-tech entrepreneurial ventures (see for instance Sahlman 1990; Gompers and Lerner 2001; Kaplan and Strömberg 2001; Denis 2004).

Nonetheless, whether access to VC financing spurs the growth of portfolio companies is a matter of empirical test. As will be documented in Sect. 7.2, the results of previous studies on this issue are not unanimous. The reason may be that these studies suffer from several methodological weaknesses. First, most of them analyze samples of firms that eventually went public. These samples are not representative of the NTBF population, since privately held firms are not considered. Moreover, they capture the moderating effect of VC financing on the relationship between the IPO and firm growth rather than the direct effect of VC financing on growth. Second, most studies resort to cross-sectional estimates and, consequently, their results are likely to be biased as they do not manage to properly control for unobserved heterogeneity across firms and reverse causality. Quite surprisingly, studies based on longitudinal datasets are rare (see Davila et al. 2003; Alemany and Martì 2005).[1] Lastly, it has been recently pointed out the relevance of the firm decision to look for external equity financing (Eckhardt et al. 2006). In other words, not all the young entrepreneurial firms are equally willing to receive VC financing and obviously, this influences the composition of the bunch of firms in which VC is able to invest in. Therefore, to evaluate the effect of VC financing on the growth of portfolio firms, it is necessary to correct for this first self-selection stage of the financing process, the stage in which NTBFs decide whether to position themselves "on the market for VC" or not (Eckhardt et al. 2006).

In this work, we resort to a hand collected 10 year long longitudinal dataset composed of 215 Italian NTBFs that operate in high-tech sectors in manufacturing and services, to analyze the effect of VC financing on firm growth in the years that

[1] For an attempt to control for this bias in cross-sectional estimates of the relation between VC financing and firm growth, see Engel (2002), Colombo and Grilli (2005).

follow the first round of financing. Italian NTBFs provide a very interesting testbed of the beneficial effects of VC financing on portfolio companies as in Italy the VC industry is quite undeveloped and VC investors operate in a quite unfavorable environment. In addition, almost all sample firms are privately held throughout the observation period. In order to capture the effect of VC financing on the subsequent growth of firms, we estimate an augmented Gibrat law type dynamic panel data model, correcting for the potential biases engendered by the NTBFs decision to actually position themselves "on the market for VC" by adapting our framework to a typical Heckman two-step procedure. We consider growth of both employees and sales. In order to control for the potentially endogenous nature of VC financing we resort to GMM-system estimation.

The results of the estimates support the view that VC financing has a dramatic positive effect on firm growth even after controlling for the self-selection of the sample.

The paper is structured as follows. In the next section, we survey the literature on the effects of VC financing on growth. In Sect. 7.3, we describe the sample of firms that are considered in the empirical analysis and we provide some descriptive statistics. In Sect. 7.4, we illustrate the models and results of the econometric analysis on the effect of VC financing on the growth of portfolio companies. Section 7.5 concludes.

7.2 Literature Review

7.2.1 The Added Value of VC Financing

The financial literature highlights several motives explaining why access to VC financing propels the growth of NTBFs.

First of all, VC investors generally focus on specific industries (see among others Gompers 1995; Amit et al. 1998; Bottazzi and Da Rin 2002). Due to their sectoral specialization, they allegedly develop context-specific screening capabilities that make them able to judge quite accurately the commercial value of entrepreneurial projects and the entrepreneurial talent of the proponents (Chan 1983; Amit et al. 1998). For an opposed view see Amit et al. (1990). Therefore, they are able to deal effectively with the adverse selection problems that would otherwise prevent great hidden value firms from obtaining the financing they need. In turn, relaxation of financial constraints leads to higher firm growth.

Second, VC firms are no silent partners (Gorman and Sahlman 1989; Barry et al. 1990). On the one hand, they actively monitor portfolio companies.[2] On the other hand,

[2] For instance, Kaplan and Strömberg (2003) show that VC firms control 41.4% of the seats of the board of directors of the US VC-backed companies that are considered in their study; in 25% of the companies they control the majority of the board seats. Bottazzi et al. (2004) document that in 66% of the deals of European VC firms the VC investor obtained one or more seats of the board of the participated company.

VC investors make use of specific financial instruments and contractual clauses (e.g., stage financing) that protect their investments from opportunistic behavior on the part of entrepreneurs and create high powered incentives for them (Sahlman 1990; Gompers 1995; Hellmann 1998; Kaplan and Strömberg 2003, 2004).

Third, VC investors allegedly perform a key coaching function to the benefit of portfolio firms (Gorman and Sahlman 1989; MacMillan et al. 1989; Bygrave and Timmons 1992; Sapienza 1992; Barney et al. 1996; Sapienza et al. 1996; Kaplan and Strömberg 2004; Colombo and Grilli 2009). In fact, they provide advising services to portfolio companies in fields such as strategic planning, marketing, finance and accounting, and human resource management, in which these firms typically lack internal competencies.[3] Moreover, portfolio companies take advantage of the network of social contacts of VC investors with potential customers, suppliers, alliance partners, and providers of specialized services like legal, accounting, head hunting, and public relation services (Lindsey 2002; Colombo et al. 2006; Hsu 2006).

Lastly, VC financing signals the good quality of a NTBF to third parties; therefore, VC-backed companies find it easier to get access to external resources and competencies that would be out of reach without the endorsement of the VC (Megginson and Weiss 1991; Stuart et al. 1999).

Finally, it is important to acknowledge that the agency relation between the VC investor and the entrepreneurs of portfolio companies may engender conflicts, leading to a deterioration of the performance of these latter companies. In fact, entrepreneurs and external investors may have different strategic visions; disagreements may absorb the entrepreneurs' effort and attention to the detriment of the pursuit of business opportunities. Even if no conflict arises, the need of VC investors to monitor managerial decisions may increase bureaucracy and formalization of decision processes, hampering flexibility and the ability of firms to timely grasp business opportunities. Furthermore, as VC investors are competent investors, they might be able to expropriate entrepreneurs of their innovative business ideas and exploit them also in their absence (Ueda 2004). The associated appropriability hazards may induce entrepreneurs to take decisions aimed at protecting their firm's technological knowledge that are detrimental to firm growth.

7.2.2 The Effect of VC Financing on the Growth of Portfolio Companies: The Empirical Literature

A growing stream of empirical literature has analyzed the effects of VC financing on the performances of portfolio companies. Here we solely focus attention on the effects on growth. Many (early) studies rely on matched pair techniques to compare

[3] Accordingly, Hellmann and Puri (2002) document that VC investors favor the recruitment of external managers, the adoption of stock option plans, and the revision of human resource policies by portfolio firms, thus contributing to their managerial "professionalization". Bottazzi et al. (2004) show that European VC firms helped portfolio companies in recruiting outside directors and senior managers in 40.8 and 48.4% of the deals they analyze, respectively.

VC-backed firms with non VC-backed ones. Most of them detect a positive impact of VC financing on firm growth (Jain and Kini 1995; Manigart and Van Hyfte 1999; Alemany and Martì 2005; Engel and Keilbach 2007); though there are some notable examples in literature of mixed results (Bürghel et al. 2000; Bottazzi and Da Rin 2002)

Several extant studies on the topic exhibit serious methodological weaknesses. First of all, some of them focus on IPO firms and this clearly leads to a selection bias, as privately held firms are not considered. Moreover, the analysis of firm growth in the period following the IPO does not allow to disentangle the effect of VC financing from that of the IPO. What one actually captures is the moderating role played by VC financing on the effect of listing on firm growth. Even more importantly, many analyses do not properly take into account the potentially endogenous nature of VC financing. In fact, access to this financing mode may be determined by both observable factors (e.g., the human capital characteristics of firms' founding team) and unobservable ones. To the extent that these unobservable factors also influence firm growth, lack of control for the endogeneity of VC financing may lead to distorted estimates of its effect on growth.

In order to deal with this problem, some cross-sectional studies adopt a two step approach inspired by the "endogenous treatment" literature (Heckman 1990; Vella and Verbeek 1999). They first consider the likelihood of obtaining VC financing through an involvement equation. Then in analyzing firm growth, they insert in the set of covariates an inverse Mill's ratio type factor calculated from the estimates of the involvement equation. Alternatively, VC financing is instrumented through the predicted probability of obtaining it. While using this methodology Engel (2002) and Colombo and Grilli (2005) document a positive effect of VC financing on firm growth in samples composed of 95,571 German firms and 506 Italian NTBFs, respectively.

Quite surprisingly, studies that rely on longitudinal datasets are rare. Alemany and Martì (2005) estimate fixed effects panel data models relating to the Spanish firms that obtained VC. Their results indicate that other things being equal, both the presence of a VC investor in the equity capital of firms and the cumulated amount of VC financing they obtained up to a given year, result in greater firm size in the same year. Davila et al. (2003) consider monthly data on employment growth for a sample composed of 494 start-ups that chose to outsource their human resource needs to a leading professional employer organization; out of them 193 are VC-backed. They resort to event study analysis. First they identify the month in which 275 VC financing events occurred; then they compare the evolution of the number of employees of these firms in a 7 month time window centered in the month in which VC financing was obtained with the evolution in the same period of the number of employees of non VC-backed firms. They find that VC-backed firms enjoy more rapid growth before but above all after obtaining VC financing.[4]

[4] Davila et al. (2003) also estimate a logit model to investigate whether the growth of the firms in the first month in which they are present in the dataset influences the likelihood of obtaining VC financing in a subsequent period. Their results suggest that firm growth does not attract VC financing.

7.2.3 The Multi-stage Financing Process

VC financing may be considered a multi-stage and multi-actor process. In this respect, Hsu (2004) highlights the role of the entrepreneurial firm in the investment decision. He finds that entrepreneurial start-ups are more willing to accept an offer and also to be paid less if the investor is a venture capitalist. The author also suggests that it's probably because start-ups look at the value added services that an investor is able to give, and thus also non-monetary aspects enters in the choice of the investor. If this article suggests that entrepreneurial firms play a key role in determining the occurrence of an equity investment, it is worth remarking that only few contributions in literature focus on this aspect. In fact, the vast majority of works looks only at the venture capitalists' selection criteria (see, e.g., Wells 1974; Fried and Hisrich 1994; Poindexter 1976; Tyebjee and Bruno 1984; MacMillan et al. 1985; MacMillan et al. 1987; Hall and Hofer 1993). The implicit line of reasoning behind this stream of literature is that the investor is the leading entity and the actual investment depends solely on its evaluation criteria.

The work by Eckhardt et al. (2006) is one of the few that combines this two perspectives, i.e., the two selection processes: the one of the entrepreneurial firm and the one of the venture capitalist. They suggest a two stage venture financing process: in the first stage, firms decide whether to look for VC financing (the firm goes "on the market for VC") or not and in the second stage, VCs select those firms to invest in. From a methodological point of view, their contribution suggests the importance of considering the process of self-selection into markets (stage 1) in order to better understand the VC selection criteria (stage 2) and the effects of investments on firm performances .

This work is much in the spirit of Eckhardt et al. (2006). We aim at looking at the impact of VC investments on the growth of NTBFs, controlling for the firm's self-selection decision of whether positioning "on the market for VC" or not. In fact, lack of controls for (un)observed heterogeneity affecting both self-selection and growth of NTBFs, may lead to biased estimations of the net effect of VC financing.

7.3 The Sample

In this work, we use a unique hand collected longitudinal dataset relating to a sample composed of 215 Italian NTBFs that are observed over a 10 year period (1994–2003). Most sample firms are privately held. They were established in 1980 or later, were independent at founding time and have remained so up to the end of 2003 (i.e., they are not controlled by another business organization even though other organizations may hold minority shareholdings). They operate in the following high-tech sectors in manufacturing and services: computers, electronic components, telecommunication equipment, optical, medical and electronic instruments, biotechnology, pharmaceuticals and advanced materials, robotics and process automation equipment, multimedia content, software, Internet services (i.e., e-commerce, ISP, and web-related services), and telecommunication services.

The sample of NTBFs was drawn from the 2004 release of the RITA (Research on Entrepreneurship in Advanced Technologies) database. Developed at Politecnico di Milano, RITA presently is the most complete source of information on Italian NTBFs. It was created in 2000 and it was updated in 2002 and 2004. The development of the database went through a series of steps. First, Italian firms that complied with the above mentioned criteria relating to age and sector of operations were identified. For the construction of the target population a number of sources were used. These included lists provided by national industry associations and regional Chambers of Commerce, on-line and off-line commercial firm directories, lists of participants in industry trades and expositions, and information provided by the national financial press, specialized magazines, and other sectoral studies. Altogether, 1,974 firms were selected for inclusion in the database. For each firm, a contact person (i.e., one of the owner-managers) was also identified. Unfortunately, data provided by official national statistics do not allow to obtain a reliable description of the universe of Italian NTBFs.[5] Second, a questionnaire was sent to the contact person of the target firms either by fax or by e-mail. The first section of the questionnaire provides detailed information on the human capital characteristics of firms' founders. The second section comprises further questions concerning the characteristics of the firms including access to external equity financing, the identity of external investors, and the evolution over time of firms' employees.

Lastly, answers to the questionnaire were checked for internal coherence by educated personnel and were compared with information obtained from firms' annual reports and other public sources. In several cases, phone or face-to-face follow-up interviews were made with firms' owner-managers. This final step was crucial in order to obtain missing data and ensure that the data were reliable.[6] In addition, financial and economic data including the evolution over time of firms' sales from 1994 onwards, and data on patent activity during firms' entire life were obtained from public sources (i.e., the AIDA and CERVED databases and the databases of patent offices, respectively).

Let us now turn to the survey-based measure of a NTBF's decision to enter into the market of VC.

To construct this measure, we first asked the firm whether it has ever actively looked for external investors (excluding family members and friends) who were disposed to acquire a stake in the equity capital of the firm. Unlike Eckhardt et al. (2006), our definition of a firm "on the VC market" does not derive solely from this,

[5] The main problem is that in Italy most individuals who are defined as "self-employed" by official statistics are actually salaried workers with atypical employment contracts. Unfortunately, on the basis of official data such individuals cannot be distinguished from entrepreneurs who created a new firm.

[6] Note that only for three firms the set of owner-managers at survey date did not include at least one of the founders of the firm.

in fact we combined it with a question useful to detect unsolicited offers. In particular, we asked NTBFs whether they ever received at least one offer from any potential equity investor or not. Consequently, we define a NTBF as being "on the market for VC" if: (i) it has ever actively looked for an equity investor and/or (ii) if it has ever received an offer by an equity investor.[7] Obviously, the use of this time-unvarying measure brings more than a limitation insofar firms may be not always on the market or always out of it. Nevertheless, it also reduces possible retrospective and subjectivity biases and, to the best of our knowledge, represents the first attempt to correct for sample self-selection in the literature on the effects of VC on firm growth.

The sample used in the present work consists of 215 RITA firms that participated in the 2004 survey. χ^2 tests show that there are no statistically significant differences between the distributions of the sample firms across industries and geographic areas and the corresponding distributions of the population of 1,974 RITA firms from which the sample was drawn ($\chi^2(4)=4.66$ and $\chi^2(3)=3.59$, respectively).

The sample is large and quite heterogeneous. Note however that there is no presumption here to have a random sample. First, in this domain representativeness is a slippery notion as new ventures may be defined in different ways (see for instance Birley 1984; Aldrich et al. 1989; Gimeno et al. 1997). Second, as was mentioned above, absent reliable official statistics, it is very difficult to identify unambiguously the universe of Italian NTBFs. Therefore, one cannot check ex post whether the sample used in this work is representative of the universe or not. Third, as in most previous studies based on the survey data, only firms having survived up to the survey date could be included in the sample.

In principle, attrition generates a sample selection bias that may distort the estimates. In fact, the likelihood of going bankrupt of VC-backed firms may exceed that of their non VC-backed counterparts as VC investors are less risk averse than other investors. The results of previous studies seem to support this argument.[8] Under these circumstances lack of control for firms that ceased activity would result in an upward bias of the effect of VC financing on firm growth. As a matter of facts, it is almost impossible to control for the selection bias. The best we can do is to check its extent. For this purpose, we focused attention on the RITA 2000 sample. This sample is composed of 401 NTBFs that were selected through a procedure similar to the one through which the RITA 2004 sample was obtained (see Colombo et al. 2004). Out of these firms, 31 were VC-backed at the beginning of year 2000. We examined the exit rate of these firms in the 2000–2003 period due

[7] Unless all received offers were systematically refused because considered unnecessary. Our aim was to include the firms that took in consideration a received (unsolicited) offer. By doing so we consider "on the market" a firm that is not looking for an investor (e.g., because of lack of time) but that is willing to accept a reasonable offer.

[8] For instance, Manigart et al. (2001) use survival data analysis techniques to compare the likelihood of survival of 565 Belgian VC-backed companies up to 9 years after the first round of VC financing with that of 565 comparable non VC-backed companies. VC-backed firms exhibit a significantly higher probability of exit due to either bankruptcy or closure of activity.

to bankruptcy or closure. 4 VC-backed firms (ceased activity in this period representing 12.9%. The corresponding percentage for non VC-backed firms is fairly close (12.2%). χ^2 tests show that the difference between the two values is not statistically significant at conventional confidence levels (χ^2 (1)=0.011 for VC). Therefore, while it is fair to acknowledge that our sample suffers from a survivorship bias, we are quite confident that this does not greatly influence the results of the estimates that will be illustrated in the following sections.

To sum up, the sample analyzed in this work has several strengths in comparison with the previous studies. As far as we know, this is the first study that relies on a large longitudinal dataset composed by privately held NTBFs which has information on a firm's positioning "on the market for VC." Moreover, the rather long observation period permits use of estimation techniques for panel data models that control quite effectively for the endogenous nature of VC financing (see Sect. 7.4.1). Information on firm-specific characteristics is also very detailed and fine-grained; hence, in testing the causality relation between VC financing and growth, we are able to insert in the set of explanatory variables several controls.

In addition, Italian NTBFs offer an interesting testbed of the alleged positive effects of VC financing on firm growth even in a rather adverse environment. In fact, the characteristics of the Italian financial system are quite unfavorable to VC financing in comparison with those of Anglo-Saxon countries. For instance, in Italy the ratio of the market value of listed firms to GDP in 2001 was 48.2% (41.7% in 2004. Source: Consob), while it was 138.0% in the USA and 151.4% in the UK (source: OECD, Financial Market Trends, October 2004).[9] Accordingly, the Italian VC industry is quite undeveloped. Early stage equity financing was almost inexistent up to the mid 1990s. It increased considerably in the 1995–2000 period, reaching a peak of 540 million € in 2000, equal to 0.046% of GDP (source: AIFI, Italian Association of Private Equity Investors). Nevertheless, not all this amount was invested in NTBFs. Since 2001, early stage equity financing experienced a dramatic decline and it almost vanished in 2004, when there were only 50 investments in 36 companies and the total invested amount was only 23 million €, that is 0.002% of GDP.[10]

Table 7.1 shows the distribution by industry, age and geographic area of sample firms according to their positioning on the VC market and their VC-backing status.

In our sample only 118 out of 215 (about 55.88% of the firms) have been "on the market for VC." Out of these 118 firms, 54 (25.12%) received VC financing.

---

[9] The difference was even larger at the beginning of the 1990s. For instance, Rajan and Zingales (2003) show that in 1990, the ratio of the market value of listed firms to GDP was 13% in Italy, while it was 54% in the USA and 84% in the UK. Conversely, the ratio of bank deposits to GDP was 40% in Italy, 33% in the UK and only 19% in the USA.

[10] These figures exclusively refer to AIFI members; so they are likely to underestimate the actual amount of VC financing. In particular, they do not include most investments made by non-financial firms. For further details on the Italian VC industry see Bertoni et al. (2006).

Table 7.1 Distribution of firms according to the positioning "on the market for VC" and the actual VC-financing; by industry, foundation year and geographical area

	Ever on the VC market?		Ever VC-financed?		
	No	Yes	No	Yes	Total
Industry					
Biotech – Pharma	1(20.00%)	4 (80.00%)	2 (40.00%)	3 (60.00%)	5 (100%)
Electronic publishing	4 (30.77%)	9 (69.23%)	6 (46.15%)	7 (53.85%)	13 (100%)
Internet & Multimedia	22 (34.38%)	42 (65.63%)	43 (67.19%)	21 (32.81%)	64 (100%)
ICT Manufacturing	25 (49.02%)	26 (50.98%)	40 (78.43%)	11 (21.57%)	51 (100%)
Robotics & Automation	12 (63.16%)	7 (36.84%)	17 (89.47%)	2 (10.53%)	19 (100%)
Software	33 (52.38%)	30 (47.62%)	53 (84.13%)	10 (15.87%)	63 (100%)
Foundation year					
1980–1984	14 (60.87%)	9 (39.13%)	18 (78.26%)	5 (21.74%)	23 (100%)
1985–1989	18 (43.90%)	23 (56.10%)	30 (73.17%)	11 (26.83%)	41 (100%)
1990–1994	22 (56.41%)	17 (43.59%)	35 (89.74%)	4 (10.26%)	39 (100%)
1995–1999	35 (43.21%)	46 (56.79%)	60 (74.07%)	21 (25.93%)	81 (100%)
2000–2003	8 (25.81%)	23 (74.19%)	18 (58.06%)	13 (41.94%)	31 (100%)
Geographical area					
North-West	54 (51.43%)	51 (48.57%)	79 (75.24%)	26 (24.76%)	105 (100%)
North-East	16 (34.78%)	30 (65.22%)	35 (76.09%)	11 (23.91%)	46 (100%)
Center	12 (37.50%)	20 (62.50%)	20 (62.50%)	12 (37.50%)	32 (100%)
South & Islands	15 (46.88%)	17 (53.13%)	27 (84.38%)	5 (15.63%)	32 (100%)
Total	97 (45.12%)	118 (54.88%)	161 (74.88%)	54 (25.12%)	215 (100%)

7.4 The Econometric Analysis

7.4.1 Specification of the Econometric Model

We resort to a typical Heckman two-step procedure in order to model the selection stage illustrated in Sect. 7.2.3 and the impact of VC financing on growth. In particular, we first estimated a probit model on the probability of firm's positioning "on the market for VC." The independent variables of this sample selection equation include founders' human capital variables, firm-specific characteristics, and other controls (see Sect. 7.4.2). Based on these estimates, we computed the inverse Mill's ratio of firm being "on the market for VC." This ratio was then inserted as a control for sample self-selection in the growth equation. This additional variable controls for the unobserved heterogeneity that affects both a firm's probability of being "on the market for VC" and its growth, allowing more consistent estimates of the parameters of the growth equation.This latter is specified as an augmented Gibrat law type dynamic growth model, where the dependent variable is the logarithm of the size of firms measured alternatively by the number of employees (including owners-managers) and sales. Regressors include the dependent variable lagged one period, the logarithm of the age of firms, a dummy variable that equal unity if at time $t-1$ or before the NTBF i got access to VC financing and the Heckman correction term. Unfortunately, as in most previous studies, we do not have information on the amount of VC financing obtained by sample firms in different rounds. Therefore we resort to a single dummy variable equal to one from the year of VC entry in order to capture the impact of VC financing on firm growth also in subsequent years. The inclusion in the growth equation of the lagged dependent variable as one of the covariates and the possible endogenous nature of the relationship between VC financing and firm size require the use of appropriate estimation techniques. In fact, as long as regressors are correlated with disturbance terms, both pooled ordinary least squares (OLS) and fixed effects within groups (WG) estimators produce biased estimates. Therefore, following the recent literature on dynamic panel data models (see Arellano and Bond 1991; Blundell and Bond 1998; Bond 2002) we resort to the generalized method of moments (GMM) procedure and estimate the growth models by the GMM-system estimator. This approach, originally proposed by Blundell and Bond (1998), extend the GMM-DIF estimator (first differenced) in that additional moment conditions are used in order to obtain more efficient estimates. In particular, other than using lagged levels of the series as instruments for first differences (as in GMM-DIF), additional information is extracted using the first differences as instruments for variables in levels.[11] This augmented GMM estimator requires the assumption of mean stationary of the series and is particularly appropriate where series are highly persistent (see Bond 2002).

7.4.2 Variables

In this subsection, we describe the independent variables of the econometric models (see Table 7.2 for definitions). As concerns the selection equation, we include a group of variables measuring the human capital of firms' founders. As regards education, we distinguish between years of university-level education in economic and managerial fields (*Ecoeduc*) and in scientific and technical fields (*Techeduc*). As to founders' work experience at the time of firm's foundation, we distinguish between years of work experience in the same sector of the new firm in the R&D, design, engineering, and production departments (*Techworkexp*), and in marketing, sale, and customer care functions (*Comworkexp*); *Otherworkexp* represents the years of work experience in other sectors. For all these variables, we calculate the average across founders, adding also the logarithm of the number of founders (*LNfounders*) in order to disentangle the truly qualitative effect of human capital

[11] In particular, considering the VC financing variable as endogenous implies the use of instruments dated t-2 for the equations in first differences and instruments dated $t-1$ for the equations in levels.

Table 7.2 Definition of explanatory variables

Variable	Description
Selection variable	
OnVCMarket	Dummy equal to one if the firm has ever been "on the market for VC"
Gibrat variables	
Employees ($t-1$)	Logarithm of the size of the company at $t-1$ measured by the number of employees
Sales ($t-1$)	Logarithm of the size of the company at $t-1$ measured by the total sales of the firm (thousand of Euro)
LAge	Logarithm of the number of years since firm's foundation at $t-1$
Founder – specific variables	
LNfounders	Logarithm of the number of founders
Techworkexp	Average number of years of technical work experience of founders in the same sector of the start-up before firm's foundation
Comworkexp	Average number of years of commercial work experience of founders in the same sector of the start-up before firm's foundation
Otherworkexp	Average number of years of work experience of founders in other sectors than the one of the start-up before firm's foundation
Techeduc	Average number of years of scientific and/or technical education of founders at university level
Ecoeduc	Average number of years of economic and/or managerial education of founders at university level
Firm – specific variables	
VC($t-1$)	One for companies that obtained VC financing at $t-1$ or before
Other controls	
VCArea	Synthetic index capturing the intensity of VC investments in the geographic area on which the NTBF is located, calculated as follows. First, we considered the total number of high-tech firms that obtained VC financing over the period 1997–2003 (source: AIFI). Let VCA_k indicate the share accounted for by geographical area k out of this number. Let A_k be the estimated shares accounted for geographical area k out of the total number of Italian NTBFs in 2003 (source: RITA Directory). Then: $VCArea_k = VCA_k/A_k$
Length observation period	Age of the firm when the survey data related to the variable OnVCMarket were collected

covariates from merely quantitative aspects. Then, since our measure of a firm positioning "on the market for VC" is time unvarying, we also included an indicator of the length of the observation period (*LenghtObservationPeriod*) calculated as the logarithm of the difference between the time when the firm answered the specific question and the founding year. This variable controls both for "age effects", i.e., a ager firm might be more likely to have ever looked for VC, and for potential retrospective bias, i.e., a firm might have difficulties in remembering events too distant in time and thus a ager firm "on the market" might be more difficult to observe. Lastly, we also included a measure of the propensity of the VC industry to invest in the geographical area (*VCArea*) in which the firm is located and industry dummies to control for industry-specific factors that may influence NTBFs' decision to position themselves "on the market for VC."

As to the growth equation, lagged variables of the logarithm of size (*Employees* $(t-1)$ and *Sales* $(t-1)$) as well as the logarithm of age (*LAge*) are introduced according to a typical Gibral law dynamic model. The independent variable of interest is *VC*$(t-1)$, which is a dummy variable denoting VC-backed firms invested (strictly) before time *t*. The equation also includes the Heckman correction term (*Selection Correction Term*) and industry dummies to control for industryspecific factors that may influence the growth of NTBFs.

7.4.3 Econometric Results

Table 7.3 shows the estimates of the Probit selection equation on the determinants of firms' positioning "on the market for VC."

The results echo those of other studies on the determinants of firm access to VC financing (see Colombo and Grilli 2005, 2009) that show that only some out of several founder-, firm-, location- characteristics significantly impact firms' probability to enter into VC market. In particular, founders' economic and managerial education and their commercial specific work experience are significantly more likely to be positioned on the VC market, while other founders' characteristics (managerial experience, technical specific and generic work experience) are found to be statistically non significant. The covariate *LNFounders* presents a positive and statistically significant coefficient. Quite reasonably, the propensity of the VC industry to invest in the same region of the NTBF is positively related to its positioning on the market for external private equity.

Table 7.4 shows the results of the estimation of the augmented Gibrat law type dynamic growth equation by GMM-system estimator. Models include a Heckman correction term for sample self-selection.

Let us first consider the effects on firm growth of the size and age variables. The coefficient of firm size is significantly smaller than unity in both the employment and sales equations. This is consistent with the stylized fact highlighted by the empirical literature on Gibrat's law (see Evans 1987; Hart and Oulton 1996; Sutton 1997; Caves 1998) that smaller firms tend to grow faster than larger ones. Conversely, the coefficient of age is negative both in the employment and sales equations, though insignificant. In other words, the contention of Jovanovic (1982) that older firms grow more slowly than younger ones is only weakly supported by our estimates (for similar results see Shanmugam and Bhaduri 2002).[12]

[12] In our sample firms are never older than 24 years, with most of them being less than 10 year old. So results cannot be generalized to older firms.

Table 7.3 The determinants of the firm positioning "on the market for VC" (Probit estimation)

	OnVCMarket	
LNfounders	0.157	***
	(0.051)	
Techworkexp	–0.002	
	(0.012)	
Comworkexp	0.015	***
	(0.005)	
Otherworkexp	–0.001	
	(0.007)	
Techeduc	0.020	
	(0.022)	
Ecoeduc	0.149	***
	(0.036)	
Length observation period	–0.007	
	(0.008)	
VCArea	0.067	***
	(0.021)	
Industry dummies	YES	
Observations	215	

Reporting marginal effects. Robust standard errors in round brackets
Significance level: ***$p<0.01$, **$p<0.05$, *$p<0.1$

More interestingly for the purpose of this paper, the estimates reveal that VC financing has an important positive impact on the growth of NTBFs. This especially applies to the growth of the number of employees. In the sales equation all VC variables exhibit positive coefficients, though insignificant in regression (3), this may partly be due to the greater volatility of sales over time.

To measure the long-run effect of VC financing on firm growth (Ê), we use a non-linear combination of the regression coefficients. In particular, the long-run effect is computed by the following expression:

$$\hat{E}_{VC(long-run)} = \frac{\hat{\beta}_k}{1-\hat{\alpha}_1}$$

This approach is equivalent to measure the cumulative distance between the size of a VC-backed firm and that of its twin non-VC-backed counterpart over time (for a similar approach in a different context see Maliranta 2005). A χ^2 test (performed by the Delta method) shows that the long-run total effect of VC financing on firm size is positive and significant, regardless of whether size is measured by the number of employees or by sales.

Table 7.4 The effects of VC financing on the growth of NTBFs (System GMM Estimations)

	Employees				Sales			
	(1)		(2)		(3)		(4)	
Constant	0.447	***	0.096		5.553	***	5.650	***
	(0.117)		(0.216)		(1.514)		(1.499)	
Employees ($t-1$)	0.837	***	0.777	***				
	(0.050)		(0.060)					
Sales ($t-1$)					0.743	***	0.718	***
					(0.092)		(0.090)	
LAge	–0.048		–0.070		–0.147		–0.194	
	(0.063)		(0.089)		(0.161)		(0.172)	
VC($t-1$)	0.352	***	0.507	***	0.253		0.409	**
	(0.075)		(0.110)		(0.213)		(0.193)	
Selection correction term			YES	**			YES	
Industry dummies	YES		YES		YES		YES	
Observations	646		646		637		637	
Number of firms	117		117		116		116	
Number of instruments	112		112		111		111	
AR(1)	–4.835	***	–4.749	***	–3.084	***	–3.142	***
AR(2)	–0.922		–0.867		–0.160		–0.161	
Sargan-Hansen	74.46		75.18		74.17		72.92	
	[104]		[103]		[103]		[102]	
Long run effect of VC	2.161	***	2.267	***	.984	*	1.451	***
	(0.479)		(0.485)		(0.556)		(0.466)	

Significance level: ***$p<0.01$, **$p<0.05$, *$p<0.1$. SYS-GMM estimates are obtained by the estimation of a two-step GMM-System model with finite sample correction (Windmeijer 2005). AR(1) and AR(2) are tests of the null hypothesis of respectively no first- or second-order serial correlation. Sargan-Hansen is a test of the validity of the overidentifying restrictions based on the efficient two-step GMM estimator. SYS-GMM estimates are based on the hypothesis of venture capital financing and additional control variables as being endogenous, which implies use of instruments dated at least $t-2$ for the equations in first differences and instruments dated $t-1$ for the equations in levels. Since the Sargan-Hansen test rejects the null hypothesis on instrument validity in the SYS-GMM sales equations, in this case instruments begin from time $t-3$ in the difference and $t-2$ in the level equations. Robust standard errors in round brackets, degrees of freedom in square brackets

The estimates show that the effect of VC financing on firm growth indeed depends on whether we control for the self-selection by including the correction term; this especially applies to firms' sales. As a matter of fact, the coefficient of VC increases in magnitude once controlling for self-selection in both employment and sales equation, as well as the long-run effects of VC. Diagnostics reassure us on the robustness of the findings. In particular, the autocorrelation tests and Sargan-Hansen test of over-identifying restrictions are passed in all regressions.[13]

To sum up, the results of the estimates clearly support the view that VC financing has a beneficial effect on the growth of both employment and sales of NTBFs. They also indicate that controlling for the self-selection matters: lack of control for it is probably to lead to a downward bias of the effects of VC on growth.

7.5 Discussion and Conclusions

The aim of this paper was to analyze empirically the effect of VC financing on the growth of NTBFs, controlling for possible sample self-selection. The extant literature emphasizes the beneficial effects that VC financing allegedly has on portfolio firms, due to the scouting, monitoring and coaching role performed by these investors, and the certification effect of their endorsement to uninformed third parties. Nevertheless, the empirical evidence on this issue is fairly limited and not unanimous. Actually, most previous econometric studies suffer from serious methodological drawbacks. The selection bias possibly engendered by exclusive consideration of firms that went through an IPO and failure to effectively control for the endogenous nature of VC financing may have led to non generalizable or distorted estimates. In addition, some recent works suggest that not all the firms are equally likely to receive VC financing. Accordingly, the effect of VC financing on the growth of portfolio firms may also depend on the characteristics of firms that actually are "on the market for VC." As a matter of fact, a large part of the NTBFs in our sample, nearly 45%, decided to stay out of the market highlighting the importance of the self-selection process.

In order to detect the positive impact on growth of VC financing, we have considered here a unique hand collected longitudinal dataset that includes 215 Italian NTBFs that operate in high-tech manufacturing and service sectors, and are observed over a 10 year period (i.e., 1994–2003). The rather long longitudinal dimension of the dataset has allowed us to estimate an augmented Gibrat law type dynamic panel data model with distributed lags using a GMM-system estimation technique that takes duly into account the endogenous nature of VC financing. As most sample firms are privately held, this dataset vdoes not suffer from the selection bias that affects samples exclusively composed of IPO firms. Furthermore, we have been able to control for the self-selection made by the firms in positioning "on the market for VC." Lastly, in Italy, the VC sector is fairly undeveloped in comparison to the USA and the UK; hence, this study offers fresh new insights on the positive role that VC could play for the development of the NTBF sector of the economy even in an adverse environment.

---

[13]As far as autocorrelation tests are concerned, AR(1) must be significantly negative and AR(2) must not be significant in order to rule out the presence of serial correlation in residuals. The Sargan-Hansen statistics tests the null hypothesis of validity of the instruments.

Our results clearly support the view that VC financing fuels firm growth. According to our estimates, after receiving the first round of VC financing portfolio firms exhibit a considerably greater growth rate measured in terms of both the number of employees and the amount of sales. Moreover, controls for sample self-selection "on the market for VC" brings the positive effect of VC on growth to become even larger.

We think that these results offer new interesting insights into the role of VC financing in fostering the growth of high-tech start-ups; moreover, they also highlight that self-selection "out of the market for VC" seem to be prominent. Quite interestingly, they clearly document that even in an unfavorable environment as the one provided by the Italian financial system, VC financing has a dramatic positive influence on NTBF growth. This evidence has important policy implications. In fact, in Europe the VC sector is far less developed than in the USA or in Israel. While an analysis of the determinants of this situation lies beyond the scope of the present work,[14] the findings illustrated here support the view that the development of the demand for and supply of VC financing should figure prominently in the innovation policy agenda of European governments.

To conclude, it is fair to acknowledge that much remains to be done in this field, especially to understand the effective positioning of the NTBFs "on the market for VC." In this respect, a fundamental research direction is the understanding of the determinants of this choice. Given the positive effect of VC financing on firm growth, why a conspicuous number of firms decide to self-select themselves out of the market?

More generally, VC selection process involves two different mutually interdependent stages: self-selection made by the firm and investment decision of the venture capitalist. The study on the interaction between these two becomes crucial for a better understanding of the effects of VC on both firm performance and, more generally, the whole economic system.

Acknowledgment We acknowledge support from the Venture Fun project promoted by the EU PRIME Network of Excellence and from the VICO project (Financing entrepreneurial ventures in Europe: impact on innovation, employment growth, and competitiveness) promoted by the Seventh Framework Programme of the European Commission.

References

Acs ZJ (2004) The value of entrepreneurial start-ups to an economy. Seminar Discussion Paper, Diebold Institute for Public Policy Studies

Aldrich HE, Kallenberg A, Marsden P, Cassell J (1989) In pursuit of evidence: sampling procedures for locating new businesses. J Bus Venturing 4:367–386

Alemany L, Martì J (2005) Unbiased estimation of economic impact of venture capital backed firms. Working paper, Università Complutense de Madrid

[14] See Da Rin et al. (2006) for an econometric study of country-specific and industry-specific factors that stimulate VC investments. For an analysis of the development of the Israel VC industry and the role of public policy see Avnimelech and Teubal (2004).

Amit R, Glosten L, Muller E (1990) Entrepreneurial ability, venture investments, and risk sharing. Manage Sci 36:1232–1245
Amit R, Brander J, Zott C (1998) Why do venture capital firms exist? Theory and Canadian evidence. J Bus Venturing 13:441–466
Arellano M, Bond S (1991) Some tests of specification for panel data: Monte Carlo evidence and an application to employment equations. Rev Econ Stud 58:277–297
Audretsch DB (1995) Innovation and industry evolution. MIT Press, Cambridge, MA
Avnimelech G, Teubal M (2004) Venture capital start-up co-evolution and the emergence of Israel's new high-tech clusters. Econ Innov N Technol 13:33–60
Barney JB, Busenitz LB, Fiet JO, Moesel DD (1996) New venture teams' assessment of learning assistance from venture capital firms. J Bus Venturing 4:257–272
Barry CB, Muscarella CJ, Peavy JW, Vetsuypens MR (1990) The role of venture capital in the creation of public companies. J financ econ 27:447–471
Berger AN, Udell GF (1998) The economics of small business finance: the roles of private equity and debt markets in the financial growth cycle. J Bank Finance 22:613–673
Bertoni F, Colombo MG, Croce A, Piva E (2006) A review of the venture capital industry in Italy. In: Gregoriou GN, Kooli M, Kraeussl R (eds) Venture capital in Europe. Elsevier, Amsterdam, pp 129–143
Birley S (1984) Finding the new firm. Proc Acad Manage Meet 47:64–68
Blundell R, Bond S (1998) Initial conditions and moment restrictions in dynamic panel data models. J Econom 87:115–143
Bond S (2002) Dynamic panel data models: a guide to micro data methods and practice. Port Econ J 1:141–162
Bottazzi L, Da Rin M (2002) Venture capital in Europe and the financing of innovative companies. Econ Policy 17:229–269
Bottazzi L, Da Rin M, Hellmann T (2004) Active financial intermediation: evidence on the role of organizational specialization and human capital. Finance working paper No. 49-2004, ECGI
Bürghel O, Fier A, Licht G, Murray G (2000) Internationalization of high-tech start-ups and fast growth. Evidence for UK and Germany. Discussion paper No. 00-35, Centre for European Economic Research (ZEW), Mannheim
Bygrave W, Timmons J (1992) Venture capital at the crossroads. Harvard Business School Press, Boston, MA
Carpenter RE, Petersen BC (2002) Capital market imperfections, high-tech investment, and new equity financing. Econ J 112:F54–F72
Caves RE (1998) Industrial organization and new findings on the turn-over and mobility of firms. J Econ Lit 36:1947–1982
Chan YS (1983) On the positive role of financial intermediation in allocation of venture capital in market with imperfect information. J Finance 35:1543–1568
Colombo MG, Grilli L (2005) Founders' human capital and the growth of new technology-based firms: a competence based view. Res Policy 34:795–816
Colombo MG, Grilli L (2009) On growth drivers of high-tech start-ups: exploring the role of founders' human capital and venture capital. J Bus Venturing, forthcoming
Colombo MG, Delmastro M, Grilli L (2004) Entrepreneurs' human capital and the start-up size of new technology-based firms. Int J Indust Organ 22:1183–1211
Colombo MG, Grilli L, Piva E (2006) In search for complementary assets: the determinants of alliance formation of high-tech start-ups. Res Policy 35:1166–1199
Da Rin M, Nicodano G, Sembenelli A (2006) Public policy and the creation of active venture capital markets. J Public Econ 90:1699–1723
Davila A, Foster G, Gupta M (2003) Venture capital financing and the growth of start-up firms. J Bus Venturing 18:689–708
Denis DJ (2004) Entrepreneurial finance: an overview of the issues and evidence. J Corp Finance 10:301–326

Eckhardt JT, Shane S, Delmar F (2006) Multistage selection and the financing of new ventures. Manage Sci 52:220–232
Engel D (2002) The impact of venture capital on firm growth: an empirical investigation. Discussion Paper No. 02-02, Centre for European Economic Research (ZEW), Mannheim
Engel D, Keilbach M (2007) Firm level implication of early stage venture capital investment: an empirical investigation. J Empir Finance 14:150–167
Evans DS (1987) The relationship between firm growth, size, and age: estimates for 100 manufacturing industries. J Ind Econ 35:567–581
Fazzari SM, Hubbard RG, Petersen BC (1988) Financing constraints and corporate investment. Brookings Pap Econ Act 1:141–205
Fried VH, Hisrich RD (1994) Toward a model of Venture Capital investment decision making. Financ Manage 23:28–37
Gimeno J, Folta T, Cooper A, Woo C (1997) Survival of the fittest? Entrepreneurial human capital and the persistence of underperforming firms. Adm Sci Q 42:750–783
Gompers PA (1995) Optimal investment, monitoring, and the staging of venture capital. J Finance 50:1461–1489
Gompers P, Lerner J (2001) The venture capital revolution. J Econ Perspect 15:145–168
Gorman M, Sahlman WA (1989) What do venture capitalist do? J Bus Venturing 4:231–248
Hall J, Hofer CW (1993) Venture capitalists' decision criteria in new venture evaluation. J Bus Venturing 8:25–42
Hart PE, Oulton N (1996) Growth and size of firms. Econ J 106:1242–1252
Heckman J (1990) Varieties of selection bias. Am Econ Rev (Papers and Proceedings) 80:313–318
Hellmann T (1998) The allocation of control rights in venture capital contracts. Rand J Econ 29:57–76
Hellmann T, Puri M (2002) Venture capital and the professionalization of start-up firms: empirical evidence. J Finance 57:169–197
Hsu DH (2004) What do entrepreneurs pay for venture capital affiliation? J Finance 59:1805–1844
Hsu DH (2006) Venture capitalists and cooperative start-up commercialization strategy. Manage Sci 52:204–219
Hubbard RG (1998) Capital-market imperfections and investment. J Econ Lit 36:193–225
Jaffee D, Russell T (1976) Imperfect information, uncertainty and credit rationing. Q J Econ 90:651–666
Jain BA, Kini O (1995) Venture capitalist participation and the post- issue operating performance of IPO firms. Managerial Decision Econ 6:593–606
Jovanovic B (1982) Selection and the evolution of industry. Econometrica 50:649–670
Kaplan SN, Strömberg P (2001) Venture capitalists as principals: contracting, screening and monitoring. Am Econ Rev 91:426–430
Kaplan SN, Strömberg P (2003) Financial contracting theory meets the real world: an empirical analysis of venture capital contracts. Rev Econ Stud 70:281–315
Kaplan SN, Strömberg P (2004) Characteristics, contracts and actions: evidence from venture capitalists analyses. J Finance 59:2177–2210
Lindsey L (2002) The venture capital Keiretsu effect: an empirical analysis of strategic alliances among portfolio firms. Working paper, Stanford University
MacMillan IC, Seigel R, Subba Narasimha PN (1985) Criteria used by venture capitalist to evaluate new venture proposals. J Bus Venturing 1:119–128
MacMillan IC, Zeman L, Subba Narasimha PN (1987) Criteria distinguishing unsuccessful ventures in the venture screening process. J Bus Venturing 2:123–137
MacMillan IC, Kulow DM, Khoylian R (1989) Venture capitalists' involvement in their investments: extent and performance. J Bus Venturing 4:27–47
Maliranta M (2005) R&D, international trade and creative destruction: empirical findings from Finnish manufacturing industries. J Ind Competition Trade 5:27–58
Manigart S, Van Hyfte M (1999) Post-investment evolution of venture backed companies. In: Reynolds P, Bygrave W, Manigart S, Mason C, Meyer G, Sapienza HJ, Shaver K (eds) Frontiers of entrepreneurship research. Babson College, Wellesley, MA, pp 419–432

Manigart S, Baeyens K, Van Hyfte M (2001) The survival of venture capital backed companies. Working paper, University of Gent
Megginson W, Weiss K (1991) Venture capitalist certification in initial public offerings. J Finance 46:879–903
Poindexter JB (1976) The efficiency of financial markets: the venture capital case. Unpublished doctorial dissertation, New York University, NY
Rajan R, Zingales L (2003) The great reversals: the politics of financial development in the twentieth century. J Financ Econ 69:5–50
Sahlman WA (1990) The structure and governance of venture-capital organizations. J Financ Econ 27:473–521
Sapienza HJ (1992) When do venture capitalists add value? J Bus Venturing 7:9–27
Sapienza HJ, Manigart S, Vermeir W (1996) Venture capital governance and value added in four countries. J Bus Venturing 11:439–469
Shanmugam KR, Bhaduri SN (2002) Size, age and firm growth in the Indian manufacturing sector. Appl Econ Lett 9:607–613
Stiglitz J, Weiss A (1981) Credit rationing in markets with incomplete information. Am Econ Rev 71:393–409
Stuart TE, Hoang H, Hybels R (1999) Interorganizational endorsements and the performance of entrepreneurial ventures. Adm Sci Q 44:315–349
Sutton J (1997) Gibrat's legacy. J Econ Lit 35:40–59
Tyebjee TT, Bruno AV (1984) A model of venture capitalist investment activity. Manage Sci 30:1051–1066
Ueda M (2004) Banks versus venture capital: project evaluation, screening, and expropriation. J Finance 59:601–621
Vella F, Verbeek M (1999) Estimating and interpreting models with endogenous treatment effects. J Bus Econ Stat 17:473–478
Wells WA (1974) Venture capital decision making. Unpublished doctorial dissertation, Carnegie Mellon University, Pittsburgh
Windmeijer F (2005) A finite sample correction for the variance of linear efficient two-step GMM estimators. J Econom 126:25–51

Part III
Learning, Innovation and Entrepreneurship

Chapter 8
Creating Exploratory Innovations by Learning from Entrepreneurial Ventures

Anu Wadhwa, Corey Phelps, and Suresh Kotha

Abstract Corporate venture capital (CVC), direct minority equity investments made by established companies in privately held start-ups, has become an important strategic tool for many large companies. In particular, firms often pursue CVC investing as a way to learn about novel technologies. Although CVC investments are inherently exploratory and have been found to enhance investing firm's innovation, research has yet to establish whether CVC investing leads to the development of exploratory innovations (i.e., innovations that embody knowledge that differs from knowledge used by the firm in prior innovation efforts). In this paper, we explore the conditions under which CVC investments lead to the creation of exploratory knowledge by corporate investors. Building on insights from the recombinatory search and interorganizational learning literatures, we argue that three characteristics of an investing firm's portfolio of start-ups will enhance its creation of exploratory knowledge. Using longitudinal data on a panel of 40 telecommunications equipment manufacturers, we find that investing firms produce more exploratory knowledge when their portfolios include start-ups that are moderately diverse, mature, and possess codified technological knowledge.

8.1 Introduction

A growing consensus in the strategic management literature suggests the development and deployment of knowledge represent a principal source of competitive advantage for firms, e.g., Eisenhardt and Martin 2000; Grant 1996; Teece et al. 1997). In particular, the creation and commercial exploitation of technological knowledge in the form

---

A. Wadhwa (✉)
College of Management of Technology, Ecole Polytechnique Fédérale de Lausanne, Lausanne, 1015, Switzerland
e-mail: anu.wadhwa@epfl.ch

D.B. Audretsch et al. (eds.), *New Frontiers in Entrepreneurship: Recognizing, Seizing, and Executing, Opportunities*, International Studies in Enterpreneurship,
DOI 10.1007/978-1-4419-0058-6_8,

of new products and services are central to the sustained economic performance of organizations (Roberts 1999). To access novel sources of knowledge and renew their competencies, established firms often augment internal R&D efforts with external initiatives such as alliances, acquisitions, and corporate venture capital (CVC) investments. While many studies have investigated the influence of alliances and acquisitions on firm innovation performance (see de Man and Duysters 2005 for a review), only recently have researchers turned their attention to assess the influence of CVC investing on firm innovation.

CVC investments are direct minority equity investments made by established companies in privately held entrepreneurial ventures (Dushnitsky 2006). CVC relationships are exploratory initiatives because they establish boundary-spanning relationships with new ventures, which often pursue novel technologies and are thus an important source of knowledge for corporate investors (Dushnitsky and Lenox 2005; Wadhwa and Kotha 2006). Although firms may seek direct financial returns from their CVC investments, strategic motives typically dominate financial incentives (Dushnitsky 2006). In particular, research shows that firms most often pursue CVC investing with the strategic objective of learning about novel technologies (Dushnitsky 2006). Consistent with this motive, recent studies show that CVC investing can enhance a corporate investor's innovativeness (Dushnitsky and Lenox 2005; Keil et al. 2007; Wadhwa and Kotha 2006).

Despite these recent studies, we still know relatively little about the conditions under which CVC investing influences investor learning and innovation (cf. Maula 2007). In particular, research into the influence of CVC on firm innovation is limited in at least one important respect: it largely ignores the *novelty* of the knowledge created and embodied in the innovations measured. This omission is surprising given that CVC relationships are typically formed for exploratory reasons. By focusing on the *amount* of innovation as the relevant dependent variable, prior research implicitly assumes that innovations resulting from CVC activity are homogeneous in terms of their resulting knowledge content. From these studies, it is difficult to determine whether investing firms generated exploitative or explorative innovations from their CVC activity. Whereas, an exploitative innovation builds on the firm's existing knowledge and represents an incremental addition to the firm's knowledge base, an exploratory innovation embodies knowledge that differs from knowledge used in prior innovation efforts and shows that the firm has broadened its technical competence (Benner and Tushman 2002; Greve 2007; Rosenkopf and Nerkar 2001). Exploratory innovation is akin to radical innovation at the firm level, since it represents innovations that embody knowledge outside a firm's extant technical competence (Greve 2007).

Understanding the origins of exploratory innovation is an important endeavor. Strategy research has emphasized that the creation of knowledge is at the core of understanding sustainable competitive advantage (Teece et al. 1997). Exploratory innovations provide firms with opportunities for strategic renewal by opening new, promising areas of technical advance and the foundation for new businesses (Kim and Kogut 1996). The production of exploratory knowledge also creates opportunities for future exploitation (Zollo and Winter 2002) and enhances long term firm survival (March 1991).

While research suggests firms typically pursue local search and produce exploitative innovations (Dosi 1988; Helfat 1994), a few studies have found that firms exhibit large variation in the scope of their search behavior and the exploratory content of their innovations (Ahuja and Lampert 2001; Rosenkopf and Nerkar 2001). Research has begun to examine how organizational design decisions such as organizational structure and vertical integration influence exploratory knowledge creation (Jansen et al. 2006; Siggelkow and Rivkin 2005). However, few studies examine the impact of external knowledge sourcing initiatives on firm exploratory knowledge creation. In particular, research has not yet examined *whether* or *when* CVC investing influences exploratory innovation.

To address these significant gaps in our understanding of CVC and firm exploration, we examine the conditions under which a CVC investor's portfolio of startup firms influences its production of exploratory technological knowledge. As such, we answer Dushnitsky's (2006) call to move beyond examining firm innovation rates and study the impact of CVC on the other aspects of firm performance. Exploratory knowledge refers to technological knowledge that is novel relative to a firm's extant knowledge stock.

Drawing on insights from interorganizational learning and recombinatory search literatures, we posit that three characteristics of a corporate investor's portfolio of start-ups will influence its exploratory knowledge creation: (1) the diversity of the corporate investors' portfolio; (2) the degree of technological knowledge codification in portfolio firms; and (3) the maturity of the portfolio firms. In so doing, we move beyond the dyadic level perspective typically employed in interorganizational learning research and examine characteristics of the collection of interfirm relationships maintained by firms. We test our hypotheses using longitudinal data on 40 telecommunications equipment manufacturers during the period 1989–2000. Our results suggest that established firms can increase their exploratory knowledge creation when they invest in moderately diverse startups with relatively mature and codified knowledge bases. These results contribute to the CVC and broader corporate entrepreneurship literatures and research into the influence of interorganizational relationships on firm innovation.

8.2 Theory and Hypotheses

To understand how and when CVC investing influences an investing firm's production of exploratory knowledge, we build on two complementary research streams: recombinatory search and interorganizational learning. Recombinatory search describes the nature of innovation. The recombinatory search literature argues that innovation is a problem-solving process in which solutions to economically valuable problems are discovered via search (Dosi 1988). Search processes leading to the creation of new knowledge, embodied in patents and new products, typically involve the novel recombination of existing elements of knowledge, problems, or solutions (Fleming 2001; Nelson and Winter 1982) or the reconfiguration of the ways in which knowledge elements are linked (Henderson and Clark 1990). Search is an uncertain and costly process and is guided by prior experience (Dosi 1988). Over time, feedback from past search efforts becomes embodied in the organizational routines that efficiently guide the innovation search activities of organizational members (Nelson and Winter 1982).

Firms create new knowledge by engaging in local and distant search (March 1991). Local search, which is synonymous with exploitation, produces recombinations of familiar and well-known knowledge elements, and is often the preferred mode of search for organizations (Cyert and March 1963; Stuart and Podolny 1996). In contrast, distant search, or exploration, involves recombinations of novel, unfamiliar knowledge and is often characterized by substantial costs and uncertainty (March 1991; Nelson and Winter 1982). Although distant search can be less efficient and less certain than local search (Fleming 2001), it increases the variance of search and the possibility of highly novel recombinations (Levinthal and March 1981; Fleming 2001). Distant search, across organizational and technological boundaries, can lead to radical innovations that create new technological opportunities and significantly influence subsequent technological change (Rosenkopf and Nerkar 2001). Despite the risks and costs involved, distant search can be critical for the development or renewal of firm competences (March 1991).

While research into recombinatory search has largely focused on *where* firms search for solutions, the interorganizational learning literature has emphasized *how* firms search. This literature argues that interfirm relationships are a mechanism for search and a medium of knowledge transfer (Huber 1991). Since knowledge is widely and heterogeneously distributed (von Hayek 1945), the exchange of knowledge is a prerequisite for recombination (Nahapiet and Ghoshal 1998). Firms that are able to search for, and identify, potentially useful elements of knowledge, conceive of how these knowledge components can be fruitfully recombined, and effectively access and assimilate this knowledge increase their chances of new knowledge creation (Galunic and Rodan 1998; Nahapiet and Ghoshal 1998). Interfirm relationships play an important role in each of these aspects of successful recombination.

Formalized interorganizational relationships are essentially social relationships that provide partners with access to each other's resources (Nahapiet and Ghoshal 1998; Stuart 2000). As such, CVC relationships can increase the amount and variety of knowledge flows available to a firm's recombination efforts, resulting in greater knowledge creation. Many characteristics of CVC relationships facilitate corporate investor access to a venture's knowledge. Before investing, corporate investors conduct rigorous due diligence on various aspects of the venture including its management team, business plan, financials, target markets, products and technology (Chesbrough 2002). As part of this evaluation, personnel from the investor's R&D group and a relevant business unit are typically involved in assessing the technology and product, which can provide valuable learning opportunities and establish relationships with venture personnel for on-going information exchange (Basu et al. 2009). Upon investment, corporate investors generally obtain either a board seat or board observer rights, which provide them with information about the venture's strategic activities and technology. These board roles are often filled by experienced business unit managers or R&D personnel who have the legitimacy and social networks within their firms to effectively channel useful information about the venture's activity to groups that can benefit from it. These individuals also frequently facilitate the development of mutually beneficial learning relationships between personnel in the venture and the corporate investor (Basu et al. 2009). Finally, corporate investors typically employ frequent, systematic performance evaluation meetings with their portfolio firms that focus on technology development and other performance indicators.

Although an interfirm relationship, such as a CVC investment, provides access to a partner's knowledge, it does not guarantee the effective detection, transfer and assimilation of this knowledge. These processes, and therefore the likelihood of successful recombination, are largely influenced by characteristics of the knowledge being accessed (Galunic and Rodan 1998; Zander and Kogut 1995). Interorganizational learning research shows that the tacitness of knowledge impedes its detection, transfer and assimilation (Simonin 1999; Sorenson et al. 2006). Tacitness typically results from the fact that much of an organization's knowledge is embedded in routines (Nelson and Winter 1982). Organizational routines develop over time as a result of learning-by-doing and embody the collective wisdom of organizational members about how to accomplish specific tasks (Nelson and Winter 1982). Well-established routines serve to effectively and efficiently guide the organizational members in the execution of specific organizational activities. Such well-honed routines can serve as templates for the effective transfer of knowledge embedded in these routines (Nelson and Winter 1982). Direct and repeatable access to an established template reduces the recipient's ambiguity about the knowledge and increases the effectiveness of its detection, transfer, and assimilation (Jensen and Szulanski 2007; Sorenson et al. 2006).

In sum, recombinatory search and interorganizational learning provide a complementary understanding of whether and when the firms are able to create exploratory knowledge through the use of CVC. Whereas, recombinatory search literature emphasizes the implications of where firms search for knowledge creation, the interorganizational learning literature identifies factors that facilitate or impede how firms search for and transfer knowledge. Recombinatory search highlights the importance of firms having access to diverse, novel domains of knowledge to expand their search space. Such access can be accomplished via CVC relationships. CVC investing represents a firm's efforts to search for new sources of innovation, access new knowledge bases, and learn about new technologies. Interorganizational learning research emphasizes the importance of the characteristics of the knowledge being accessed to the success of its recombination. CVC relationships that provide a corporate investor access to ventures with codified knowledge and well-developed (i.e., mature) routines should be better able to detect, transfer, and assimilate this knowledge, resulting in an increased recombinatorial success.

We examine the influence the composition of a corporate investor's portfolio of startups has on its exploratory knowledge creation. Doing so allows us to move beyond the dyadic level perspective typically employed in interorganizational learning research and examine characteristics of the collection of interfirm relationships maintained by firms. Taking a portfolio perspective is consistent with the centralized and dedicated way minority equity investing is typically managed in established firms (Dushnitsky 2006). Focusing on the portfolio of the new ventures rather than individual dyadic relationships also follows directly from our theoretical perspective. When firms invest in multiple startups over time, they develop a portfolio of new ventures and gain access to a search space comprised of the portfolio firms' knowledge. We argue that the nature of knowledge embedded in an investor's portfolio of start-ups has important implications for its production of exploratory innovations. Our examination of the recombinatory search and interorganizational learning literatures suggests that three aspects of a corporate investor's portfolio will influence its exploratory knowledge creation: the diversity of the portfolio firms, the extent to which their knowledge is codified, and the maturity of their knowledge stock.

8.2.1 Diversity

The recombinatory search literature emphasizes the importance of access to diverse sources of knowledge for the creation of exploratory knowledge. Diversity increases the number and variety of combinatorial possibilities and the potential for highly novel solutions (Fleming 2001). Searching for diverse knowledge challenges existing cognitive structures and beliefs about cause-effect relationships, which can promote new associations and lead to highly novel insights and solutions (Simonton 1999). By searching diverse and novel knowledge, firms can develop multiple conceptualizations of problems and solutions and can potentially apply solutions from one domain to problems in another (Hargadon and Sutton 1997). Searching diverse, nonredundant domains of knowledge can stimulate intensive experimentation of new combinations, leading to highly novel innovations (Ahuja and Lampert 2001).

The diversity of a CVC investor's portfolio of venture investments reflects the degree to which its portfolio firms are similar to, or different from, one another, based on their technologies and industry membership. A focused portfolio limits the scope of knowledge to which a corporate investor has access to, and thus limits its potential for exploratory knowledge creation. In contrast, a CVC investor with a more diverse portfolio has access to a broader, nonredundant set of knowledge components, which can lead to an enhanced exploratory innovation.

Although some degree of diversity is valuable for exploratory knowledge creation, too much can be detrimental. The ability of firms to attend to and comprehend the interactions among diverse knowledge components is diminished due to limited experience and cognitive capacity (Fleming and Sorenson 2001). A firm must expend greater effort and resources to understand and integrate dissimilar knowledge. This can result in costly, excessive and inconclusive experimentation and ultimately diseconomies of scale in innovation efforts (Ahuja and Lampert 2001). Integrating novel knowledge from diverse sources also often requires changing existing patterns of communication and social exchange (Kogut and Zander 1992), which is difficult in established organizations. As knowledge components become increasingly diverse, the likelihood of their successful recombination declines, with excessive diversity negatively impacting innovation (Fleming and Sorenson 2001). Thus, we expect that a moderate level of portfolio diversity will be most valuable to a corporate investor's exploratory knowledge creation.

Hypothesis 1 (H1): *The diversity of a firm's portfolio of new ventures will have a ∩-shaped relationship with the firm's exploratory knowledge creation.*

8.2.2 Portfolio Codification

The transmission of knowledge across firm boundaries is difficult, especially when the knowledge to be transferred is tacit (Teece 1981). Knowledge is tacit when it has not been codified using an agreed upon, formal and symbolic language (Kogut and Zander 1992). Tacit knowledge diffuses less rapidly and less effectively than articulated and codified knowledge (Kogut and Zander 1992). The difficulty in transferring tacit knowledge will affect its recombination potential. First, since tacit knowledge is less likely to be detected, it may be challenging for scientists and engineers to identify important knowledge elements and novel combinations of these elements (Galunic and Rodan 1998). Additionally, because tacit knowledge is often prohibitively expensive or even impossible to transfer and assimilate (Zander and Kogut 1995), its likelihood of recombination is further reduced (Galunic and Rodan 1998). Thus, the tacitness of knowledge reduces exploratory knowledge creation by decreasing its potential for recombination.

CVC investors may face such problems in their quest for exploratory knowledge. The technological knowledge residing in their portfolio firms may be embedded in routines and may not have been formalized or codified. Consequently, an investing firm may not be able to detect which elements of the startup's knowledge make for useful recombinations with their own existing knowledge. Even if the investor is able to identify potentially promising knowledge elements for recombination, the tacitness of the venture's knowledge will decrease the investor's ability to transfer and assimilate the knowledge.

Firms can codify their technological knowledge by patenting it (Griliches 1990; Katila and Mang 2003). Since a patent includes a detailed explanation (using well-understood, formal and symbolic language) of a novel and valuable solution to a technical problem, a patent indicates a firm has articulated its technological knowledge and demonstrated the potential utility of the knowledge (Katila and Mang 2003)[1]. Thus, the extent to which a CVC investor's portfolio of startups has a

[1]A patent also provides formal intellectual property rights on the commercial use of the knowledge embodied in the patent. The assignment of such property rights to a firm increases its ability to appropriate the returns from its investment in the patented knowledge. This fact does not affect the validity of our argument that patenting increases the codification of knowledge. If the patented knowledge is recombined with other knowledge by another firm (e.g., corporate investor) in a novel, non-obvious and useful way, it may do so and obtain its own patent (Griliches 1990). A patent may increase the marginal cost of knowledge transfer due to the payment of a license fee by the recipient to the inventor, but a patent is neither necessary nor sufficient for this to occur.

codified knowledge base, as indicated by its patents, will increase its likelihood of exploratory knowledge creation via recombination.

> Hypothesis 2 (H2): *The degree of codified knowledge in a firm's portfolio of new ventures will be positively related to its exploratory knowledge creation.*

8.2.3 Portfolio Maturity

Successful recombinations typically involve knowledge components that are salient, proximal, readily accessible and well understood (Fleming 2001). Since emerging and novel technologies are inherently uncertain, their technical feasibility, scalability, and economic potential are ambiguous (Dosi 1988). These aspects of the technology may simply be unknown due to its immaturity or only tacitly understood by a few individuals, none of whom have a complete, integrative understanding of the technology. Given that organizational routines are developed and refined through extensive experience and substantial efforts at articulation (Huber 1991), the organizational routines associated with an immature, emerging technology tend to be poorly developed. Such routines are unlikely to aid in the transfer and assimilation of technological knowledge (Jensen and Szulanski 2007). Finally, early stage technologies are untested and typically exist only in prototypical form. Such prototypes elicit a variety of equivocal interpretations and serve as poor templates for imitation (Henderson 1998). Thus, recombining immature technological knowledge is problematic because it is difficult to identify and understand which of the knowledge elements are potentially valuable for recombination or how to recombine them (Sahal 1985), and which one can be effectively transferred and assimilated (Galunic and Rodan 1998).

In the CVC context, a young venture pursuing an emerging technology is subject to uncertainties arising from the technology itself. Early-stage ventures typically possess untested, early-stage technologies. In such ventures, the cause and effect relationships of what constitutes a potentially comercializable product are ambiguous and the interactions between the startup's technology and other existing technologies also remain to be articulated. In contrast, in a more mature venture the technology tends to be more developed, reflecting a more advanced and refined knowledge base. With maturity comes a better understanding of the benefits and shortcomings of the technology. Corporate investors who invest in mature ventures should be better able to appraise the technologies being developed by these ventures, better estimate their recombinant value, and find it easier to transfer and assimilate such knowledge. The maturation of the venture and its technology allows for increased time and effort to codify aspects of the technological knowledge, increasing the ease to which it can be detected and transferred. Maturity also provides for greater learning about and experience with the technology, increasing the reliable and effective routinization of the knowledge (Huber 1991). CVC relationships can provide direct and repeatable access to such knowledge, thus reducing the investor's ambiguity about the knowledge and increasing the effectiveness of its detection, transfer and assimilation (Jensen and Szulanski 2007; Sorenson et al. 2006). In sum, access to the knowledge of mature ventures will greatly improve a corporate investor's potential for exploratory knowledge creation.

Hypothesis 3 (H3): *The maturity of a firm's portfolio of new ventures will be positively related to its exploratory knowledge creation.*

8.3 Research Context and Sample

The global telecommunications equipment industry (SIC 366: "Communications Equipment") is the setting for this study. Firms in this industry produce and market hardware and software that enable the transmission, switching and reception of voice, images, and data over both short and long distances using digital, analog, wireline and wireless technology. We chose this empirical context for two reasons. First, in the last three decades this industry has experienced substantial changes in technology and competition (Amesse et al. 2004), which resulted in frequent CVC activity among incumbents (Dushnitsky 2006). Second, because we use patent data for multiple measures, we study an industry in which firms actively patent their inventions (Griliches 1990). Ample evidence suggests telecommunications equipment firms routinely and systematically patent their inventions (Hagedoorn and Cloodt 2003; Levin et al. 1987).

Many practical considerations influenced the construction of our sample. To control for unobserved differences in firm exploratory knowledge creation, we required sufficient time varying data on the same set of firms. We chose the period 1989–1999. We chose 1989 as the initial year because it coincides with the beginning of a wave of increasing CVC investment among telecom firms (Dushnitsky 2006). Also, financial data on many non-U.S. sample firms were unavailable prior to this time. Given the lag between the application date of a patent and its granting, we ended the sample in 1999. We excluded the year 2000 because it exhibited a major spike in VC investments that could bias our results. Nearly 99% of all patent applications are decided upon by the USPTO within 5 years of application (Hall et al. 2001), eliminating the possibility that our patent data are right censored. Given the 1 year lag between the independent and dependent variables, 1999 is the final year in which we observe CVC investments.

We limited the sample frame to public firms to ensure the availability and reliability of financial data. We used the VentureXpert database to construct our sample of corporate investors. Corporate investors are defined as non-financial public firms who invested capital in private, entrepreneurial firms, either directly or through their venture funds. VentureXpert is the official database of the National Venture Capital Association (NVCA). We identified corporate investors from the telecommunications equipment industry that made at least one CVC investment during the sample period, 1989–1999. Our sample consists of an unbalanced panel of 40 publicly traded telecommunications equipment manufacturers and 419 firm-year observations. Descriptive information on the investment targets of the 40 corporate investors is presented in Table 8.1.

Table 8.1 Characteristics of Ventures Receiving CVC Investments

	Sector distribution		Age at first financing (years)		Age at first CVC financing (years)		Number of investors in round			Nationality		
Industry sector	#	%	Mean	Median	Mean	Median	Mean	Median	% syndicated	Country	#	%
Biotechnology	1	0.3	3.0	3.0	4.0	4.0	7.0	7.0	100.0	Belgium	2	0.56
Communications & media	109	30.8	1.8	0.8	3.9	3.0	5.7	4.5	86.9	Canada	3	0.85
Computer hardware	34	9.6	1.4	0.8	3.5	2.9	5.8	6.0	96.6	Denmark	1	0.28
Computer software & services	89	25.1	2.0	0.6	3.6	3.0	5.0	4.0	88.3	France	1	0.28
Consumer related	8	2.3	3.8	1.8	4.9	2.0	8.8	5.0	100.0	Germany	2	0.56
Industrial/energy	2	0.6	2.8	2.8	5.5	5.5	7.8	6.0	80.0	Israel	3	0.85
Internet specific	63	17.8	1.3	0.9	2.8	2.8	4.8	3.0	81.9	South Korea	1	0.28
Medical/health	2	0.6	2.2	2.2	2.0	2.0	2.5	2.5	50.0	United Kingdom	2	0.56
Other products	8	2.3	1.9	0.4	6.6	6.0	3.6	3.0	72.7	United States	339	95.76
Semiconductors/ other elect.	38	10.7	1.2	0.5	3.6	3.0	8.6	7.0	97.9			
Total	354	100.0	1.7	0.8	3.6	3.0	5.7	5.0	88.32	Total	354	100.00

8.4 Data and Measures

We used patent data to assess the sample firms' technological knowledge because patents are perhaps the most valid and robust indicators of knowledge creation (Trajtenberg 1987). One way that knowledge creation is instantiated is in the form of inventions (Schmookler 1966). Inventions provide a trace of an organization's knowledge creation activities and patents provide a measure of novel invention that is externally validated through the patent examination process (Griliches 1990). While patents measure only a codifiable portion of a firm's technological knowledge, they correlate with measures that incorporate tacit knowledge, such as experts' ratings of firms' technical competencies (Narin et al. 1987), new product introductions (Brouwer and Kleinknecht 1999), and innovation counts (Basberg 1987). Hagedoorn and Cloodt (2003) showed patents are a valid and reliable measure of innovation in the telecom equipment industry.

We used U.S. patents, obtained from Delphion, for many reasons. Using patents from a single country maintains consistency, reliability and comparability across firms (Griliches 1990). U.S. patents are a very good data source because of the rigor and procedural fairness used in granting them, the strong incentives for firms to get patent protection in the world's largest market, the high quality of services provided by the USPTO, and the U.S.'s reputation for providing effective IP protection (Pavitt 1988; Rivette 1993).

We used the date of application, instead of the grant date, to assign granted patents to firms because it more precisely captures the time of knowledge creation (Griliches 1990). Given that patents are often assigned to subsidiaries, which may change their names or merge, we carefully aggregated patents to the firm level (Griliches 1990). We initially identified all divisions, subsidiaries, and joint ventures of each sample firm (using Who Owns Whom and The Directory of Corporate Affiliations) as of 1980. We then traced each firm's history to account for name changes, division names, divestments, acquisitions, and joint ventures to obtain information on the timing of these events. This process yielded a master list of entities that we used to identify all patents belonging to sample firms for the period of study.

We collected data on CVC investments from the VentureXpert database and obtained firm financial data from Compustat, annual reports, SEC filings, The Japan Company Handbook, Worldscope and Global Vantage. We obtained data on acquisitions and alliances through systematic and exhaustive searches of the SDC M&A database, SDC alliance database, Factiva, Lexis-Nexis, and Dialog.

8.4.1 Dependent Variable

We define *exploratory knowledge creation* as the degree to which a firm creates technological knowledge that is novel relative to its extant knowledge stock. Following prior research (Benner and Tushman 2002; Rosenkopf and Nerkar 2001), we measured exploratory knowledge creation using patent citation data. The extent to which a firm reuses elements of knowledge (e.g., patent citations) with which it has experience reflects that it is practicing local search and exploiting its extant knowledge base. The extent to which a firm deviates from this practice and utilizes citations it has no experience with is indicative of exploration (Benner and Tushman 2002; Katila and Ahuja 2002).

We assessed the exploratory knowledge creation of corporate investor *i* in year *t* by classifying and tabulating all citations included in the firm's patents applied for in year *t* (and subsequently granted). Each citation was traced to determine if the firm had used the same citation or if the citation was to a patent developed by the firm during the 7 years prior to the focal year[2]. Thus, each citation was classified as being new or used. Exploratory knowledge creation was operationalized as the number of new citations that appear in the list of all citations contained in firm *i*'s patents applied for in year *t*.[3]

8.4.2 Independent Variables

In constructing our portfolio measures, we include all ventures in which a firm invested in the 4 years prior to and including the focal year. Since CVC relationships typically endure for more than 1 year, constructing portfolios using only investments announced in the focal year would implicitly assume that the knowledge flows and learning benefits from these ventures are limited to 1 year. With the exception of publicly reported events such as an IPO, it is often difficult to observe when a venture exits a firm's portfolio. We assumed that ventures remain in a firm's portfolio for 4 years from the date of initial investment for two reasons. First, we were able to identify the exit dates for 82 of the 354 portfolio firms in the sample and found that the average time between initial CVC investment and portfolio exit for these 82 firms was nearly 4 years. Second, prior research on the influence of interfirm relationships such as alliances and acquisitions has found that the effect of these relationships on firm innovation endures for 3–5 years (Ahuja and Katila 2001; Stuart 2000). We use the subscript $it-1$ below to

[2]We use a 7-year window to reflect that knowledge decays over time (Griliches 1990) and the intertemporal transfer of knowledge within organizations is quite difficult (Nerkar 2003). Prior research has used a 4–7 year period as the time for which a firm's technical knowledge remains current (Ahuja 2000; Stuart and Podolny 1996).

[3]To illustrate this measure, consider the following example. Assume that a corporate investor applied for (and was granted) one patent in the focal year and that this patent cited ten prior art patents. If six of these citations did not appear in the list of prior art citations from the firm's patents granted in the previous 7 years and did not cite any of these same patents, then the value of exploratory knowledge creation for the focal firm-year would be 6.

indicate the independent variables for firm i are lagged 1 year relative to the dependent variable.

Portfolio Diversity. We measured the diversity in firm i's portfolio of CVC investments by using the VentureXpert Industry Classification codes ("VEIC" codes)[4] assigned to the ventures. This variable is computed as a reverse-scaled Herfindahl Index:

$$\text{Portfolio diversity}_{it-1} = \left[1 - \sum_{j=1}^{N} \left(P_j^2\right)\right] / PSit - 1,$$

where P_j is equal to the number of portfolio firms in industry j in which firm i invested during the 4 years prior to and including year $t-1$, divided by the total number of portfolio firms in which firm i invested over the 4 year window (PS_{it-1}). This variable ranges between 0 and 1. Lower values denote specialization (i.e., portfolio firms have the same VEIC code), and the higher values imply greater diversity.

Portfolio Knowledge Codification. We measured *Portfolio Knowledge Codification* as the average number of patents assigned to the portfolio firms in which firm i invested during the 4 years prior to and including year $t-1$. The extent to which a venture has patented its technical inventions reflects the degree to which its technological knowledge is codified (Griliches 1990; Katila and Mang 2003).

Portfolio Maturity. We assessed the age of a portfolio firm as the number of months since founding at the end of year $t-1$. *Portfolio maturity* for investor firm i was computed as the average age of all portfolio firms in which firm i invested during the 4 years prior to and including year $t-1$.

8.4.3 *Control Variables*

Size. Prior research has proved inconclusive in determining whether small or large firms are more innovative (Cohen and Levin 1989). Since this inconclusiveness may be due to the presence of both negative and positive effects of size on innovation performance (Cohen and Levin 1989), we control for the influence of firm size using the natural log of sales (in $US million) for firm i year $t-1$.

[4] VEIC codes are a proprietary industry classification system developed by Venture Economics, the initial developer and provider of the VentureXpert database. These codes are similar to three digit SIC codes.

R&D. A firm's annual R&D expenditures represent the formal investments in knowledge creation (Griliches 1990), and contribute to its ability to learn and acquire knowledge from external sources (Cohen and Levinthal 1989). We control for the influence of *R&D* on exploration using R&D intensity (R&D expenditures divided by sales) of firm i in year $t-1$.

Slack. Organizations having significant slack resources may participate in more exploratory search than their slack-deprived counterparts (Singh 1986), which can result in an enhanced innovative performance (Nohria and Gulati 1996). We control for the slack resources of firm i in year $t-1$ using its current ratio (current assets divided by current liabilities, measured at year end).

Age. As firms age, they tend to exploit their existing technological competencies rather than exploring new and unfamiliar technologies (Sorensen and Stuart 2000). We operationalize firm age as the number of years from the date of founding of firm i to year $t-1$.

Portfolio Size. If firms invest in dissimilar ventures, a larger portfolio of new ventures may provide a corporate investor with access to more technological diversity. The effect of portfolio size may be confounded with the effect of portfolio diversity. Accordingly, we control for the natural log of the number of portfolio firms in which firm i invested during the 4 years prior to and including year $t-1$.

Portfolio Involvement. A higher degree of involvement with a portfolio firm will provide a corporate investor greater access to the venture's knowledge and a higher degree of social interaction between personnel from the two firms, both of which can improve interorganizational learning (Beckman and Haunschild 2002). We control for this potential confounding effect using a measure of portfolio involvement. To construct our measure, we counted (a) the number of commercial agreements (i.e., alliances) formed between the corporate investor and its portfolio firms, and (b) the number of instances in which the investor obtained a seat on the board of directors of its portfolio firms. Firm i's *portfolio involvement* is the average number of its alliances and board seats with its portfolio firms.

Acquisitions & Alliances. External knowledge sourcing activities, such as CVC, acquisitions and alliances are often complementary and correlated within firms (Arora and Gambardella 1990). Thus, the effect of acquisitions and alliances on exploratory knowledge creation may be confounded with the effect of CVC investments. Since research shows that firm innovation is affected by acquisitions (Ahuja and Katila 2001) and alliances (Ahuja 2000), we control for both acquisitions and alliances. We control for the number of acquisitions completed by firm i during the 4 years prior to and including year $t-1$. We used straight-line depreciation to account for the declining effect of an acquisition on exploration over time. We also control for the number of alliances, excluding those involving portfolio firms, formed by firm i during the 4 years prior to and including year $t-1$. We used straight-line depreciation to account for the declining effect of alliances on exploration over time.

Technological Diversity. Increasing technological diversity may increase the potential for innovation due to internal spillovers (Garcia-Vega 2006), and may increase a firm's ability to identify, evaluate, and absorb knowledge from external sources (Cohen and Levinthal 1989). We measure firm i's technological diversity in year $t-1$ using the adjusted Herfindahl index (Hall 2002):

$$\text{Technological diversity}_{it-1} = \left[1 - \sum_{j=1}^{J}\left(\frac{N_{jii}}{N_{it}}\right)\right] \times \frac{N_{it}}{N_{it} - 1},$$

where N_{it-1} is the total number of patents obtained by firm i in the 4 years prior to and including year $t-1$. N_{jit-1} is the number of patents in primary technology class j in firm i's 4 year knowledge base. This variable may take on values between 0 (no diversity) and 1 (maximum diversity).

Total Patent Citations. Firms whose patents contain a large number of citations are at a greater risk of having a higher number of exploratory citations. To control for the size of the risk set, we control for the total number of citations contained in corporate investor i's patents in year t.

Presample Exploratory Citations. To control for unobserved heterogeneity in firm exploratory knowledge creation, we follow the pre-sample information approach of Blundell et al. (1995) and calculate the variable *Presample Exploratory Citations* as the sum of exploratory citations contained in the patents obtained by firm i in the 4 years prior to its entry into the sample.

Nationality. We use dummies indicating the regional origin of a corporate investor to control for regional effects on exploration. *USA & Canada* is coded 1 when the firm is headquartered in the U.S. or Canada. *Europe* is coded 1 when the firm is headquartered in Europe. *Asia* is the omitted category.

8.4.4 Model Specification and Estimation

The dependent variable in this study is a count variable and takes on only non-negative integer values. The use of linear regression to model such data can result in inefficient, inconsistent, and biased coefficient estimates (Long 1997). While Poisson regression is appropriate to model count data, our data were significantly overdispersed, violating a basic assumption of the Poisson estimator (Hausman et al. 1984). We use a negative binomial estimator to model the count data. The negative binomial model is a generalization of the Poisson model and allows for overdispersion by incorporating an individual, unobserved effect into the conditional mean (Hausman et al. 1984). The negative binomial panel estimator accommodates explicit control of persistent individual unobserved effects through both fixed and random effects. In this study, unobserved heterogeneity refers to the possibility that unmeasured differences among observationally equivalent firms affect their exploratory innovation. Unobserved heterogeneity may also stem from unmeasured, systematic time period effects. Failing to control for unobserved heterogeneity can result in specification error (Heckman 1979).

We employed two strategies to control for unobserved heterogeneity. First, we included year fixed effects to control for systematic period effects such as differences in macroeconomic conditions that may affect all sampled firms' exploration. Second, we employed individual firm effects to control for unobserved, temporally stable firm differences in exploration. We use both firm fixed and random effects specifications in alternative estimations of our model. Since the random effects specification assumes that the unobserved firm effect is uncorrelated with the regressors, we used a Hausman (1978) test to check this assumption. Hausman tests were insignificant for three of the five models described below, supporting the use of a random effects specification. Since the Hausman test did not converge for the final two models, we also report results of the full model using fixed effects for comparison.

8.5 Results

Table 8.2 presents descriptive statistics and correlations. Table 8.3 displays the negative binomial panel regression results. Although not reported, all models include year dummy variables. In 8.3, Model 1 is the baseline model (control variables only). Models 2–5 sequentially introduce portfolio diversity, square of portfolio diversity, portfolio knowledge codification, and portfolio maturity, respectively, to test hypotheses 1 through 3. Model 5 represents the fully specified random effects model. We also report results for the full model using firm fixed effects (Model 6). We report one-tailed significance levels for all hypothesized variables and two-tailed tests for control variables.

Hypothesis 1 predicted an inverted U-shaped relationship between the portfolio diversity and exploratory knowledge creation. In Model 2, portfolio diversity is positive and statistically significant ($\beta=0.398$, $p<0.05$). When portfolio diversity squared is entered (Models 3–5), it exhibits a consistently negative and significant effect (Model 5, $\beta=-10.176$, $p<0.05$), providing evidence of an inverted U-shaped effect. Thus, we find support for Hypothesis 1. The maximum value of exploratory knowledge generation occurs when portfolio diversity = 0.097, which is within the sample range of 0.00–0.25[5].

Hypothesis 2 predicted a positive effect of portfolio knowledge codification on exploratory knowledge creation. In Models 4 and 5, portfolio knowledge

---

[5]We computed the optimum using marginal effects. The marginal effect of variable j is $e^{\beta x}\beta_j$, where X is the set of all covariates and β_j is the regression coefficient for variable j (Cameron and Trivedi 1998). We computed the marginal effects for Portfolio Diversity and its square by setting all other covariates to their sample means.

codification is positive and statistically significant (Model 5, $\beta=0.015, p<0.001$). Thus, we find support for Hypothesis 2. In order to assess the magnitude of the effect, we employed the estimated semi-standardized coefficient ($e\beta X$) to calculate the effect of a one standard deviation change in portfolio knowledge codification (see Cameron and Trivedi 1998: 82). A one standard deviation increase in portfolio knowledge codification yields a 6.4% increase in exploratory knowledge creation.[6]

Hypothesis 3 proposed a positive effect of portfolio maturity on exploratory knowledge creation. Results from the full model (Model 5) show that portfolio maturity is statistically significant ($\beta=0.001$, $p<0.05$). Thus, we find support for hypothesis 3. An increase of one standard deviation in portfolio maturity yields a 3.5% increase in exploratory knowledge creation.[7] Results from using firm fixed effects (Model 6) are consistent with the results employing random effect (Model 5) for each hypothesis.

Eight of the 13 control variables are consistently significant. Larger firms create more exploratory knowledge as do firms that spend more on R&D. Moreover, the total number of citations contained in a firm's patents positively affects its exploratory knowledge creation, measured as the number of new citations among these total citations. While the number of alliances has no significant effect, the results suggest the number of acquisitions significantly increases exploratory knowledge creation. Firm technological diversity and the number of presample new citations, fixed effects controls for unobserved heterogeneity, both exhibit consistently positive and significant effects. Firms based in the U.S., Canada and Europe exhibit significantly less exploratory knowledge creation than firms based in Japan and South Korea. Finally, we find that portfolio size has no discernible effect in the baseline model, but exhibits a consistently negative effect on exploratory knowledge creation after controlling for portfolio diversity.

8.6 Discussion

The purpose of this study was to identify and empirically test the conditions under which CVC investing influences the corporate investor's exploratory knowledge creation. This is an important question since exploratory knowledge creation helps firms discover and pursue new opportunities and generates the potential for future exploitation. The extant research on CVC and firm innovation has ignored the novelty of knowledge created and embodied in the innovations measured. Drawing on recombinatory search and interorganizational learning literatures, we argued

---

[6]Calculation: $\exp[\beta \times \text{S.D. of PF\_CODIFICATION}] - 1 = \exp[0.015 \times 4.12] - 1 = \exp 0.0618 - 1 = 1.064 - 1 = 0.064$.

[7]Calculation: $\exp[\beta \times \text{S.D. of PORTFOLIO MATURITY}] - 1 = \exp[0.001 \times 34.55] - 1 = \exp 0.035 - 1 = 1.035 - 1 = 0.035$.

Table 8.2 Descriptive statistics and correlations ($n=419$)

	Mean	S.D.	Min	Max	(1)	(2)	(3)	(4)	(5)
(1) Exploratory knowledge creation$_{it}$	1949.5	2412.9	0.0	10532.0	1				
(2) Size$_{it-1}$	8.4	2.3	0.5	11.5	0.609	1			
(3) R&D$_{it-1}$	0.1	0.2	0.0	3.3	−0.09	−0.38	1		
(4) Slack$_{it-1}$	2.3	2.3	0.4	24.2	−0.3	−0.64	0.272	1	
(5) Age$_{it-1}$	46.7	39.1	0.0	152.0	0.467	0.558	−0.14	−0.28	1
(6) M&A$_{it-1}$	7.5	10.2	0.0	62.5	0.479	0.418	−0.08	−0.2	0.545
(7) Alliances$_{it-1}$	33.5	38.4	0.0	230.8	0.741	0.603	−0.1	−0.27	0.484
(8) Portfolio size$_{it-1}$	0.7	0.8	0.0	4.0	0.071	0.203	−0.03	−0.15	0.054
(9) Portfolio involvement$_{it-1}$	0.2	0.7	0.0	10.0	0.004	0.112	0.024	−0.02	−0.03
(10) Firm technological diversity$_{it-1}$	0.8	0.3	0.0	1.0	0.35	0.595	−0.21	−0.39	0.427
(11) Total Citations$_{it}$	2961.7	3718.4	0.0	16599.0	0.983	0.599	−0.09	−0.29	0.461
(12) Presample new citations$_{i}$	3277.6	4450.8	0.0	16908.0	0.652	0.599	−0.13	−0.28	0.598
(13) USA/Canada	0.6	0.5	0.0	1.0	−0.37	−0.41	0.063	0.177	−0.5
(14) Europe$_{i}$	0.2	0.4	0.0	1.0	0.132	0.296	−0.06	−0.18	0.581
(15) Portfolio diversity$_{it-1}$	0.0	0.1	0.0	0.3	0.072	0.16	−0.06	−0.15	0.048
(16) Portfolio diversity$^{2}_{it-1}$	0.0	0.0	0.0	0.1	0.074	0.148	−0.06	−0.13	0.044
(17) Portfolio codification$_{it-1}$	1.1	4.1	0.0	48.0	0.121	0.124	−0.01	−0.08	−0.06
(18) Portfolio maturity$_{it-1}$	24.7	34.6	0.0	156.0	0.085	0.077	0.061	0.021	0.011

(6)	(7)	(8)	(9)	(10)	(11)	(12)	(13)	(14)	(15)	(16)	(17)	(18)
1												
0.573	1											
0.205	0.146	1										
0.053	0.087	0.194	1									
0.289	0.323	0.131	0.036	1								
0.463	0.742	0.101	0.02	0.346	1							
0.436	0.626	0.044	−0.01	0.376	0.679	1						
−0.22	−0.27	0.127	−0.06	−0.37	−0.32	−0.22	1					
0.438	0.167	−0.06	−0.06	0.202	0.105	0.145	−0.56	1				
0.022	0.07	0.56	0.116	0.155	0.081	0.038	0.024	−0.05	1			
0.003	0.057	0.418	0.11	0.147	0.078	0.043	0.005	−0.05	0.974	1		
0.06	0.104	0.162	0.323	0.106	0.118	0.05	0.06	−0.07	0.117	0.112	1	
0.213	0.093	0.555	0.189	0.155	0.098	0.044	0.078	−0.06	0.368	0.307	0.307	1

Table 8.3 Random and fixed effects negative binomial panel regression

	Random effects	Random effects	Random effects	Random effects	Random effects	Fixed effects
Variables	Model 1	Model 2	Model 3	Model 4	Model 5	Model 6
Constant	–3.213***	–3.215***	–3.143***	–3.089***	–3.063***	–3.957***
	[0.395]	[0.390]	[0.392]	[0.387]	[0.388]	[0.338]
$Size_{it-1}$	0.440***	0.435***	0.439***	0.448***	0.453***	0.520***
	[0.043]	[0.042]	[0.043]	[0.043]	[0.043]	[0.043]
$R\&D_{it-1}$	0.587*	0.581*	0.570^{+}	0.630*	0.606*	0.792*
	[0.288]	[0.287]	[0.292]	[0.278]	[0.285]	[0.321]
$Slack_{it-1}$	0.038^{+}	0.035	0.03	0.029	0.027	0.033
	[0.022]	[0.022]	[0.023]	[0.022]	[0.022]	[0.024]
Age_{it-1}	0.004	0.005^{+}	0.004	0.004	0.004	0.007**
	[0.003]	[0.003]	[0.003]	[0.003]	[0.003]	[0.002]
$M\&A_{it-1}$	0.006*	0.007**	0.007**	0.007**	0.007**	0.004^{+}
	[0.002]	[0.002]	[0.002]	[0.002]	[0.002]	[0.002]
$Alliances_{it-1}$	0.000	0.000	0.000	0.000	–0.001	–0.001
	[0.001]	[0.001]	[0.001]	[0.001]	[0.001]	[0.001]
Portfolio $size_{it-1}$	–0.03	–0.048^{+}	–0.087*	–0.095**	–0.122**	–0.145***
	[0.025]	[0.027]	[0.037]	[0.035]	[0.039]	[0.042]
Portfolio $involvement_{it-1}$	0.041*	0.039*	0.045*	0.018	0.021	0.036^{+}
	[0.017]	[0.018]	[0.018]	[0.019]	[0.019]	[0.020]
Firm technological $diversity_{it-1}$	1.086***	1.080***	1.060***	0.987***	0.971***	0.734**
	[0.290]	[0.288]	[0.287]	[0.286]	[0.285]	[0.280]
Total $citations_{it}$	0.000***	0.000***	0.000***	0.000***	0.000***	0.000***
	[0.000]	[0.000]	[0.000]	[0.000]	[0.000]	[0.000]
Presample new $citations_{i}$	0.000^{+}	0.000^{+}	0.000^{+}	0.000*	0.000*	

	[0.000]	[0.000]	[0.000]	[0.000]	[0.000]	
USA/Canada	–0.672***	–0.625***	–0.606***	–0.649***	–0.673***	
	[0.181]	[0.178]	[0.177]	[0.178]	[0.178]	
$Europe_i$	–0.636**	–0.604*	–0.591*	–0.599**	–0.647**	
	[0.235]	[0.236]	[0.235]	[0.232]	[0.234]	
Portfolio $diversity_{it-1}$		0.398*	1.642*	1.686*	1.977**	2.411**
		[0.205]	[0.788]	[0.767]	[0.780]	[0.870]
Portfolio $diversity^2_{it-1}$			–7.925$^+$	–8.174*	–10.176*	–12.287*
			[4.828]	[4.699]	[4.816]	[5.434]
Portfolio $codification_{it-1}$				0.017***	0.015***	0.014***
				[0.004]	[0.004]	[0.004]
Portfolio $maturity_{it-1}$					0.001*	0.001$^+$
					[0.000]	[0.001]
Firm effects	RANDOM	RANDOM	RANDOM	RANDOM	RANDOM	FIXED
Year effects	YES	YES	YES	YES	YES	YES
Observations	419	419	419	419	419	419
Degrees of freedom	23	24	25	26	27	24
Log likelihood	–2893.05	–2891.18	–2889.83	–2882.37	–2880.53	–2493.204
Likelihood ratio test		3.75$^+$	6.45*	21.36***	25.05***	22.47***
Wald Chi 2	2153.71***	2168.36***	2166.66***	2261.63***	2267.76***	1751.65***

Standard errors in brackets; ***$p<0.001$, **$p<0.01$, *$p<0.05$, $^+p<0.1$; Two-tailed tests for control variables and one-tailed test for hypothesized variables that three characteristics of a corporate investor's portfolio of startups – diversity, codification, and maturity – enhance the investor's exploratory knowledge creation.

Overall, we found strong support for all three theoretical predictions. First, we found that diversity in an investor's portfolio of startups exhibits a curvilinear effect, first increasing and then decreasing the investor's exploratory knowledge creation. Second, our results suggest the level of codification in the knowledge base of portfolio firms has a positive effect on the investor's exploratory knowledge creation. Finally, we found that the maturity of a corporate investor's portfolio firms positively influences its exploratory knowledge creation. Taken together, these results suggest that *where* firms search for innovative solutions to valuable problems and *how* they search for these solutions have important implications for their ability to create exploratory knowledge.

This study contributes to the corporate entrepreneurship literature by developing a framework that explains the impact of CVC investing, an important external venturing activity, on exploratory innovation in established organizations. Prior research on CVC and investor innovation performance (Dushnitsky and Lenox 2005; Keil et al. 2007; Wadhwa and Kotha 2006) has not examined whether or when CVC investments are instrumental in the creation of exploratory knowledge. However, Schildt et al. (2005) investigated a related question. They constructed a sample of CVC investor – startup firm dyads and examined whether investors received exploratory or exploitative knowledge from their portfolio firms. Their results were substantially constrained by their measurement of explorative and exploitative interorganizational learning and were inconclusive.[8] Our study contributes to CVC research and the broader corporate entrepreneurship literature by identifying the conditions under which CVC investments can contribute to investor exploratory innovation.

Our study is the first to empirically examine the influence of a corporate investor's portfolio of startups on its exploratory innovation performance. Moving beyond the dyadic level perspective typically employed in interorganizational learning research, we examine characteristics of the collection of CVC relationships maintained by corporate investors. Doing so allows us to better understand how CVC investing affects investor innovation performance. Recent research on strategic alliances has also recognized the importance of examining the nature of alliance portfolios rather than the formation, management and outcomes of dyadic relationships (Lavie 2007).

This research also contributes to the recombinatory search literature. This literature has emphasized the propensity of firms to engage in local search, which leads to

[8]Schildt et al. (2005) measured explorative learning as investor firm patents that cited the portfolio firm, but did not self-cite any investor patents. They measured exploitative learning as investor patents that cited both the portfolio firm and the investor. In their study, only 7 out of 998 CVC relationships had patents that could be classified as explorative or exploitative. Their results are also subject to a right censoring bias and may fail to reflect the learning benefits associated with CVC because the average citation lag is 3–4 years (cf. Dushnitsky 2006: 424).

incremental, exploitative innovations. Few studies have examined how and when firms overcome the predisposition towards local search and develop exploratory innovations. Our study shows that a moderate level of diversity in a firm's recombinatory search space enhances the likelihood of exploratory innovation. Increasing levels of diversity in the search space increase the probability that the corporate investor is exposed to diverse stimuli and varied sources of knowledge, thus increasing the possibilities for highly novel recombinations. However, we find that too much diversity ultimately reduces exploratory innovation. Prior research has found similar effects of diversity on new product introductions (Ahuja and Katila 2001).

Additionally, we found the presence of mature and codified novel knowledge in a firm's search space increases the firm's ability to develop exploratory innovations. Prior research has emphasized that distant search can have uncertain, costly and temporally distal outcomes (Fleming 2001; Nelson and Winter 1982). Our results suggest that when firms engaging in distant search via CVC investments access mature and codified knowledge, they are able to reduce the uncertainty and difficulty of detecting and transferring this novel knowledge, and subsequently improve their exploratory knowledge creation. This study shows that even though CVC investments are low commitment initiatives by corporate investors in developing new competencies (Basu et al. 2009), they can be the effective means of recombinatory search.

8.7 Limitations and Future Research

Although promising, this study has certain limitations. First, we were unable to observe knowledge flows between corporate investors and their portfolio firms. Following much of the research on interfirm relationships and firm innovation, we infer these flows based on the characteristics of the partner firms. Prior interfirm learning research has used cross-citations between the patents of partners to observe knowledge flows (e.g., Gomes-Casseres et al. 2006). Since nearly 50% of our sample startups did not have any patents upon investment, it was impossible to measure knowledge flows using patent citations.

Second, the use of patents to proxy for knowledge creation has limitations. Patents do not capture all knowledge created in an organization. Additionally, firms may patent exploratory inventions in anticipation of partnering to appropriate the greater economic value associated with such highly novel inventions (Brouwer and Kleinknecht 1999). The findings of this study may be influenced by such unobserved appropriation concerns. The use of a year lag between collaboration and patenting reduces the likelihood of such a bias. Firm effects also mitigate this bias by controlling for unobserved heterogeneity.

A third limitation concerns the generalizability of the findings. Given that firms in different industries exhibit different patenting behaviors, we limited this study to a single industry. Scholars have argued that in high technology industries with rapid technological change, such as telecom equipment, few organizations are able to build new competences without using external knowledge (Leonard-Barton 1995).

This suggests that the findings of this study may apply to other high technology industries. However, it is important that researchers test the generalizability of the findings in other industries.

8.8 Conclusion

In many industries, the creation of technological knowledge is essential for firm survival and competitive advantage (Teece et al. 1997). The results of this study highlight the importance of CVC investments for corporate investors' exploratory knowledge creation. We examined the influence of three characteristics of a firm's portfolio of new ventures in stimulating exploratory knowledge creation. Our results suggest that it is important for corporate investors to spread their equity investments among moderately diverse startups that are relatively mature and possess codified technological knowledge. Exploring how characteristics of portfolio firms drive relative differences in knowledge creation in corporate investors contributes to our knowledge of innovative outcomes of CVC investments, and provides empirical evidence of the strategic benefits of CVC.

References

Ahuja G (2000) Collaboration networks, structural holes, and innovation: A longitudinal study. Adm Sci Q 45:425

Ahuja G, Katila R (2001) Technological acquisitions and the innovation performance of acquiring firms: A longitudinal study. Strategic Management J 22:197

Ahuja G, Lampert CM (2001) Entrepreneurship in the large corporation: A longitudinal study of how established firms create breakthrough inventions. Strategic Management J 22(6/7):521

Amesse F, Latour R, Rebolledo C, Séguin-Dulude L (2004) The telecommunications equipment industry in the 1990s: from alliances to mergers and acquisitions. Technovation 24:885–897

Arora A, Gambardella A (1990) Complementarities and external linkages: the strategies of large corporations in biotechnology. J Ind Econ 38(4):361–379

Basberg BL (1987) Patents and the measurement of technological change: a survey of the literature. Res Policy 16:131–141

Basu S, Phelps C, Kotha S (2009) Towards understanding who makes corporate venture capital investments and why. Forthcoming. Journal of Business Venturing

Beckman CM, Haunschild PR (2002) Network learning: the effects of partners' heterogeneity of experience on corporate acquisitions. Adm Sci Q 47:92–124

Benner M, Tushman ML (2002) Process management and technological innovation: a longitudinal study of the paint and photography industries. Adm Sci Q 47:92–1724

Blundell RR, Griffith R, Van Reenen J (1995) Dynamic count data models of technological innovation. Econ J 105:333–344

Brouwer E, Kleinknecht A (1999) Innovative output, and a firm's propensity to patent. An exploration of CIS micro data. Res Policy 28:615–624

Cameron AC, Trivedi PK (1998) Regression analysis of count data. Cambridge Press, Cambridge

Chesbrough HW (2002) Making sense of corporate venture capital. Harv Bus Rev 80(3):4–11

Cohen WM, Levin RC (1989) Innovation and market structure. In: Schmalensee R, Willig R (eds) Handbook of industrial organization. Elsevier, New York, pp 1060–1107
Cohen R, Levinthal D (1989) Innovation and learning: the two faces of R&D. Econ J 99:569–596
Cyert RM, March JG (1963) A behavioral theory of the firm. Prentice-Hall, Englewood Cliffs
de Man AP, Duysters GM (2005) Collaboration and innovation: a review of the effects of mergers, acquisitions and alliances on innovation. Technovation 25(12):1377–1387
Dosi G (1988) Sources, procedures and microeconomic effects of innovation. J Econ Lit 26:1120–1171
Dushnitsky G (2006) Corporate venture capital: past evidence and future directions. In: Casson M (ed) Oxford handbook of entrepreneurship. Oxford University Press, New York, pp 387–431
Dushnitsky G, Lenox MJ (2005) When do incumbents learn from entrepreneurial ventures? Corporate venture capital and investing firm innovation rates. Res Policy 34(5):615–639
Eisenhardt KM, Martin JK (2000) Dynamic capabilities: what are they? Strat Manag J 21:1105–1121
Fleming L (2001) Recombinant uncertainty in technological search. Manage Sci 47:117
Fleming L, Sorenson O (2001) Technology as a complex adaptive system: evidence from patent data. Res Policy 30:1019–1039
Garcia-Vega M (2006) Does technological diversification promote innovation? An empirical analysis for European firms. Res Policy 35:230–246
Galunic DC, Rodan S (1998) Resource recombinations in the firm: knowledge structures and the potential for Schumpeterian innovation. Strat Manag J 19:1193–1201
Gomes-Casseres B, Hagedoorn J, Jaffe AB (2006) Do alliances promote knowledge flow? J Financ Econ 80(1):5–33
Grant RM (1996) Prospering in dynamically-competitive environments: organizational capability as knowledge integration. Organ Sci 7(4):375–387
Greve HR (2007) Exploration and exploitation in product innovation. Ind Corp Change 16:945–975
Griliches Z (1990) Patent statistics as economic indicators. J Econ Lit 28(4):1661–1707
Hagedoorn J, Cloodt M (2003) Measuring innovative performance: is there an advantage in using multiple indicators? Res Policy 32:1365–1379
Hall BH (2002) A note on the bias in the Herfindahl based on count data. In: Jaffe A, Trajtenberg M (eds) Patents, citations, and innovation. MIT Press, Cambridge, MA, pp 149–156
Hall B, Jaffe, AB, Trajtenberg M (2001) The NBER Patent Citations Datafile: Lessons, Insights and Methodological Tools. NBER Working Paper No. 8498 (October 2001)
Hargadon A, Sutton RI (1997) Technology brokering and innovation in a product development firm. Adm Sci Q 42:716–749
Hausman J, Hall B, Griliches Z (1984) Econometric models for count data with and application to patents-R&D relationship. Econometrica 52:909–938
Hausman JA (1978) Specification tests in econometrics. Econometrica 46(6):1251–1271
Heckman JJ (1979) Sample selection bias as a specification error. Econometrica 47(1):153–161
Helfat CE (1994) Evolutionary trajectories in petroleum firm R&D. Manage Sci 40(12):1720–1747
Henderson K (1998) The role of material objects in the design process: a comparison of two design cultures and how they contend with automation. Sci Technol Human Values 23: 139–174
Henderson R, Clark K (1990) Architectural innovation: the reconfiguration of existing product technologies and failure of established firms. Adm Sci Q 35:9–30
Huber GP (1991) Organizational learning: the contributing processes and the literature. Organ Sci 2:88–115
Jansen JJP, Van Den Bosch FAJ, Volberda HW (2006) Exploratory innovation, exploitative innovation, and performance: effects of organizational antecedents and environmental moderators. Manage Sci 52(11):1661–1674

Jensen, Robert J, Szulanski, Gabriel (2007) Template Use and the Effectiveness of Knowledge Transfer Management Sci 53: 1716–1730
Katila R, Ahuja G (2002) Something old, something new: a longitudinal study of search behavior and new product introduction. Acad Manage J 45(6):1183
Katila R, Mang P (2003) Exploiting technological opportunities: the timing of collaborations. Res Policy 32(2):317–332
Keil T, Maula M, Schildt H, Zahra SA (2007) The effect of governance modes and relatedness of external business development activities on innovative performance. Strat Manag J 29(8):895–907
Kim JJ, Kogut B (1996) Technological platforms and diversification. Organ Sci 7:283–301
Kogut B, Zander U (1992) Knowledge of the firm, combinative capabilities, and the replication of technology. Organ Sci 3:383–397
Lavie D (2007) Alliance portfolios and firm performance: a study of value creation and appropriation in the U.S. software industry. Strat Manag J 28(12):1187–1212
Leonard-Barton D (1995) Wellsprings of knowledge. Harvard University Press, Boston, MA
Levin RC, Klevorick AK, Nelson RR, Winter SG (1987) Appropriating the returns from industrial research and development. Brooking Pap Econ Act 3:783–820
Levinthal DA, March JG (1981) A model of adaptive organizational search. J Econ Behav Organ 2:307–333
Long JS (1997) Regression models for categorical and limited dependent variables. SAGE, Thousand Oaks, CA
March JG (1991) Exploration and exploitation in organizational learning. Organ Sci 2(1):71–87
Maula M (2007) Corporate venture capital as a strategic tool. In: Landstrom H (ed) Handbook of research on venture capital. Edward Elgar, UK
Nahapiet J, Ghoshal S (1998) Social capital, intellectual capital and the organizational advantage. Acad Manage Rev 23(2):242–266
Narin F, Noma E, Perry R (1987) Patents as indicators of technological strength. Res Policy 16:143–155
Nelson R, Winter S (1982) An evolutionary theory of economic change. Belknap, Cambridge, MA
Nerkar A (2003) Old is gold? The value of temporal exploration in the creation of new knowledge. Manage Sci 49(2):211–229
Nohria N, Gulati R (1996) Is slack good or bad for innovation? Acad Manage J 39(5):1245
Pavitt K (1988) Uses and abuses of patent statistics. In: van Raan AFJ (ed) Handbook of quantitative studies of science and technology. Elsevier, Amsterdam, pp 509–536
Rivette KG (1993) Corporate patent portfolios. Price Waterhouse, New York
Roberts PW (1999) Product innovation, product-market competition and persistent profitability in the US pharmaceutical industry. Strat Manage J 20:655–670
Rosenkopf L, Nerkar A (2001) Beyond local search: boundary-spanning, exploration, and impact in the optical disk industry. Strat Manage J 22(4):287
Sahal D (1985) Technological guideposts and innovation avenues. Res Policy 14(2):61
Schildt H, Maula MVJ, Keil T (2005) Explorative and exploitative learning from external corporate ventures. Entrep Theory Prac 29(4):493–515
Schmookler J (1966) Invention and economic growth. Harvard University Press, Cambridge, MA
Siggelkow N, Rivkin JW (2005) Speed and search: designing organizations for turbulence and complexity. Organ Sci 16:101–122
Simonin BL (1999) Ambiguity and the process of knowledge transfer in strategic alliances. Strat Manage J 20(7):595
Simonton DK (1999) Origins of genius. Oxford University Press, New York
Singh JV (1986) Performance, slack, and risk taking in organizational decision making. Acad Manage J 29:562–585
Sorensen J, Stuart T (2000) Aging, obsolescence, and organizational innovation. Adm Sci Q 45(1):81

Sorenson O, Rivkin JW, Fleming L (2006) Complexity, networks and knowledge flow. Res Policy 35:994–1017
Stuart T, Podolny J (1996) Local search and the evolution of technological capabilities. Strat Manage J 17:21–38
Stuart TE (2000) Interorganizational alliances and the performance of firms: a study of growth and innovation rates in a high-technology industry. Strat Manage J 21:791
Teece D (1981) The market for know-how and the efficient international transfer of technology. Ann Am Acad Pol Soc Sci 458:81–95
Teece DJ, Pisano G, Shuen A (1997) Dynamic capabilities and strategic management. Strat Manage J 18(7):509–533
Trajtenberg M (1987) Patents, citations, and innovations: tracing the links. Working paper no. 2457. National Bureau of Economic Research. Washington, DC
von Hayek F (1945) The use of knowledge in society. Am Econ Rev XXXV(4):519–530
Wadhwa A, Kotha SB (2006) Knowledge creation through external venturing: evidence from the telecommunications equipment manufacturing industry. Acad Manage J 49:819–835
Zander U, Kogut B (1995) Knowledge and the speed of the transfer and imitation of organizational capabilities. Organ Sci 6:76–92
Zollo M, Winter SG (2002) Deliberate learning and the evolution of dynamic capabilities. Organ Sci 13(3):339–351

Chapter 9
Business-University Alliances and Innovation in New and Adolescent Technology Ventures

Ken Colwell and Donna Marie DeCarolis

Abstract The dynamic resource based view introduces the concept of capability lifecycles. Applying this theory to new and adolescent technology ventures, we propose and test a model of the sources of heterogeneous knowledge capabilities that impact innovation. We suggest that the characteristics of the top management of these ventures impacts business-university alliance formation – a critical knowledge capability that affects innovation. Building on prior research, we also examine the source of firm specific knowledge through geographical munificence. Our results suggest that there are paths to knowledge capability development and innovation and that *people* are critical to the building of collaborative relationships, not merely being in the right *location.*

In new and adolescent technology companies, there can be no more pressing strategic issue than developing capabilities for new product development in competitive environments. While technological opportunities abound, converting those opportunities into products and revenues comes with a high risk of failure. In science-based industries, such as biotechnology, the challenge of building strong capabilities is even more acute due to rapid advances in knowledge and the long development time for new products.

Business-university alliances are a powerful way for new and adolescent technology firms to facilitate research and development. Universities provide state of the art research as they nurture scientists who devote their careers by seeking new advances in existing technologies and explore new science and emerging technologies. Building relationships with research organizations such as universities provides firms with access to unique knowledge and capability development (Powell et al. 1996). With notable exception (George et al. 2002), there is little scholarly investigation in the strategy or entrepreneurship literatures on the variables that might impact business-university alliances.

K. Colwell (✉) and D.M. DeCarolis
LeBow College of Business, Drexel University, Philadelphia, PA, USA
e-mail: kcolwell@miami.edu

D.B. Audretsch et al. (eds.), *New Frontiers in Entrepreneurship: Recognizing, Seizing, and Executing, Opportunities*, International Studies in Enterpreneurship,
DOI 10.1007/978-1-4419-0058-6_9,

We propose and test a model of the sources of knowledge capabilities that includes business university alliances and builds prior empirical research on knowledge building in new and adolescent technology ventures (DeCarolis and Deeds 1999). While it is understood that the heterogeneous innovative capabilities are critical to competitive advantage as underscored by the resource based and knowledge based view of firm behavior (Barney 1991; Grant 1996), the paths to develop those capabilities are not clearly understood. The dynamic resource based view provides a provocative framework for understanding how firm heterogeneity of capabilities arise (Helfat and Peteraf 2003) through a conceptual model of a capabilities lifecycle (CLC).

We suggest that the CLC framework is applicable to new and adolescent technology ventures. In particular, the CLC encompasses the dual components of teams and routines and how they work to create capabilities. Our concern is with the first two stages of the capabilities lifecycle – founding and development as they are the most appropriate to new and adolescent technology ventures.

Strategic alliances with universities represent an organizational process that is shaped by the firm's knowledge posture (Eisenhardt and Martin 2000; Eisenhardt, Santos 2002). Assuming that every firm is unique in its array of assets and capabilities (Wernerfelt 1984; Barney 1991), then there will be differences in the capacities of firms to collaborate with the universities and to assimilate external knowledge. Different capabilities imply different approaches to and sources of externally generated knowledge.

We add to the strategic alliance literature through the incorporation of the CLC framework and in particular, the impact of the *top management team* in the formation of business-university alliances. Our primary set of research questions focuses on business-university alliances. Specifically, (1) what are the factors that make some firms more adept than others at exploiting university innovations; and (2) does the sourcing of knowledge from universities have a positive impact on innovation?

The contribution of this model is its focus on the roles that management, alliances and location play in cultivating organizational knowledge and innovation. We propose that firm specific intellectual capital and university alliances are related to innovation in technology new ventures. We further propose that top management team characteristics will influence the proclivity to partner with universities in the quest for new knowledge. Finally, extending previous work on organizational knowledge and innovation (DeCarolis and Deeds 1999), we propose that the location of the firm will also influence the acquisition of firm specific intellectual capital and university alliance activity.

We test our model in the context of the biotechnology industry, a particularly rich research setting for studying the sourcing of organizational knowledge. The biotechnology industry is comprised mostly of small, newly formed companies focused on particular drug discovery processes and therapeutic areas. Firms in this industry often collaborate with other firms and universities to discover and develop new products or license early stage technologies from universities in order to commercialize them (Liebeskind et al. 1996). In addition, there are well-documented clusters of geographic "hot spots" for biotech activity, and biotechnology companies represent the second largest networked industry in the USA after the defense industry (Oliver 2000).

In the next section, we describe how university research is a critical component of private sector innovation. We then proceed to build the theoretical background of our model and develop the hypotheses. This is followed by a description of our methodology, model, analysis and results. Finally, we close with a discussion of our findings.

9.1 Business-University Alliances and Capability Development

The Bayh-Dole Act of 1980 sparked an increase in university patenting of new inventions and subsequent commercialization of these inventions in the forms of licensing and university spin-offs. Prior to the Bayh-Dole Act, the federal government retained the ownership of patents from federally funded research. Thousands of inventions remained in the university laboratories as the federal government could not commercialize these technologies for which they had assumed ownership. With the passage of the Bayh-Dole Act, universities became the owners of inventions created under federally funded research. In return, universities are expected to file for patent protection and are motivated to commercialize laboratory innovations either through licensing or university spin-offs.

University generated knowledge is critical to firm innovation. Cohen et al. (2002) found that university research affects the industrial R&D in manufacturing industries. In particular, their findings suggest that "non-market" knowledge flows, such as publications and conferences, are the most significant vehicles of knowledge transfer from university to firm. They also found that the greatest effects of public and university research were found in the pharmaceutical industry.

University research is critical to industrial research efforts as it both motivates new research and development platforms and contributes to the completion of existing products (Cohen et al. 2002). In fact, universities produce cutting edge research that has frequently proven to be the catalyst for transforming industries and societies. It is therefore not surprising that collaboration with university scientists increases innovative activity. Evidence suggests, for example, that co-authorship of scientific articles among university and firm scientists has a positive impact on firm innovative efforts (Zucker et al. 2002).

Companies seek out alliances with universities for several reasons. First, companies may be ill-equipped to generate certain types of knowledge or inventions, particularly those that are based on nascent scientific areas. Second, universities provide access to talented faculty and students. This could be valuable not only within an alliance itself, but also for future staffing opportunities. Third, companies seeking university based knowledge and inventions, desire collaborative relationships with academic scientists, relationships in which professors are engaged in the strategic direction of the alliance (Etzkowitz 2000; George et al. 2002; McMillan et al. 2000).

In the strategy and entrepreneurship literatures, there has been a great deal of theoretical and empirical research on the use of alliances for innovative activity (Deeds and Hill 1996; Powell et al. 1996; Kale et al. 2000; George et al. 2002). University research is a critical component of innovation in technologically dynamic industries. Yet, this is an area of strategic alliance research that is not frequently addressed yet represents a critical area for technology intensive firms. With notable exception (George et al. 2002), there is little research on the variables that influence the formation of business-university alliances and the outcomes of those alliances We build on this literature by focusing on the sourcing of knowledge from universities. The model presented below seeks to extend this body of literature on business-university alliances, their sources and their impact on innovation.

9.2 Model Development

Our model is based on the dynamic resource based CLC framework (Helfat and Peteraf 2003) which depicts capabilities as emanating from teams and evolving over time as an organization develops through various stages. In particular, we suggest that innovative capabilities in technology intensive industries for new and developing firms are related to university alliances which are in turn related to the characteristics of the top management team. We further suggest that innovative capabilities are influenced by firm specific knowledge that is related to the munificence of firm location.

9.3 Top Management Team and Business-University Alliances

The resource based view proposes that competitive advantage is largely attributed to heterogeneity of capabilities and resources (Barney 1991; Helfat and Peteraf 2003). Subsequent theoretical development augments the idea that resources and capabilities evolve, and in fact, are dynamic (Teece et al. 1997; Zollo and Winter 2002). The dynamic resource based view (Helfat and Peteraf 2003) introduces the concept of capability life cycle (CLC) which enables a deeper understanding of the sources of firm heterogeneity and the paths that capabilities take over time. Building on the work of Zollo and Winter (2002) and Teece et al. (1997), the CLC distinguishes between operational capabilities – those involving the performance of an activity such as manufacturing and dynamic capabilities – those that build, integrate or reconfigure operational capabilities. Yet, both types of capabilities, operational and dynamic, include two sets of routines: those to perform individual tasks and those that coordinate individual tasks. The coordination of tasks implies team efforts and thus, the CLC perspective "...depicts the evolution of an organizational capability that resides within a team" (Helfat and Peteraf 2003:999).

Moreover, the CLC framework outlines the stages of a capability: founding, development and maturity; as well as six additional stages (retirement, retrenchment, renewal, replication, redeployment, and recombination) that may take place in differing patterns over time. The founding and development stages as they relate to capability development are most relevant to the present context.

The CLC framework emphasizes the importance of the founding team to capability development. The founding team has a particular set of human and social capital, and cognitive perspectives. In addition, they also may bring "team" skills if they have previously worked together. Together, these founding team characteristics establish the initial endowments for capability building (Helfat and Peteraf 2003). Further, in the development stage, capabilities develop as the top management team begins to flesh out alternatives for capability development. The CLC framework proposes that capabilities will take different paths that depend on the characteristics of the teams and the conditions of the firm. Helfat and Peteraf (2003) suggest, for example, that teams composed of individuals that are predisposed to innovation strategies are more likely to pursue emerging technologies.

This framework for understanding capability development is also related to the stream of research in entrepreneurship that explores the composition of the founding and ensuing teams in new ventures and various outcomes (Cooper et al. 1994; Nelson 2003)

We apply the tenants of the CLC to our idea that the top management team matters to university-firm alliance formation in new and adolescent technology ventures. The managerial assets – the wisdom, skills, values and cognitive structures – of the top management team shape the organizational processes and strategic initiatives that will drive firm performance.

External sourcing of knowledge is one such strategic initiative. A managerial propensity to obtain the requisite and cutting edge knowledge that is needed to compete in technologically dynamic industries from internal vs. external sources may influence the innovative output of the firm. In technology intensive firms, the need to acquire and assimilate knowledge is critical to new product development. As described above, university knowledge is often cutting edge and provides extensive opportunities for firms to capitalize on and to extend that knowledge through alliances.

From the CLC perspective, the founding team that is critical in building capabilities would have a significant impact on how a new venture creates new product development capabilities. Alliances with universities represent a path to capability development and that path may be more pronounced when the founding team has human capital experience and social capital ties with academia.

Top management teams represent unique assets for each firm (Castanias and Helfat 2001). Upper echelons theory (Hambrick and Mason 1984) suggests that the psychological and cognitive orientations of the firm's top management team exhibit a strong influence on the strategic direction and ultimately the performance of the firm. Empirical research in this area utilizes demographic characteristics of the top management team as indicators of psychological and cognitive orientations. The upper echelons theory proposes that TMT values, skills, attitudes and cognitive structures impact firm strategies and performance. Further, the theory suggests that the demographic characteristics of the TMT may capture unobservable psychological traits. Ensuing empirical research on the upper echelons theory examined observable characteristics of the TMT and their relationship to strategic decision-making and firm performance (i.e., Bantel and Jackson 1989; Wiersema and Bantel 1992; Hambrick 1994; Hambrick et al. 1996). While much of this empirical work has focused on established firms, some studies have applied upper echelons theory to new ventures. Eisenhardt and Schoonhoven (1990) found that team size, team common experience and heterogeneity were linked to higher growth.

However, the results of a number of studies that focused on the relationship between TMT characteristics and firm performance have been mixed (i.e., Boeker 1997; Macmillan et al. 1985). These inconsistent findings have led some to doubt the premises of upper echelons theory (West and Schwenk 1996). Later work has suggested that moderating or mediating variables between TMT characteristics and performance best capture this relationship. Carpenter (2002) found support for his hypothesis that the strategic context moderates the TMT-performance link in large to medium sized firms.

Expanding on the previous empirical work on TMT and relating it to organizational knowledge, we suggest that two demographic traits – functional background and education – of the TMT and CEO are particularly relevant in the context of this study and mediate the relationship between TMT characteristics and performance.

Functional background of the TMT is considered an important observable characteristic in the work on upper echelons theory (Brothers et al. 2000; Hitt and Tyler 1991). Functional background includes the training and experience of the CEO or TMT such as in finance, accounting, law, or marketing. Interestingly, the role of the CEO or top manager is often viewed as a "generalist" position, given that they are responsible for the whole organization. Yet, CEO's arrive at these positions from specific functional specializations (Gupta 1984). The training and educational orientation of individuals will to a certain extent influence how they perceive and understand situations. For example, functional background was found to influence the strategic choices of top management in that they emphasize the function with which they have experience (Boeker 1997). Brothers et al. (2000) found that managers with functional experience in management pursued more aggressive strategies when compared managers with functional experience in finance and accounting.

Educational background of the TMT may impact the strategic choices of a firm. There are several reasons why we propose that educational backgrounds of both the CEO and TMT in biotechnology companies will impact the strategic decision making. First, CEO's with a scientific background and training may have a greater understanding of the nature of the technology in their firm and the unique competencies of their scientists. This insight allows them to evaluate resource complementarities in terms of potential alliance partners. Second, in this context, these CEO's may have the scientific acumen to recognize the future value of university technology and the ability to recognize external alliance opportunities through their assessment of potential partners' competencies. They certainly also possess the particular cognitive schema and language to communicate effectively with university scientists and technology transfer offices. Third, CEOs and TMTs with scientific functional and educational experience may have access to social capital through the networks they have created throughout their careers. Social capital consists of the good will and reciprocity that an individual may expect from a network of contacts (Adler and Kwon 2002). Thus, we argue that university alliance formation may be a function of the functional and educational backgrounds of the CEO and TMT.

Hypothesis 1: *The educational and professional experience of new and adolescent technology ventures' top management team will have a direct relationship to university alliance formation.*

9.3.1 Geographic Location, Intellectual Capital and Business-University Alliances

"Hot spots" of innovation are defined as geographically clustered firms within industries that begin as start-up firms, grow more rapidly than other industry participants and have similar immobile physical resource requirements in the long run (Pouder and St. John 1996). There are many examples of such "hot spots" around the world: the biotechnology industry in San Diego and North Carolina, the ceramics industry in Corning, New York, and Sassuolo, Italy and the computer industry in Austin, Texas. It is suggested that "hot spots" are generated when a few firms in the same industry in an area become successful and so a ripple effect occurs. Suppliers, qualified workers and investors are drawn to the area and become readily available. New firms are born, some of which are spin-offs from the original firms. Agglomeration economies (i.e., the net benefits of a firm being in a location will increase with the number of firms in that location) allow for lower costs and superior resources for clustered firms. There is then a resource advantage for a firm being located in a cluster.

In the instance of biotechnology firms, the munificence of the geographic environment is manifested not just in terms of available pools of knowledgeable workers, but also in the form of access to local university researchers, university research projects and a cluster of similar firms. Being embedded in a hot spot of industry specific knowledge flowing from universities and other firms facilitates innovation. Hot spots provide opportunities for inter-organizational knowledge flows and communications. The proximity of firms to competitors, suppliers, and a qualified labor pool increases the flow of knowledge across firm boundaries. Social interactions, both formally and informally, stimulate information exchange about such topics as competitor's plans, developments in process technologies and recent developments within the local university's laboratories. Interaction among employees of different firms and organizations from the same industry located in a geographic cluster may be facilitated through membership in local political and religious organizations, involvement in local art, athletic and community groups, residing in the same neighborhoods (Yates 1984) and through local industry events such as trade and professional association meetings (Almeida and Kogut 1999; Saxenian 1990).

Patents represent a firm's intellectual stock of knowledge. Patents are the physical, codifiable manifestations of innovative ideas, techniques, products and processes. Patents embody the knowledge of employees. Firms embedded in hot spots of innovation are exposed to opportunities for knowledge flow among the individuals and organizations in that area. As new ideas enter firms, they are assimilated, combined with existing knowledge and many times, this new knowledge is contained in a patent. Recent empirical evidence suggests that geographic location influences knowledge development (Henderson et al. 1998). These observations lead to the following hypothesis.

Hypothesis 2a: *Location in a "hot spot" will have a direct and positive relationship to the accumulation of new and adolescent technology ventures' specific intellectual capital.*

We also suggest that geographic location will have an impact on university alliance formation. Close proximity of universities to knowledge intensive organizations increases opportunities of information sharing, informal meetings, and joint participation in regional and university based events (Audretsch et al. 2005). Industry executives may become more familiar with local university inventions through university technology transfer offices (Mansfield and Lee 1996). These observations lead to the following hypothesis:

Hypothesis 2b: *Location in a "hot spot" will have a direct and positive relationship to business- university alliance formation.*

9.4 Business-University Alliances, Intellectual Capital and Innovation

A common indicator of performance in emerging high technology industries is a firm's products under development or products in the pipeline. Financial analysts and potential investors will monitor and assess the products being pursued by firms. The strength of a firm's pipeline is considered a valuable indicator of its future potential. This is particularly true in emerging industry contexts where new ventures and even established companies struggle to commercialize the products in uncertain market and technological environments. Prior research has demonstrated an empirical link between the alliances and research productivity (Shan et al. 1994; Deeds and Hill 1996).

A firm's stock of intellectual capital and flows of university alliance knowledge should be related to its innovative performance. According to the resource-based, knowledge-based and dynamic capabilities frameworks, the unique accumulation of organizational knowledge leads to competitive advantage. Business-university alliances provide the opportunity for firms and universities to combine skills in unique ways thus improving the capacity for product development. Similarly, the firm's stock of intellectual capital, manifested in its patenting activity, should result in innovative ideas.

The knowledge based view suggests that it is the knowledge embodied in products, processes and strategies that facilitate competitive advantage. Organizational knowledge evolves in particular ways and travels through certain trajectories (Dosi 1997). A firm's stock of knowledge (Dierickx and Cool 1989; DeCarolis and Deeds

1999) is critical to competitive advantage. Patents represent a firm's intellectual stock of knowledge. Patents are physical, codifiable manifestations of innovative ideas, techniques, products and processes that embody the knowledge of employees. These observations lead to the following hypothesis.

Hypothesis 3: *A new and adolescent venture's stock of intellectual capital will be directly and positively related to innovative performance.*We further suggest that university-industry alliances bring special value to a firm. University knowledge is typically cutting edge basic science as research coming from these institutions is generated in a relatively risk free atmosphere. University research not only suggests new R&D projects to industry but also enables the completion of existing industrial research projects (Cohen et al. 2002). It has also been shown that university research has a substantial impact on the industrial R&D in a few industries, particularly the pharmaceutical industry.

In technologically dynamic industries, firms are compelled to reach beyond their boundaries to access knowledge. External linkages such as technology related strategic alliances provide access to evolving knowledge, both product and process. Deeds and Hill (1996) and Shan et al. (1994) found a positive relationship between the number of a firm's strategic alliances and the research productivity of the firm. Particularly in technologically dynamic markets, alliances provide opportunities for co-discovery and co-development of complex and emerging technology and risk sharing (Kogut 1988). These observations lead to the following hypothesis.

Hypothesis 4: *New and adolescent firms' business- university alliances will be directly and positively related to innovative performance.*

9.5 Methodology

9.5.1 Research Setting

The biotechnology industry provides an appropriate context for our investigation into the determinants of the sourcing and accumulation of organizational knowledge. While it is a knowledge intensive and dynamic industry, it has also been characterized as having a knowledge base that is still "immature" (Pisano 1996). Since the field is nascent and new discoveries are constantly being made, firms must constantly acquire new knowledge in order to compete and survive. The biotechnology industry has been the setting for a number of strategic alliance studies in the past decade (i.e., Powell et al. 1996; Walker et al. 1997). Arora and Gambardella (1990) found that the universities, new biotechnology firms and established companies have complementary skills and resources that encourage collaboration. Baum et al. (2000) found that collaborating with universities is related to firm success in the biotech industry. Moreover, the research and development process for new products takes well over 10 years at a cost of about $800 million. Food and Drug Administration

(FDA) approval is required and the approval process is highly uncertain. It is estimated that of every 10,000 molecules that are discovered, one will eventually make it through the development process (clinical trials) and achieve FDA approval. This enhances the imperative to access university knowledge as a means to secure those technologies with commercial potential.

Our period of study ran from 1992 to 2002. 2002 was the latest date for which all of the data was available. We wanted to examine the effects of knowledge accumulation over time, so we collected data for a decade prior to this date.

9.5.2 Model and Sample

The sample for this study is biotechnology firms that were publicly traded in US markets during the study period of 1992–2002. We used COMPUSTAT to find all of the firms in the biotechnology industry sector that were listed on a U.S. stock market at the end of 2002. We excluded firms based in foreign countries due to the difficulties in obtaining data about them. Several others were eliminated from the sample because of unavailable data. The most common reason for exclusion was missing SEC filings. The characteristics of this sample are presented in Table 9.1.

In order to test our hypotheses regarding the relationships between firm location, the characteristics of top management teams, formation of university alliances and firm innovation, a structural equation model was developed. Structural equation modeling (SEM) is a cross-sectional statistical modeling technique that compares the covariance matrix of a series of parameters with a theoretical relationship between them. SEM differs from ANOVA and regression techniques chiefly in its ability to model the relationships between multiple parameters simultaneously (Hoyle 1995). SEM has become more prevalent in the strategic management literature in recent years due to the increasing theoretical sophistication of researchers' models (Shook et al. 2004).

We specified our SEM using the maximum likelihood estimation (MLE) procedure of AMOS 4 (Arbuckle 1999). MLE models do not assume that the indicator variables of the model are normally distributed. Such assumptions are frequently violated in practice (Shook et al. 2004).

Table 9.1 Sample characteristics

Sample size	218
Avg. firm age[a]	14.08 years
Avg. time to IPO	6.09 years
Avg. firm size[a]	411 employees

[a]As of 12/31/2002

9.5.3 *Operational Measures*

We used a variety of archival sources to operationalize our constructs of top management team characteristics, firm-specific intellectual assets, and geographic munificence.

9.5.4 *Top Management Team Characteristics*

We operationalized the extent to which the firm's TMT has the skills and knowledge to understand and access university scientific technology by collecting the following data:

the professional background of the CEO; the percentage of top management team members who possess a Ph.D. or other terminal degree; the percentage of board members who possess a Ph.D. or other terminal degree; the percentage of board members who are professors; the percentage of outside (non-employee) board members. This information was gathered from the firm's 2002 SEC filings. In most cases, the proxy statement contained the required information. If the proxy statement was not available or did not contain the required information, the firm's 2002 annual report (SEC 10 K report) was used.

9.5.5 *Firm-Specific Intellectual Assets*

Firm specific intellectual assets may be captured by the firm's patent filings. The scientific momentum of a biotechnology firm is evidenced by its patent portfolio. We operationalized firm-specific intellectual assets as the *number of patents* assigned to the firm during the study period of 1992–2002. These data were gathered from the US Patent Office patent database.

9.5.6 *Geographic Munificence*

Following DeCarolis and Deeds (1999), we considered the presence of critical resources in a firm's proximity a measure of geographic munificence. To measure the supply of skilled human assets, we used the number of graduate students in the region in four areas: Chemistry, Biological Sciences, Medical, and Other Life Sciences (National Science Foundation 2003). As an indicator of commercialization activity and the availability of capital, we also measured the total value of venture capital investments in biotech firms in the region during the study period. These data were obtained from the VentureXpert database. The region used for all of these measures was the firm's U.S. Census Metropolitan Statistical Area (MSA).

9.5.7 University Alliance Formation

We used *RECAP*, a biotechnology alliance database, to obtain the rate of university alliance formation per year during the study period of 1992–2002. We included both R&D alliances and licensing activities to ensure that we captured the array of research knowledge collaborations that link the biotechnology firms and universities.

9.5.8 Innovation Performance

The level of firm innovation was measured as the number of a biotechnology firm's products in the pipeline as of the end of 2002. The information was obtained from the RECAP database.

9.5.9 Control Variables

We controlled for firm size (number of employees), firm age, and firm R&D expenditures. These data were gathered from COMPUSTAT.

9.6 Results

The structural equation model depicted in Fig. 9.1 estimates the path coefficients reflecting the hypothesized relationships between the variables. There are two types of SEM variables – observed (endogenous) and latent (exogenous). By convention, observed variables are represented in SEM diagrams as squares, while latent variables are depicted as circles. In our model, there are two latent variables, Geographic Munificence and TMT Characteristics. The TMT Characteristics variable (Fig. 9.2) is derived from the observed variables regarding the firm's top management team described in the previous section. Similarly, the Geographic Munificence variable (Fig. 9.3) is derived from the geographic munificence variables described in the previous section.

There are a number of fit indices that can be calculated to demonstrate the overall fit of the model to the data. The best of these are measures of incremental fit – the degree to which the model is superior to the null hypothesis of no covariance among the variables. They are forced to take values between 0 and 1, with a value of 0 indicating no covariance and 1 indicating perfect fit between the model and the data. We report two fit indices in Fig. 9.1. The Incremental Fit Index (IFI) estimates the relative improvement per degree of freedom of the model when compared to the null hypothesis.

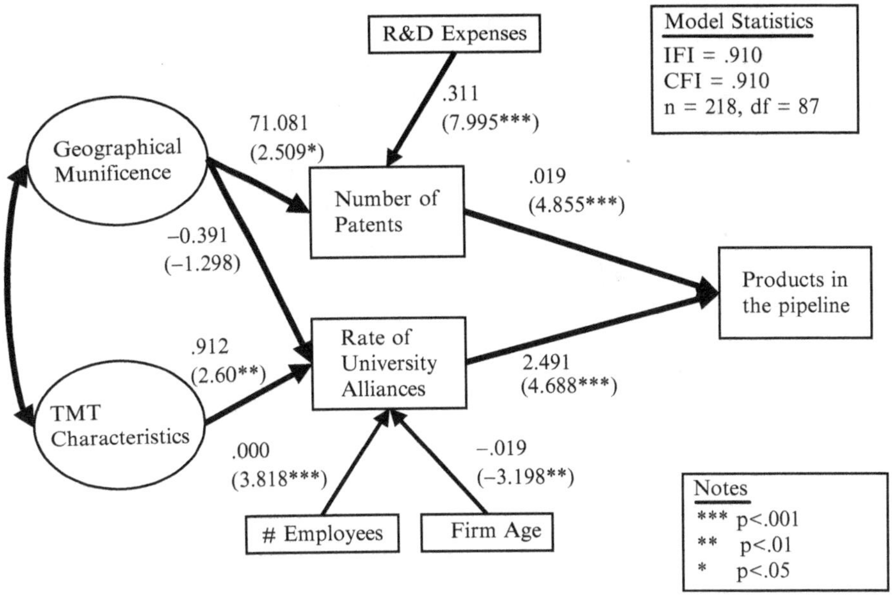

Fig. 9.1 Sources of organizational knowledge structural equation model

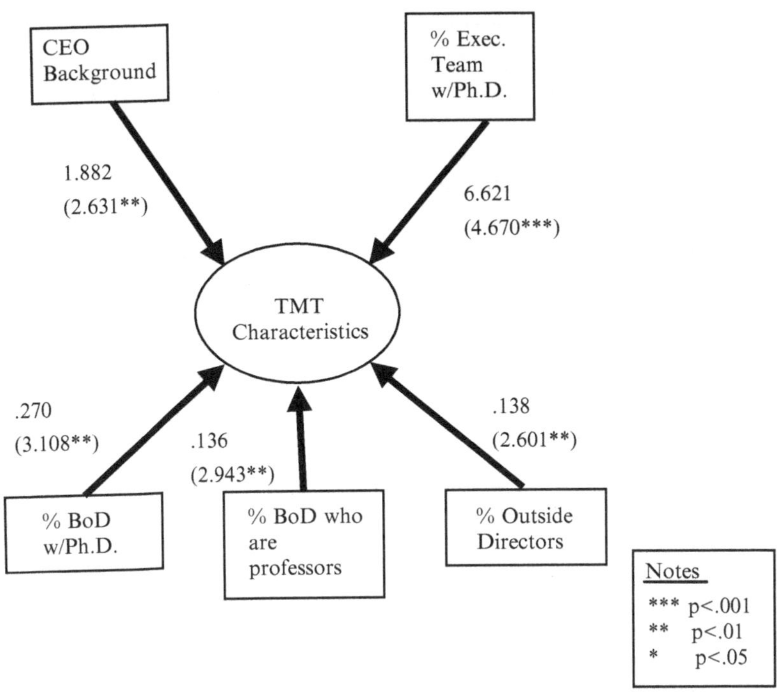

Fig. 9.2 The TMT characteristics construct

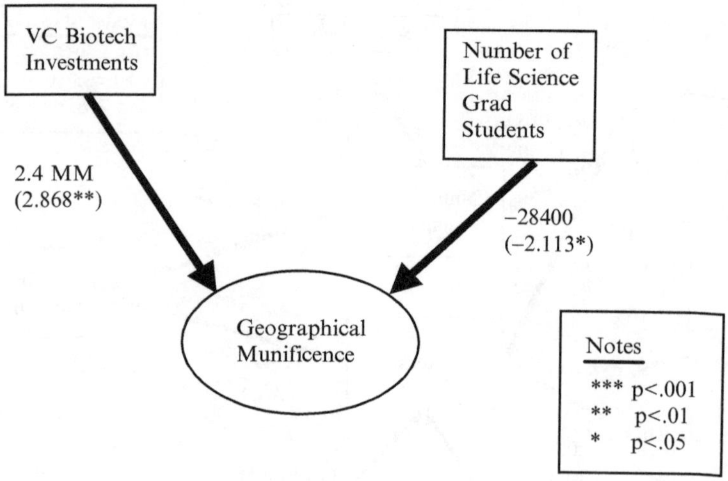

Fig. 9.3 The geographical munificence construct

The Comparative Fit Index (CFI) estimates the relative reduction in lack of fit of the model when compared with the null hypothesis. These indices are less sensitive to changes in sample size than the other commonly used measures of SEM fit such as chi-square (Hoyle 1995).[1] The IFI and CFI of our model are 0.910 and 0.909, respectively. There are no theoretical or empirical critical values for any of the SEM fit indices; however, our index values compare well to the 0.90 "rule of thumb" critical value often reported by researchers. Table 9.2 shows the means, standard deviations and zero-order correlations of all the observed variables.

Our first hypothesis predicted a relationship between the composition of the top management team and the formation of business-university alliances. This hypothesis was *supported.* The professional background of the CEO, the percent of the executive team who hold terminal degrees, the percent of board members who hold terminal degrees, whose primary occupation is professor and who are not otherwise employed by the firm are all had a significant positive relationship with the TMT characteristics latent variable. These relationships are depicted in Fig. 9.2. TMT characteristics have a highly significant positive relationship with the rate of university alliance formation ($t=2.60$, $p<0.01$).

In Hypothesis 2a, we suggested a relationship between geographic location and firm-specific intellectual capital. This hypothesis was *supported.* The total amount of biotech venture deals during the study period and the total number of medical/life science graduate students in the firm's MSA both had a significant positive relationship with the Geographic Munificence latent variable. These relationships are depicted in Fig. 9.3. Geographic Munificence had a significant positive relationship with patenting activity ($t=2.509$, $p<0.05$).

[1]The chi-square of the overall model was 392.61, $p<0.0001$.

Table 9.2 Descriptive statistics and zero-order correlations among model variables

		Mean	SD	1	2	3	4	5	6	7	8	9	10	11	12	13
1	# Patents	38.4	95.8	1.00												
2	Rate of university alliances	0.4647	0.693	0.062	1.00											
3	Products in pipeline	5.31	6.03	0.321***	0.303***	1.00										
4	CEO background	2.81	2.04	.106	–0.048	0.054	1.00									
5	# Execs with Ph.D.	2.53	2.04	0.139*	0.232**	0.244***	0.198**	1.00								
6	% Directors with Ph.D.	0.3484	0.24	0.024	0.080	0.108	0.017	0.215**	1.00							
7	% Outside directors	0.7627	0.15	0.050	0.078	0.076	0.035	0.167*	–0.01	1.00						
8	% Directors who are professors	0.1147	0.13	0.074	0.143*	0.193**	0.216**	0.163*	0.212**	0.154*	1.00					
9	VC investment	2.09	2.06	0.204**	0.061	0.033	0.109	0.157*	0.007	0.088	0.055	1.00				
10	# Grad. students	67,181	42,110	–0.09	–0.004	0.048	0.125	–0.029	0.057	–0.055	0.102	–0.147*	1.00			
11	Firm age	14.08	7.4	0.105	–0.168*	0.056	–0.050	–0.078	–0.131	–0.055	0.008	–0.146*	0.069	1.00		
12	# Employees	411	1077	0.463***	0.209**	0.282***	–0.075	0.113	0.066	0.128	0.125	0.050	–0.047	0.239***	1.00	
13	R&D expenses	52.6184	141.39	0.503***	0.162*	0.363***	0.008	0.177**	0.066	0.117	0.135*	0.102	–0.032	0.094	0.819***	1.00

*$p<0.05$
**$p<0.01$
***$p<0.001$

On the other hand, Hypothesis 2b predicted that geographic location would influence university alliance formation. This hypothesis was *not supported.* The relationship between geographical munificence and university alliance formation was negative and insignificant. It appears that being located in a hot spot of innovation contributes to a firm's accumulation of knowledge stocks but not to its proclivity to partner with universities. Despite the presence and availability of university researchers in the life sciences, and strong commercialization activity, biotech firms located in "hot spots" did not form more alliances than the other biotech firms.

Our third hypothesis predicated a positive relationship between firm-specific intellectual capital and products in the pipeline. Not surprisingly, this hypothesis was *supported.* Patents were positively related to products in the pipeline ($t=4.855$, $p<0.001$).

Hypothesis 4 predicted a positive relationship between the university alliance formation and products in the pipeline. This hypothesis was also *supported.* The rate of university alliance formation had a positive significant relationship with products in the pipeline ($t=4.688$, $p<0.001$).

9.7 Discussion and Conclusions

The research questions that we addressed in this paper focused on the variables that impact the sourcing and accumulation of organizational knowledge and the relationship between that knowledge and innovation performance in high tech ventures. We suggested that business-university alliance formation and firm research represent, respectively, external and internal knowledge acquisition routines, and are both critical firm capabilities. Since relationships with universities can be a vital source of innovation for firms in technologically dynamic industries, a major part of our focus was on the antecedents and impacts of business-university alliances. We proposed that the background of the top management team would influence the university-firm collaboration, and that university alliances would lead to an increased firm innovation.

Our empirical findings suggest that the composition of the top management team does matter in terms of university-firm collaboration and, ultimately, innovation performance. TMT members that have scientific and research backgrounds are related to higher rates of university alliance formation. In addition, more business-university alliances lead to more products in the pipeline for biotechnology firms. This is a critical finding for both universities and technologically intensive firms. The commercialization of university intellectual property is of vital interest to universities, faculty inventors and firms. The risk and expense of R&D, particularly in the biotechnology sector, may lead the firms to be increasingly interested in the universities as sources of intellectual property. Our findings not only confirm that business-university alliances are fruitful endeavors for biotech firms, but also point to some factors that facilitate these critical relationships. Having more outside board members, particularly professors, leads to a greater rate of university alliance formation. Having more TMT members with terminal degrees such as Ph.D.'s and

MD's does as well. Finally, having a CEO with an academic or R&D background also results in more university alliances. Firms interested in collaborating with university researchers may find these results to be relevant to their staffing decisions.

Coupled with the influence of the top management team in the sourcing and accumulation of knowledge, we also suggested that location matters to both university alliance collaboration and the accumulation of intellectual capital in the form of patents. We predicted that being immersed in a location of abundant scientific and commercialization activity would facilitate university alliances for biotechnology firms. This did not turn out to be the case. While the TMT matters to university alliance formation, we found no evidence that geographical location does. This finding suggests that *people* are critical to the building of formal collaborative relationships, not merely being in the right *place*. The notion that people make the difference in university collaboration is also interesting when compared to our other finding that location does impact internal knowledge accumulation in the form of patents.

As Audretsch et al. (2005) point out; there are several ways in which knowledge spillovers from universities can occur. Being embedded in a hot spot enhances the likelihood that knowledge spillovers will occur in the form of trained graduates who can enhance the internal R&D efforts. Additional formal and informal spillovers occur in hot spots due to the presence of startups and other members of the new venture community such as venture capitalists. These factors seem to affect the accumulation of internal knowledge in organizations, as evidenced by its codification in patent approvals. On the other hand, munificent location does not seem to be sufficient to access university knowledge spillovers from scientific research in the form of collaboration with university scientists.

In the theoretical articulation of dynamic capabilities lifecycle, there are multiple paths to critical firm capabilities such as new product development. Our finding that patents and university alliance activity both impact innovation performance as measured by products in the pipeline provides empirical support for this claim. Models that correlate one potential pathway, for example R&D spending, to innovative output may miss the fact that different firms may choose different paths to the same end based on their existing resource stocks as well as their strategic posture.

Against this backdrop, it is perhaps not too great an intuitive leap to assume that successful collaboration with universities and geographic location can both lead to a sustained competitive advantage for a firm, particularly in a research-intensive industry such as biotechnology.

9.7.1 Limitations and Areas for Future Research

Our model and data are not without limitations. We examined only the biotechnology industry, and our results may not be generalizable to the other industry contexts. Our sample consists of only publicly traded firms, which may create a survivor bias by excluding smaller, newer firms. Furthermore, we correlate a dynamic flow of knowledge over a 10-year period (university alliance and patent accumulations) with a static stock of innovations (products in the pipeline) at one period of time. Although our analysis shows a strong correlation between these variables, the model does not distinguish which particular knowledge leads to a specific innovation. Longitudinal studies that specify this relationship may be a useful extension of this work.

Another interesting extension of this work would be to explore why top management teams with science and research backgrounds form more alliances with universities. There are a number of socio-cognitive factors that are all reasonable possibilities. For example, the difference could be due to strategic intent. TMT members with scientific backgrounds may be more likely to see the strategic value in university collaboration, and seek such relationships more often. Another possibility is that TMT members with scientific backgrounds may have existing relationships with university researchers and other forms of social capital that facilitate collaboration. Lastly, TMT members with scientific backgrounds may possess the ability to communicate effectively with researchers across the university-commercial divide. Since this ability is notably lacking among many on both sides of the divide, TMT members who fit in with both communities may have an advantage in forming alliances with universities.

References

Adler PS, Kwon S (2002) Social capital: prospects for a new concept. Acad Manage Rev 27(1):17–41

Almeida P, Kogut B (1999) Localization of knowledge and the mobility of engineers in regional networks. Manage Sci 45(7):905–918

Arbuckle JL (1999) AMOS 4.0. http://www.spss.com/amos/

Arora A, Gambardella A (1990) Complementarity and external linkages: the strategies of the large firms in biotechnology. J Ind Econ 38:361–379

Audretsch DB, Lehmann EE, Warning S (2005) University spillovers and new firm location. Res Policy 34:1113–1122

Bantel K, Jackson S (1989) Top management and innovations in banking: does the composition of the top team make a difference? Strateg Manage J 10:107–134

Barney J (1991) Firm resources and sustained competitive advantage. J Manage 17:99–120

Baum JA, Calabrese T, Silverman B (2000) Don't go it alone: alliance network composition and startups' performance in Canadian biotechnology. Strateg Manage J 21:267–294

Boeker W (1997) Strategic change: the influence of managerial characteristics and organizational growth. Acad Manage J 40(1):151–171

Brothers KD, Brouthers LE, Werner S (2000) Influences on strategic decision-making in the Dutch financial services industry. J Manage 26(5):863–883

Carpenter MA (2002) The implications of strategy and social context for the relationship between top management heterogeneity and firm performance. Strateg Manage J 23(3):275–284

Castanias RP, Helfat CE (2001) The managerial rents model: theory and empirical analysis. J Manage 27:661–679

Cohen W, Nelson R, Walsh J (2002) Links and impacts: the influence of public research on industrial R&D. Manage Sci 48(1):1–23

Cooper AC, Gimeno-gascon FJ, Woo CY (1994) Initiel Human and Financial Capital as Predictors of New Venture Performance Journal of Business Venturing 9:371–395

DeCarolis D, Deeds D (1999) The impact of stocks and flows of organizational knowledge on firm performance: an empirical investigation of the biotechnology industry. Strateg Manage J 20:953–968

Deeds DL, Hill CWL (1996) Strategic alliances and the rate of new product development: an empirical study of entrepreneurial biotechnology firms. J Bus Venturing 11(1):41–56

Dierickx I, Cool K (1989) Asset stock accumulation and sustainability of competitive advantage. Manage Sci 35(12):1504–1513

Dosi G (1997) Opportunities, incentives and the collective patterns of technological change. Econ J 107(444):1530–1547

Eisenhardt KM, Martin JA (2000) Dynamic capabilities: what are they? Strateg Manage J 21:1105–1121

Eisenhardt K, Santos F (2002) Knowledge-based view: a new theory of strategy? In: Pettigrew A, Thomas H, Whittington R (eds) Handbook of strategy and management. Sage Publications, London

Eisenhardt KM, Schoonhoven CB (1990) Organizational growth: linking founding team, strategy, environment and growth among U.S. semiconductor ventures, 1978–1988. Adm Sci Q 35(3):504–529

Etzkowitz H (2000) The second academic revolution: MIT and the rise of entrepreneurial science. Gordon & Breach, London

George G, Zahra SA, Wood DR (2002) The effects of business-university alliances on innovative output and financial performance: a study of publicly traded biotechnology companies. J Bus Venturing 17(6):557–590

Grant R (1996) Toward a knowledge based theory of the firm. Strateg Manage J 17(Special Issue):109–122

Gupta AK (1984) Contingency linkages between strategy and general manager characteristics: a conceptual examination. Acad Manage Rev 9(3):399–413

Hambrick DC (1994) Top management groups: a conceptual integration and reconsideration of the "team" label. Res Organ Behav 16:171–215

Hambrick D, Mason P (1984) Upper echelons: the organization as a reflection of its top managers. Acad Manage Rev 9(2):193–206

Hambrick DC, Cho TS, Chen M-J (1996) The influence of top management team heterogeneity on firm's competitive moves. Adm Sci Q 41(4):659–684

Helfat C, Peteraf M (2003) The dynamic resource based view: capability lifecycles. Strateg Manage J 24:997–1010

Henderson R, Jaffe AB, Trajtenberg M (1998) Universities as sources of commercial technology: a detailed analysis of university patenting. Rev Econ Stat 80(1):119–128

Hitt MA, Tyler BB (1991) Strategic decision models: integrating different perspectives. Strateg Manage J 12(5):327–351

Hoyle RH (1995) Structural equation modeling: concepts, issues, and applications. Sage Publications, Thousand Oaks

Kale P, Singh H, Perlmutter H (2000) Learning and protection of property assets in strategic alliances: building relational capital. Strateg Manage J 21(3):217–238

Kogut B (1988) Joint ventures: theoretical and empirical perspectives. Strateg Manage J 9(4):319–332

Liebeskind JP, Oliver AL, Zucker L, Brewer M (1996) Social networks, learning and flexibility: sourcing scientific knowledge in new biotechnology firms. Organ Sci 7:428–443

MacMillan I, Siegel R, Narasimha PN (1985) Criteria used by venture capitalists to evaluate venture proposals. J Bus Venturing 1(1):119–129

Mansfield E, Lee J-Y (1996) The modern university: contributor to industrial innovation and recipient of industrial R&D support. Res Policy 25:1047–1058

McMillan S, Narin F, Deeds D (2000) An analysis of the critical role of public science in innovation: the case of biotechnology. Res Policy 29:1–8

National Science Foundation, Division of Science Resources Statistics (2003) Graduate Students and Postdoctorates in Science and Engineering: Fall 2001, NSF 03-320, Project Officer, Joan S. Burrelli. Arlington, VA

Nelson T (2003) The persistence of founder influence: management, ownership and performance effects at initial public offering. Strateg Manage J 10:125–141

Oliver RW (2000) The coming biotech age: the business of biomaterials. McGraw-Hill, New York

Pisano GP (1996) Learning-before-doing in the development of new process technology. Res Policy 25(7):1097–1130

Pouder R, St. John C (1996) Hot spots and blind spots: geographic clusters of firms and innovations. Acad Manage Rev 21(4):1192–1225

Powell WW, Koput KW, Smith-Doerr L (1996) Interorganizational collaboration and the locus of innovation: networks of learning in biotechnology. Adm Sci Q 41:116–146

Saxenian A (1990) Regional networks and the resurgence of Silicon Valley. Calif Manage Rev 33(1):89–112

Shan W, Walker G, Kogut B (1994) Interfirm cooperation and startup innovation in the biotechnology industry. Strateg Manage J 15:387–394

Shook CL, Ketchen DJ, Hult GT, Kacmar KM (2004) An assessment of the use of structural equation modeling in strategic management research. Strateg Manage J 25:397–404

Teece D, Pisano G, Shuen A (1997) Dynamic capabilities and strategic management. Strateg Manage J 18(7):509–533

Walker G, Kogut B, Shan W (1997) Social capital, structural holes and the formation of an industry network. Organ Sci 8:109–125

Wernerfelt B (1984) A resource-based view of the firm. Strateg Manage J 5(2):171–180

West CT, Schwenk CR (1996) Top management team strategic consensus, demographic homogeneity and firm performance: A report on resounding nonfindings. Strateg Manage J 17(7):571–578

Wiersema M, Bantel K (1992) Top management team demography and corporate strategic change. Acad Manage J 35(1):91–120

Zollo M, Winter SG (2002) Deliberate learning and the evolution of dynamic capabilities. Organ Sci 13:339–351

Zucker LG, Darby MR, Armstrong JS (2002) Commercializing knowledge: university science, knowledge capture, and firm performance in biotechnology. Manage Sci 48(1):138–153

Part IV
Open Innovation and New Entrepreneurship

Chapter 10
A Test of Lazear's Theory of Entrepreneurship in the Open Source Software Virtual Community*

Paola Giuri, Francesco Rullani, and Salvatore Torrisi

Abstract This paper studies the emergence of entrepreneurs and their skill profile in the open source software (OSS) community. We test the hypothesis that entrepreneurs, carrying out complex, multitask activities, have more balanced skill sets compared with individuals who are less involved in project management activities. Our empirical analysis employs the SourceForge dataset containing information on 77,039 individuals working in 54,229 OSS projects. We estimate logit and ordered logit models to explore the likelihood that an individual is a project founder or manager. Our main regressors include individual attributes like skill level and diversity, and project-level controls. Results support our hypothesis.

10.1 Introduction

According to Schumpeter, the entrepreneurial function "does not necessarily consist in either inventing anything or otherwise creating the conditions which the enterprise exploits. It consists in getting things done" (Schumpeter 1942, p. 132). From this perspective, entrepreneurship does not consist exclusively in the creation of a new company or business, but also in the management and coordination of innovative combinations of human capital and other inputs with the purpose of "getting things done."

Our analysis draws on this broad view of entrepreneurship to look at the emergence of entrepreneurs and their skill profile in the open source software (OSS)

P. Giuri and S. Torrisi (✉)
Department of Management, University of Bologna, via Capo di Lucca 34, 40126, Bologna, Italy
e-mail: torrisi@unibo.it

F. Rullani
INO, Copenhagen Business School, Kilevej 14A, 3rd floor, office 3.41, 2000, Frederiksberg, Denmark

*A shorter version of this paper has been published in *Information Economics and Policy* 2008 with the title "Explaining leadership in virtual teams: the case of open source software."

D.B. Audretsch et al. (eds.), *New Frontiers in Entrepreneurship: Recognizing, Seizing, and Executing, Opportunities*, International Studies in Enterpreneurship,
DOI 10.1007/978-1-4419-0058-6_10,

community. In this particular context, we define entrepreneurs as both founders and managers of open source projects.

Various empirical accounts of the OSS community suggest that many projects rely on a quite well-defined division of labor between "core developers" and project leaders, who control the evolution of the base code, and a wider "periphery" of contributors who provide feedbacks that are critical for product quality improvement (the "obscure developers" as defined by Dalle and Jullien (2003)).

In large projects such as Linux or Apache, there is a quite clear decision-making chain. For example, Linus Torvalds, the founder of the Linus project, has the right to decide which changes enter the official Linux releases, whereas core developers of the Apache Group approve changes to the source code by voting (Mockus et al. 2000). Even in these large projects, however, developers contribute on a voluntary basis, choosing which tasks to undertake and how much effort to devote. Project founders and leaders then must be able to manage a virtual team in a regime of "distributed authority" (Mateos-Garcia and Steinmueller 2003).

Several OSS projects are participated by a small number of active, highly committed programmers (Ghosh and David 2003). Most probably, in small projects, the division of labor is more blurred than in large ones and the coordination efforts of project leaders are quite limited. But, this does not imply that these projects do not need any project management. On the contrary, the lack of management and coordination is probably a major source of failure of many OSS projects. In this setting, it is crucial to understand the forces that lead to the emergence of project managers among OSS participants.

The knowledge of these forces is still limited[1] and we aim to fill this gap in the literature by analyzing the association between the roles played by individuals in the projects with their skill profile. In line with the theory of occupational choice elaborated by Lazear (2002, 2004), we expect that OSS entrepreneurs must possess a diversified skill set that is needed to select the inputs provided by various participants, motivate contributors, and coordinate their efforts while specialists, such as pure developers, are supposed to be endowed with a more focused skill set.

We test this hypothesis by controlling for various individual and project characteristics such as project size and the degree of modularity of the development process. Modular, flexible design and manufacturing systems are based on multiskilled teams and have to be coordinated by novel management approaches that differ from traditional ones. Spatial dispersion of team members and computer-mediated interaction, which are typical of "virtual teams," pose additional challenges to project management and require individuals focusing on this type of activity (Martins et al. 2004). Project team managers must be "able to articulate project goals and to assign responsibilities with specific schedules and work deadlines. They have to be flexible and willing to delegate responsibilities to other group members and help developing links among participants thus favoring mutual trust" (Kayworth and Leidner 2000: 189).

[1] An example of research in this sense is Dahlander (2007).

Our empirical analysis employs a dataset containing information on 77,039 individuals working in 54,229 projects hosted by the SourceForge.net (*SF.net* henceforth) website from November 1999 to January 2003.

The SF.net dataset provides information on the role of each user registered with a project (i.e., developer, project manager, web designer, content manager, "all-hands persons," etc.). For our purposes, we grouped these roles into broader role categories implying increasing levels of managerial task complexity. The dataset also contains information that can lead to the identification of the founders of each project started after September 2000.

We explore the likelihood that an individual plays multitask, managerial roles by estimating an ordered logit model. Our main regressors include individual attributes such as skill level and diversity, the average project size, and the average number of subprojects per project as a proxy for project modularity, plus a series of controls. We also perform logit estimations of the probability to be a founder of the project, conditional to individual level characteristics.

The results support the hypothesis that entrepreneurs, carrying out complex, multitask activities, have more balanced skill sets compared with individuals who are less involved in project management activities.

The paper is organized as follows. Section 2 discusses the background literature and the research hypothesis. Section 3 illustrates the data used in the empirical analysis, descriptive statistics, and the econometric estimations. Section 4 concludes.

10.2 Theory and Research Hypotheses

10.2.1 The OSS Context

The organization of OSS projects can benefit from recent advances in the analysis of "virtual teams". These have been defined as "teams whose members use technology to varying degrees in working across locational, temporal, and relational boundaries to accomplish an interdependent task" (Martins et al. 2004, p. 808). This stream of the literature recognizes that virtual teamwork has become widespread in several activities, especially in knowledge-intensive industries. For instance, Kanawattanachai and Yoo (2002)) show that over 60% of professional employees work in virtual teams. But, despite the growing number of papers produced in over 10 years, "there is a lack of clarity on what we know" on virtual teams (Martins et al. 2004). An area that has attracted limited research efforts so far (e.g., Kayworth and Leidner 2000) is about leadership in virtual environments. Drawing on a large survey of the management literature, Martins et al. (2004) note that relevant for future research are issues such as the way leaders define roles, motivate, and evaluate participants' performance, and how the degree of virtualness affects the patterns of leader–member exchange (p. 821).

OSS represents an ideal testing ground for analyzing virtual teams and indeed several papers have addressed their attention to the organization of OSS projects and the motivations of participants (see, for instance, Harhoff et al. 2003; von Hippel 2001; Lerner and Tirole 2002).

The OSS model of innovation involves a large community that shares values (generalized reciprocity and meritocracy), conduct rules, and institutions (such as priority, peer review principles, and the refuse of formal development methodologies and management systems). These social norms and institutions conform to the concepts of self-organization and gift economy (e.g., Raymond 1999, 2001; Di Bona et al. 1999).

The increasingly large number of programmers who offer their voluntary contribution to OSS projects has spurred a stream of research which focuses primarily on specific OSS projects, especially large ones. For instance, Koch and Schneider (2000)) have analyzed the CVS (concurrent versions system) of the GNOME project (an OSS project dedicated to a desktop environment for users and an application framework for developers) and found that only a small number of programmers work together on the same file. The number of codevelopers increases with the size of the file and more active programmers work more for large files compared with less active programmers. Similarly, Mockus et al. (2000) found that in the case of the Apache server project, the top 15 developers contributed more than 83% of changes to Apache source code and only 25 developers submitted changes on a regular basis during the period 1995–1999. The 15 most active "core developers" corresponds approximately to the Apache Group, the organization responsible for the management of the Project. These project maintainers are primarily devoted to developing or reviewing new functionalities to the base code and, to a lesser extent, to fixing defects. The periphery of less active contributors is made of non-core developers (about 250 people during the time window of Mockus et al.'s analysis) which, relative to core developers, are more active in bugs or problem-related changes (patches). The most external part of the Apache server's periphery is made of a wider community of over 3,000 users who only report bugs (Mockus et al. 2000).

We should remember, however, that the majority of OSS projects are small and much less organized than that described above. For example, Krishnamurthy (2002) has analyzed the top 100 mature projects in Sourceforge and found that the median number of codevelopers was only 4. These projects then generate only limited informal exchange among users and therefore require less coordination. But, the leaders of small projects, most probably, carry out different activities and have to work hard to attract new contributors. To some extent, then project leaders represent a critical resource for both large and small OSS projects.

It is worth to note that coordinating and managing an OSS project appears to be a particularly challenging task compared with other settings like a traditional firm. As Lerner and Tirole (2002) pointed out, OSS leaders have to carry out some critical tasks: (a) to provide a "vision" that is provided through a critical mass of code that demonstrates their expertise and credibility; (b) to attract new programmers by posing challenging issues and, at the same time, leaving to potential contributors significant opportunities for future improvements to the initial code; (c) to ensure an efficient division of the project into modules and to allow contributors to perform their tasks independently from the rest of the contributors; (d) to avoid that conflicting views and approaches among participants lead to dropouts and forking (p. 21).

When does critical role materialize in OSS projects? We submit to empirical test the view that the emergence of entrepreneurs in OSS teams is associated with the skill profile of team members. In our empirical analysis, we also control for characteristics of the project like size and modularity.

10.2.2 Lazear's Theory of Entrepreneurship

The economics and strategic management literature of the 1980s and the 1990s has examined different ways in which skill level and diversity may affect firm performance.

First, skill heterogeneity implies that firms can experiment complex combinations of skills that are difficult to imitate (Lippman and Rumelt 1982). Second, skill diversity allows a more flexible strategic adaptation to changing external environment (Galunic and Rodan 1998). Skill heterogeneity provides firms with more comprehensive problem solving ability and creative conflict resolution (Sutton and Hargadon 1997; Galunic and Rodan 1998). The cognitive diversity resulting from interaction among people with different perspectives makes it possible to identify and formulate a wider array of problems and to find a larger set of alternative solutions (Bantel and Jackson 1989)[2].

More recently, the literature has stressed that the level of capabilities and skills is also particularly important for newly established firms. Well-balanced founding teams (or highly skilled single founders) are able to attract financial resources, customers, and collaborators (see, for instance, Bhidé 2000; Baron and Hannah 2002). In the case of OSS, skilled core developers are more likely to attract new users, because their software addresses relevant problems that are not met by commercial products or because it raises technical puzzles that are challenging to the community of developers. This in turn helps the project to evolve and become more productive. OSS projects then are not very different from the traditional entrepreneurial sector, where new ventures have to overcome the "liability of newness" and must convince potential stakeholders to pool their resources to support new ideas and to grow.

Our main hypothesis is that individuals, who choose to found a project and/or to become project leaders (either deliberately or as the result of internal "myopic" selection process), must possess a balanced skill set. They are not necessarily the

[2] Empirical papers on the benefits of heterogeneous workforce mainly provide evidence of positive or curvilinear (inverted U-shape) relations between skill diversity and performance. See Bantel and Jackson (1989), Hamilton et al. (2003), Laursen et al. (2005), Carbonell and Rodriguez (2006). See also Hambrick et al. (1996) on the impact of heterogeneity of top management teams on firms competitive actions.

most skilled among project members neither they need to have a comparative advantage in specific skills. Our hypothesis draws on the Lazear's theory of entrepreneurship (Lazear 2002, 2004).

Unlike other theories of entrepreneurship which view entrepreneurs as technical specialists, in the Lazear's model of occupational choice entrepreneurs are "generalists", i.e., multiskilled individuals. Using a dataset of Stanford Master of Business Administration alumni, Lazear finds supports to the "jack-for-all-trades" theory. In line with the entrepreneurship literature, Lazear (2002) defines entrepreneurs as those individuals who have established the business and "are usually responsible for the conception of the basic product, hiring the initial team, and obtaining at least some early financing" (p. 3).

Other scholars have also found support to this theory drawing different data sets. For example, Wagner (2003, 2006), using data on the German population and a survey of new entrepreneurs, and Astebro (2006), drawing on data from Canada, have found that the likelihood of being an entrepreneur is higher for individuals with more balanced skill and working experience.

One may wonder why we need a theory of entrepreneurship to explain OSS project founders and leaders and whether OSS entrepreneurs are really the equivalent of entrepreneurs in business enterprises. We believe that OSS founders and project leaders share some important characteristics with entrepreneurs. First, as we discuss later, in most cases project managers are also founders of OSS projects. Moreover, they play a leading role, by coordinating the efforts of different members and finalizing the results of the development team. In fact, Lazear (2002) tested his model by using two different definitions of entrepreneur. The first definition described before refers to new business founders, wheras the second one includes individuals who take responsibility for the organizations' direction, or major business function. This category includes senior or high-level managers. Lazear finds that these individuals too have a balanced skill set and therefore the "jack-for-all-trades" view can be applied not only to founders of new initiatives but also to individuals who occupy high-level managerial positions within the organization.

10.3 Empirical Analysis

10.3.1 Data

Our empirical analysis uses a rich dataset containing information on the role, skill profiles and activities of individuals registered with an OSS project. The dataset has been built from data provided by SF.net (http://sourceforge.net) from November 1999 to January 2003. *SF.net al*so provides complementary data on several characteristics of the project participated by the individual members.

Our version of the dataset consists of 65,535 projects and 544,669 individuals. These individuals include both people registered with one or more projects (i.e., participants who are supposed to be "active" contributors) and individuals who registered with the SF.net website but have not become member of any specific project, i.e., users who download software and signal bugs or post questions to the project forums. The total number of people registered with a project (project members) in our dataset is 90,255. Of these, 26,314 provide data on skills. Our sample excludes all "inactive" projects, i.e., projects with no registered users as to January 2003 or not labeled as "active" by the SF.net staff.

We end up with a sample of 77,039 individuals who registered with 54,229 projects. Data on skills are available for only 23,560 individuals registered with 26,254 projects. Information about project founders could be built for 66,944 users, i.e., only those registered after September 2000 or that have founded a group after that date.

A main limitation of the SF.net dataset is that it excludes some large OSS projects such as Apache and Linux, although other large and popular projects are included. Moreover, a large number of projects are inactive (Howison and Crowston 2004). To account for these drawbacks we control for the size of projects and level of activity of individuals and projects.

10.3.2 *Definition of Variables*

10.3.2.1 Dependent Variables: The Roles of Project Members

The main contribution of this paper is about the skill profiles of founders and project members playing managerial roles. The SF.net dataset specifies the role of the member registered with each project at the end of the covered period, i.e., January 2003. As individuals can be registered with more than one project, they can also perform different roles in different projects. Over 22% of individuals in our sample are registered with more than one project (the average number of projects participated by the sample individual is 1.39). Matching individuals and projects yields 106,823 individual–role pairs. Obviously, the number of pairs is larger than that of individuals (77,039) because, as mentioned before, an individual may perform different roles in different projects of which he/she is a member. Appendix reports the distribution of all pairs by type of role.

Developer is the most frequent role (28.09% of cases), followed by project manager (10.57%). Other roles like all-hands person, web designer, tester, graphic, are much less frequent, wheras in about half cases project members are not assigned any specific role.

For our purposes, we grouped the 19 roles listed in Appendix into four categories characterized by increasing levels of managerial task complexity (variable ROLE4). At the lower end of the complexity range, there is obviously "No role". In all likelihood individuals in this category have a very limited commitment in a specific project. The category "Other roles" (Other) includes secondary, supporting tasks such as web design, test, editorial/content writer, and consultant. The category "Developer" (DEV), the most frequent across project members, includes members who carry out core project activities which may imply high levels of technical sophistication but limited managerial complexity. The category Project Manager (PM) represents, by definition, the tasks with the highest level of managerial complexity. Project managers may be responsible for specific project modules and subprojects or the whole project.

Table 10.1 summarizes the distribution of the four categories of roles in our dataset. The first column shows the frequency of each role amongst the individuals in our sample.

As each individual may perform different roles in different projects, we want to see the level of managerial complexity of tasks carried out by individuals across all projects of which they are members. To this end, we consider all roles each individual performs in all projects he/she participates and build a second classification which differs from ROLE4 for one category that represents individuals who play the role of project manager in one project and other roles in other projects. More precisely, the fifth category includes "PM & Other", "PM & Dev" and "PM & Other & DEV."

Table 10.2 shows the distribution of individuals across the five categories above (ROLE5). The share of individuals with No role (44.59%) is lower than in the previous classification, suggesting that most individuals registered with more than one project focus their activities on one project, in particular while playing no specific role in other projects. Individuals with Other roles are 10.24% of the sample. Developers are again the most frequent category of project members (31.91%). Project managers account for 10.49% of individuals, whereas multirole individuals (category 5) account for 2.78% of the sample individuals.

Table 10.1 Distribution of pairs by role category (ROLE 4)

	Role	*N*	%
1	No role	54,879	51.37
2	Other roles (Other)	10,647	9.97
3	Developer (DEV)	30,009	28.09
4	Project Manager (PM)	11,288	10.57
	Total pairs	106,823	100

Table 10.2 Distribution of individuals by role category (ROLE 5)

	Role	*N*	%	% Founders[a]
1	No role	34,351	44.59	82.37
2	Other roles	7,885	10.24	30.36
3	Developer (DEV)	24,581	31.91	23.55
4	Project Manager (PM)	8,081	10.49	70.21
5	PM &/or Other &/or DEV	2,141	2.78	81.98
	Total individuals	77,039	100	55.48

[a]The number of individuals for which information about the founder state is available is 66,944

We use this ordered classification of member roles to estimate the association between several individual and project-level characteristics and the probability that a participant becomes involved in activities that imply increasing levels of managerial complexity.

The results discussed in this paper focus on individuals as unit of analysis and therefore ROLE5 is used as dependent variable.

From SF.net we also built, for a sample of 66,944 users, a dummy variable called FOUNDER which is equal to 1 if an individual founded at least one SF.net project and equal to 0 otherwise[3]. The last column of Table 10.2 shows the share of individuals who founded a project in each role category. It is worth noting that 70% of project managers and 82% of individuals who perform multiple roles (project managers and other roles) are also project founders. By contrast, only 24% of developers and 30% of individuals with other roles founded at least a project. Surprisingly, about 82% of people with no role are a project founder. However, we found that on average these individuals (and their projects) have an extremely low level of activity (bugs, patched, messages, etc.) compared with individuals with a specified role. These individuals represent the large number of OSS participants who enter the community by founding a project and remain inactive thereafter. Thus, they are very different from individuals who play a specific role in active projects.

The variable FOUNDER is used as dependent variable in logit estimations of the probability to found an OSS project associated to several individual level characteristics.

10.3.2.2 Key Regressors: Skill Level and Diversity of Individuals

A key variable in our analysis is represented by skills. At the time of registration with SF.net, the website users are asked to self-assess their experience in 33 types of different skills which can be grouped into three main areas of expertise: programming languages (e.g., C/C++ and Python), application-specific skills (e.g., networking, security, etc.), and "people" skills proxied by the knowledge of spoken languages. Registered individuals can also update the information relative to their skills at any time. Unfortunately, the dataset does not tell whether and when registered users have updated their skills since registration and this gives rise to problems of endogeneity. Although the mix and the level of skills declared at the time of registration may change over time, skills are likely to change slowly over time relative to roles and this moderates the endogeneity of this variable.

Another possible drawback of these measures is that they might be affected by self-assessment biases. However, we believe that this is not a serious problem in our case, because the information supplied by developers can be made public to other developers who can check its reliability. Since, as noted by Lerner and Tirole

---

[3] The variable captures the requests made to SF.net to found a project. Thus, it captures the initial act of foundation irrespectively of its postentry performance.

(2002), expected delayed benefits arising from signaling represent an important incentive to contribute to the OSS community, individuals who register with SF.net have strong reasons to provide information as close as possible to the reality. Moreover, there are no reasons to believe that a potential bias due to self-reporting should affect particular types of developers or projects.

Drawing on this information, we build the following measures of skills at the individual level.

EXPERIENCE. This variable is computed as the average level of experience of the skills of each individual. The level of experience in each skill is measured on a 5-point Likert scale, i.e., 1 = less than 6 months; 2 = 6 months to 2 years; 3 = 2–5 years; 4 = 5–10 years; 5 = more than 10 years.

N_SKILLS. This variable indicates the number of different skills mastered by the individual member. It is a proxy for the variety of skills of the individual.

HERF. This variable measures the degree of skill diversification of the project member. To build this measure, we first define the share of each skill i on the total skills experience of the individual j:

$$s_{ij} = \left(S_{ij} * e_{ij}\right) * l_{ij} \, / \sum_{i=1}^{n} \left(S_{ij} * e_{ij}\right) * l_{ij}$$

where $S_{ij} = 1$ when individual j reports skill i, and 0 otherwise, e_{ij} represents the experience of the skill i of the individual j (see EXPERIENCE above) and l_{ij} is a weight based on the individual's expertise in that skill (also self-assessed and measured on a 5-point Likert scale ranging from "Want to Learn" to "Wrote it").

We then computed the Herfindahl index of skills for each individual as follows:

$$Herf_j = \sum_{i=1}^{n} s_{ij}^2$$

This measure allows to weight each skill of the individual by its experience (and expertise) in each of the skills. For a more intuitive interpretation of the variables based on the Herfindahl indexes in our analysis, we use the 1-HERF. The index ranges from 0 (min skill diversification) to 1 (max skill diversification).

D_MISSING_SKILLS. Dummy equal to 1, if the individual does not report her/his skills.

D_VIEW_SKILLS. Dummy variable equal to 1 if the individual agrees that his/her skills can be published on the SF.net website.

10.3.2.3 Individual-Level Controls

TIME_REG. Number of months the individual has been registered with SF.net.

D_MAIL. Dummy equal to 1, if the e-mail address of the individual is reported in the dataset.

D_MAIL_COM. Dummy equal to 1, if the e-mail address of the individual has a .com suffix, considered as a proxy for the affiliation to a commercial organization.

N_MESSAGES. Number of messages posted by the individual to project forums hosted by SF.net from November 1999 to January 2003.

N_MAINCONTR_SUB. Number of main contributions (bugs, patches, and feature requests) submitted by the individual to SF.net projects from November 1999 to January 2003.

N_MAINCONTR_ASS. Number of main contributions (bugs, patches, and feature requests) assigned to the individual from November 1999 to January 2003.

N_OTHERCONTR_SUB. Number of other contributions (like support requests, among others) submitted by the individual to SF.net projects from November 1999 to January 2003.

N_OTHERCONTR_ASS. Number of other contributions (like support requests, among others) assigned to the individual from November 1999 to January 2003.

D_NL. 13 dummy variables for the natural language the individual declares to speak.

10.3.2.4 Project-Level Controls

SIZE. An important factor that can explain the emergence of managerial roles is the size and internal organization of the project. In order to estimate the net effect of the skill profiles on the probability to assume a managerial role, we need to control for these project characteristics in our econometric analysis. These variables are instead not included in the estimation of the probability to become a project founder, which is obviously independent of ex-post characteristics of the project.

We expect that the likelihood that a project member plays managerial roles is positively affected by the size of the project. This is because with the increase in the number of participants, coordination and integration of different inputs become more complex tasks which call for expert project managers.

Our measure of project size is the number of members registered with the project in which the individual is registered at January 10, 2003. If the individual is registered to more than one project, this is the average size of the projects at which he/she is registered.

NSUB_PROJECTS. This is a measure of modularity which is defined as a "strategy for organizing complex products and processes efficiently". Modularity relies on system architectures that define the set of modules and their respective functions, the interfaces that allow modules to interact (compatibility), and the standards that are used to test the modules' compliance with the design rules (Baldwin and Clark 1997). In the case of OSS, the architecture of the system typically consists of a core structure (e.g., the kernel of the GNU/Linux operating system) and a series of modules that are developed independently of one another. In large projects, such as Linux kernel or Apache server, a significant level of modularity is achieved through a sharp distinction between the core product architecture and more "external" features that are "located in modules that can be selectively compiled and configured" (Mockus et al. 2000, p. 4).

Our proxy for the project modularity is the cumulated number of subprojects with at least one opened task launched by all projects with which the individual is registered from November 1999 to January 2003. It captures the organizational modularity of the project, viz., how many different tasks (e.g., code production, construction of the website) the development activity has been divided. If the individual is registered to more than one project, this is the average number of subprojects opened in all projects in which he/she is registered.

N_FILE_REL. Number of files releases (new versions of the software) from the date of registration of the project to January 2003. If the individual is registered to more than one project, this is the average number of files released of the projects in which he/she is registered.

D_LI_GPL_LGPL. Dummy equal to 1, if the main license initially adopted by the projects participated by the individual is GPL or LGPL. The dummy is equal to 0, if the main license is BSD, Public Domain, Artistic license, Apache license, MIT license, or Others. If the individual is registered with more than one project, this variable indicates whether these types of license are adopted by at least one of the projects.

D_NL_ENG. Dummy equal to 1, if the official spoken language is English in at least one of the projects of the individual and it is 0 otherwise.

D_PL_ C/C++. Dummy equal to 1, if the programming language is C/C++ in at least one of the projects of the individual, and it is 0 otherwise (Java, Php, Perl, Python, Visual Basic, Unix Shell, Others).

D_OS_LINUXPOSIX. Dummy equal to 1, if the operating system is Linux or Posix in at least one of the projects of the individual, and it is 0 otherwise (Microsoft, MacOS, Independent, Others).

D_MISSING_CHAR. Dummy equal to 1, if the information on the projects' license, programming language and operating system is missing in the dataset, and equal to 0 otherwise. If the individual is registered with more than one project, this variable indicates the share of projects for which this information is missing among those he/she is registered with.

In terms of data reliability, it should be noticed that at the moment of the analysis, we had no means to identify individuals who registered more than one time to the SF.net website, having thus multiple user ids. However, we checked for the influence of this phenomenon in our sample, and it seems having only a marginal effect. The other point that is worth to take into account is that the activities represented by the dataset, such as file releases or subprojects, are recorded since the date of their creation. However, for some of them, we have no record of their development, and just observe their status for January 2003. This means that we can take into account only the net effects of the changes happened before that date.

10.3.3 Descriptive Statistics

As mentioned before, the key variables of this paper are the role of individuals, their skill profile, and the organization of the project in which they are active.

Table 10.3 summarizes the descriptive statistics of all variables at the individual level. Table 10.4 shows the mean and standard deviation of the main individual level variables for each of the five role profiles.

It is worth to observe that there are substantial differences in the individual skill profile across different roles. First, the average level of skills of individuals (EXPERIENCE) increases from category 1 (No role) to 5 (PM_Oth_DEV) from

Table 10.3 Descriptive statistics – key regressors and controls

Variable	Mean	S D.	Min	Max
EXPERIENCE[a]	2.770	0.734	1	5
1-HERF[a]	0.724	0.216	0	0.97
N_SKILLS[a]	6.605	3.607	1	29
D_MISSING_SKILLS	0.694	0.461	0	1
D_VIEW_SKILLS	0.134	0.341	0	1
TIME_REG	18.556	10.530	1	40
N_PROJECTS	1.387	0.995	1	52
D_MAIL	0.197	0.398	0	1
D_MAIL_COM	0.082	0.274	0	1
N_MESSAGES	2.875	23.924	0	1,758
N_MAINCONTR_SUB	1.430	8.852	0	1,034
N_MAINCONTR_ASS	1.473	15.262	0	976
N_OTHERCONTR_SUB	0.490	2.636	0	448
N_OTHERCONTR_ASS	0.621	75.474	0	19,052
SIZE	5.937	9.300	1	102
NSUB_PROJECTS	0.692	1.730	0	45
N_FILE_REL	4.673	11.773	0	444
D_NL for English	0.813	0.390	0	1
D_NL for German	0.063	0.244	0	1
D_NL for French	0.035	0.184	0	1
D_NL for Italian	0.013	0.113	0	1
D_NL for Spanish	0.018	0.132	0	1
D_NL for Portuguese	0.010	0.100	0	1
D_NL for Russian	0.010	0.099	0	1
D_NL for Polish	0.005	0.074	0	1
D_NL for Chinese	0.005	0.072	0	1
D_NL for Japanese	0.005	0.073	0	1
D_NL for Swedish	0.006	0.076	0	1
D_NL for Dutch	0.007	0.085	0	1
D_NL for Other	0.009	0.094	0	1
D_LI_GPL_LGPL	0.809	0.393	0	1
D_OS_LINUXPOSIX	0.636	0.481	0	1
D_PL_ C/C++	0.610	0.488	0	1
D_NL_ENG	0.818	0.386	0	1
D_MISSING_CHAR	0.239	0.405	0	1

Number of observations = 77,039

[a]For the variables using information about skills, the number of observations is 23,560

Table 10.4 Profile of individuals by role

Variable	(1) No role	(2) Other	(3) DEV	(4) PM	(5) PM_ Other_DEV	Total
EXPERIENCE[a]	2.756	2.754	2.764	2.823	2.815	2.770
	(0.736)	(0.759)	(0.737)	(0.713)	(0.681)	(0.734)
1-HERF[a]	0.710	0.713	0.730	0.740	0.770	0.724
	(0.226)	(0.221)	(0.212)	(0.200)	(0.175)	(0.216)
N_SKILLS[a]	6.351	6.579	6.664	6.879	7.540	6.605
	(3.555)	(3.682)	(3.582)	(3.617)	(3.746)	(3.607)
D_MISSING_SKILLS	0.728	0.677	0.704	0.607	0.428	0.694
	(0.445)	(0.468)	(0.456)	(0.488)	(0.495)	(0.461)
D_VIEW_SKILLS	0.106	0.154	0.135	0.184	0.318	0.134
	(0.308)	(0.361)	(0.341)	(0.387)	(0.466)	(0.341)
TIME_REG	20.420	16.362	16.402	18.040	23.422	18.556
	(10.975)	(9.867)	(9.743)	(9.917)	(9.299)	(10.530)
N_PROJECTS	1.208	1.333	1.459	1.407	3.531	1.387
	(0.618)	(0.988)	(1.036)	(0.921)	(2.286)	(0.995)
D_MAIL	0.144	0.194	0.211	0.288	0.554	0.197
	(0.351)	(0.395)	(0.408)	(0.453)	(0.497)	(0.398)
D_MAIL_COM	0.059	0.085	0.088	0.122	0.223	0.082
	(0.235)	(0.279)	(0.283)	(0.327)	(0.416)	(0.274)
N_MESSAGES	1.545	3.166	2.893	5.642	12.505	2.875
	(11.678)	(20.333)	(25.224)	(37.809)	(63.531)	(23.924)
N_MAINCONTR_ SUB	0.702	1.559	1.684	2.127	7.089	1.430
	(3.998)	(10.096)	(9.240)	(9.733)	(28.407)	(8.852)
N_MAINCONTR_ASS	0.473	1.149	1.682	2.982	10.631	1.473
	(7.114)	(10.449)	(15.663)	(21.842)	(49.413)	(15.262)
N_OTHERCONTR_ SUB	0.338	0.545	0.378	0.883	2.517	0.490
	(1.263)	(5.612)	(1.900)	(2.413)	(6.304)	(2.636)
N_OTHERCONTR_ ASS	0.352	0.512	0.216	0.478	10.544	0.621
	(44.365)	(24.202)	(8.936)	(11.581)	(412.051)	(75.474)

Number of observations = 77,039. Standard errors in parenthesis
[a]For the variables using information about skills the number of observations is 23,560

2.76 to 2.82. Roles with more complex managerial tasks (4 and 5) show also a greater variety of skills (N_SKILLS) and a more diversified skill profile (HERF). Project managers are also more likely to report their skills and to agree to publish his/her skills on the web, which suggests a higher commitment to the project and an interest to signal their profile to the OSS community.

The statistics on the other individual level variables suggests that individuals with managerial roles are more likely to have a company affiliation (conditional of having been able to retrieve their e-mail address from the dataset). On average, they are more active in the OSS community relative to other roles, as indicated by the larger average number of messages sent to forums, and of submitted and assigned contributions.

Table 10.5 Skill profile of founders by role

	N		EXPERIENCE		N_SKILLS		1-HERF	
	Founder	No_ Founder	Founder	No_ Founder	Founder	No_ Founder	Founder	No_ Founder
No role	6,769	979	2.75	2.73	6.40	6.10	0.71	0.70
			(0.72)	(0.81)	(3.57)	(3.51)	(0.22)	(0.23)
Other roles	1,206	1,113	2.73	2.74	7.09	5.91	0.74	0.68
			(0.73)	(0.80)	(3.84)	(3.41)	(0.21)	(0.24)
Developer	2,520	3,961	2.74	2.74	6.91	6.43	0.74	0.72
			(0.69)	(0.76)	(3.70)	(3.46)	(0.20)	(0.22)
Project Manager	2,556	418	2.81	2.82	6.96	6.48	0.74	0.71
			(0.71)	(0.72)	(3.61)	(3.68)	(0.20)	(0.22)
PM_Other_ DEV	1,009	133	2.81	2.81	7.67	6.67	0.78	0.72
			(0.66)	(0.77)	(3.74)	(3.82)	(0.17)	(0.21)
Total	14,060	6,604	2.76	2.74	6.74	6.30	0.73	0.71
			(0.71)	(0.77)	(3.66)	(3.49)	(0.21)	(0.23)

Standard errors in parenthesis. For this table we used a sample of 20,664 individuals for which we have information on skills and on founder status (whether they have founded a project or not)

In order to provide a deeper understanding of the skill profile of founders and project managers, Table 10.5 compares the skill profile of individuals who founded a project with individuals who did not found any project for the total sample and for each role category.

The last row of the table shows that on average founders have a more diversified skill profile and a higher skill level than non-founder individuals, but this difference is very small. However, when we compare the skill profile of founders and non-founders by role category, we observe two interesting patterns. First, the level of skills (EXPERIENCE) of founders and non-founders is the same or almost the same in each role category.

Second, the number and degree of diversification of skills is always greater for founders with respect to non-founder in each role category, and this difference tends to increase in managerial roles. This suggests that founders who also assume managerial and other roles have the most diversified skill profile, if compared with founders with no managerial roles or non-founder with managerial roles.

Table 10.6 finally presents the correlation between the main regressors.

10.3.4 Regression Results

We first analyze the association between individual and project-level characteristics and the individuals' role by running ordered logit estimations. In the first set of regressions, the dependent variable is ROLE5, a categorical and ordered variable,

Table 10.6 Correlations between main regressors

Variable	*[1]*	*[2]*	*[3]*	*[4]*	*[5]*	*[6]*	*[7]*	*[8]*	*[9]*	*[10]*	*[11]*	*[12]*	*[13]*	*[14]*	*[15]*
[1] EXPERIENCE	1														
[2] 1-HERF	−0.69*	1													
[3] N_SKILLS	0.80*	−0.33*	1												
[4] D_VIEW_SKILLS	0.53*	−0.30*	0.56*	1											
[5] TIME_REG	0.14*	−0.07*	0.13*	0.08*	1										
[6] D_MAIL	0.18*	−0.09*	0.17*	0.14*	0.20*	1									
[7] D_MAIL_COM	0.10*	−0.05*	0.10*	0.09*	0.11*	0.60*	1								
[8] N_MESSAGES	0.06*	−0.03*	0.06*	0.06*	0.06*	0.15*	0.11*	1							
[9] N_MAINCONTR_SUB	0.07*	−0.03*	0.07*	0.06*	0.10*	0.28*	0.18*	0.15*	1						
[10] N_MAINCONTR_ASS	0.06*	−0.02*	0.04*	0.03*	0.08*	0.19*	0.13*	0.24*	0.39*	1					
[11] N_OTHERCONTR_SUB	0.09*	−0.04*	0.08*	0.06*	0.11*	0.24*	0.16*	0.14*	0.23*	0.21*	1				
[12] N_OTHERCONTR_ASS	0.01*	−0.01*	0.01*	0.01*	0.01	0.02*	0.02*	0.04*	0.04*	0.11*	0.10*	1			
[13] SIZE	−0.03*	0.03*	−0.04*	−0.01*	−0.03*	0.05*	0.04*	0.03*	0.04*	0.04*	0.02*	0.00	1		
[14] NSUB_PROJECTS	0.03*	−0.01*	0.04*	0.04*	0.01*	0.07*	0.05*	0.05*	0.06*	0.04*	0.02*	0.00	0.35*	1	
[15] N_FILE_REL	0.03*	−0.01*	0.01*	0.02*	0.05*	0.19*	0.12*	0.09*	0.09*	0.09*	0.08*	0.00	0.37*	0.22*	1

$^{*}p<0.05$

which takes on five values corresponding to the five roles described above, which are characterized by increasing levels of managerial task complexity.

Table 10.7 reports the results of these estimations. As a primary goal of this paper is the relationship between skill profile and individual's roles, we estimate three model specifications which correspond to different measures of skills. The first specification includes EXPERIENCE, in the second one we add N_SKILLS, and in the third we used HERF in place of N_SKILL. We run these three regression specifications by progressively adding to the main skill variables (columns 1–3) individual-level controls (columns 4–6), the main project-level regressors, SIZE and NSUB_PROJECTS (columns 7–9), and finally project-level controls (columns 10–12).

In line with the Lazear's theory, we find that the number of skills and the level of skill diversification (HERF) have positive and significant coefficients, and that 1-HERF marginal effects on "managerial" roles is larger than N_SKILLS.[4] These results support the hypothesis that individuals who carry out multitask jobs and take managerial responsibilities have more balanced skill sets compared with individuals who play more specialized tasks.

The level of skills instead is less important as a predictor of roles. The coefficient of EXPERIENCE is positive and significant only in the regressions without other individual and project-level variables (columns 1–3), whereas it becomes insignificant in all other specifications. The descriptive statistics also show that, although the average level of skills is increasing with the managerial complexity of roles, the differences between the means across roles are very small. Project or team managers then do not necessarily need to be more skilled than specialized team members, but they must possess broader skill sets to coordinate different activities.

As far as individual-level variables are concerned, individuals who carry out managerial roles appear more open to the community, as shown by the positive and significant coefficient of D_VIEW_SKILL and of N_MESSAGES.

An interesting set of results concerns the level of activity associated with project managers. Individuals who perform these roles submit (and are assigned) larger number of key tasks, such as bugs and patches (N_MAINCONTR_ASS and N_MAINCONTR_SUB), compared with other roles. They are also likely to submit "minor" tasks, such as support requests (N_OTHERCONTR_SUB), but are unlikely to be assigned this type of tasks (N_OTHERCONTR_ASS). This is consistent with the view that in the OSS setting, project managers delegate minor activities, such as support request processing, to other project members. The significance of N_OTHERCONTR_ASS however decreases when all controls are included in the regressions.

SIZE and N_SUBPROJECTS are both positive and significant (columns 7–9), confirming that larger projects and projects organized in different modules require higher levels of coordination and managerial tasks. As expected, larger projects and

[4] The same variables have a negative marginal effect on other roles such as "No role" and "Other roles."

Table 10.7 Results of the ordered logit estimations

Variable	(1)	(2)	(3)	(4)	(5)
EXPERIENCE	0.070*** (0.017)	0.068*** (0.017)	0.065*** (0.017)	0.024 (0.017)	0.024 (0.017)
D_MISSING_SKILLS	−0.164*** (0.048)	0.083 (0.054)	−0.338*** (0.051)	−0.152*** (0.050)	0.016 (0.055)
N_SKILLS		0.038*** (0.004)			0.028*** (0.004)
1-HERF			0.584*** (0.057)		
D_VIEW_SKILLS				0.257*** (0.025)	0.216*** (0.025)
TIME_REG				−0.031*** (0.001)	−0.031*** (0.001)
D_MAIL				0.656*** (0.026)	0.651*** (0.026)
D_MAIL_COM				−0.024 (0.033)	−0.023 (0.033)
N_MESSAGES				0.003*** (0.001)	0.003*** (0.001)
N_MAINCONTR_SUB				0.007*** (0.002)	0.007*** (0.002)
N_MAINCONTR_ASS				0.005*** (0.001)	0.005*** (0.001)
N_OTHERCONTR_SUB				0.064*** (0.011)	0.064*** (0.011)
N_OTHERCONTR_ASS				−0.000* (0.000)	−0.000* (0.000)
NSUB_PROJECTS					
SIZE					
N_FILE_REL					
Constant cut 1	−0.276*** (0.048)	−0.03 (0.053)	0.133** (0.063)	−0.65*** (0.051)	−0.487*** (0.055)
Constant cut 2	0.136*** (0.048)	0.383*** (0.053)	0.546*** (0.063)	−0.217*** (0.051)	−0.054 (0.055)
Constant cut 3	1.828*** (0.049)	2.077*** (0.054)	2.239*** (0.063)	1.537*** (0.051)	1.701*** (0.056)
Constant cut 4	3.512*** (0.052)	3.762*** (0.057)	3.924*** (0.066)	3.26*** (0.054)	3.425*** (0.059)
Observations	77,039	77,039	77,039	77,039	77,039
Log Pseudolikelihood	−9,9379.83	−99314.78	−99,325.41	−97,122.59	−97,089.07
Wald chi2	588.56	688.67	680.5	4,175.35	4,217.37

*$p<0.10$, **$p<0.05$, ***$p<0.01$. Robust standard errors in parenthesis.

Regressions from column (4) to column (12) include dummies for the natural language of the individual (*D_NL*)

Regressions from column (10) to column (12) also include the following dummies: *D_NL_ENG, D_OS_LINUXPOSIX, D_PL_ C/C++, D_LI_GPL_LGPL, D_MISSING_CHAR*

(6)	(7)	(8)	(9)	(10)	(11)	(12)
0.022 (0.017)	0.015 (0.017)	0.015 (0.017)	0.012 (0.017)	0.027 (0.017)	0.026 (0.017)	0.024 (0.017)
−0.306*** (0.053)	−0.206*** (0.050)	−0.040 (0.055)	−0.361*** (0.053)	−0.062 (0.051)	0.109* (0.055)	−0.214*** (0.054)
		0.028*** (0.004)			0.029*** (0.004)	
0.466*** (0.059)			0.470*** (0.059)			0.462*** (0.060)
0.221*** (0.025)	0.241*** (0.025)	0.201*** (0.025)	0.205*** (0.025)	0.196*** (0.025)	0.154*** (0.026)	0.160*** (0.026)
−0.031*** (0.001)	−0.030*** (0.001)	−0.030*** (0.001)	−0.030*** (0.001)	−0.024*** (0.001)	−0.024*** (0.001)	−0.024*** (0.001)
0.652*** (0.026)	0.619*** (0.026)	0.614*** (0.026)	0.615*** (0.026)	0.499*** (0.027)	0.493*** (0.027)	0.495*** (0.027)
−0.023 (0.033)	−0.037 (0.033)	−0.036 (0.033)	−0.036 (0.033)	−0.021 (0.034)	−0.020 (0.034)	−0.021 (0.034)
0.003*** (0.001)	0.002*** (0.001)	0.002*** (0.001)	0.002*** (0.001)	0.002*** (0.000)	0.002*** (0.000)	0.002*** (0.000)
0.007*** (0.002)	0.006*** (0.002)	0.005*** (0.001)	0.006*** (0.002)	0.005*** (0.001)	0.005*** (0.001)	0.005*** (0.001)
0.005*** (0.001)	0.005*** (0.001)	0.005*** (0.001)	0.005*** (0.001)	0.005*** (0.001)	0.005*** (0.001)	0.005*** (0.001)
0.064*** (0.011)	0.070*** (0.012)	0.069*** (0.012)	0.069*** (0.012)	0.066*** (0.012)	0.066*** (0.012)	0.066*** (0.012)
−0.000* (0.000)	−0.000 (0.000)	−0.000* (0.000)	−0.000* (0.000)	−0.000 (0.000)	−0.000 (0.000)	−0.000 (0.000)
	0.078*** (0.004)	0.078*** (0.004)	0.078*** (0.004)	0.056*** (0.004)	0.056*** (0.004)	0.056*** (0.004)
	0.023*** (0.001)	0.024*** (0.001)	0.024*** (0.001)	0.020*** (0.001)	0.020*** (0.001)	0.020*** (0.001)
				0.004*** (0.001)	0.004*** (0.001)	0.004*** (0.001)
−0.341*** (0.064)	−0.483*** (0.051)	−0.322*** (0.055)	−0.171*** (0.065)	0.138** (0.058)	0.304*** (0.062)	0.445*** (0.071)
0.092 (0.064)	−0.035 (0.051)	0.126** (0.055)	0.277*** (0.065)	0.611*** (0.058)	0.776*** (0.062)	0.918*** (0.071)
1.847*** (0.065)	1.743*** (0.052)	1.905*** (0.056)	2.056*** (0.065)	2.432*** (0.059)	2.598*** (0.062)	2.740*** (0.071)
3.571*** (0.067)	3.46*** (0.055)	3.623*** (0.059)	3.774*** (0.068)	4.157*** (0.060)	4.324*** (0.064)	4.466*** (0.073)
77,039	77,039	77,039	77,039	77,039	77,039	77,039
−97,089.94	−96,163.69	−96,131.02	−96,130.73	−93,980.63	−93,946.51	−93,949.66
4,223.24	5,598.86	5,642.31	5,651.67	10,148.81	10,189.7	10,188.32

modular design allow for a greater division of labor between specialists and more multitalented, general-purpose individuals. These results hold when controls, such as the type of license, programming languages, operating systems, and the project spoken language, are included. It is also worth noting that, when we compute the marginal effect, N_SUBPROJECT exerts a greater influence than SIZE, suggesting that managerial roles are important, especially for coordinating and integrating different inputs and people working on different modules.

We also controlled for project performance by including the number of new file releases of the project software and found that this is positively correlated with high managerial roles.

We also perform a second set of estimations that analyze the association between individual-level characteristics and the probability that an individual founded a project. We carry out logit estimations and the dependent variable is FOUNDER. Like in the previous set of estimations, we estimate three model specifications which correspond to different measures of skills. However, in these regressions, we only perform models 1–6 including individual variables. We do not run regressions including project-level regressors relative to the founded projects, which are not antecedent to the decision to found a project. For the same reason, we also exclude from this analysis all variables that measure the level of activity of individuals in the projects of which they are members.

The results of these regressions are reported in Table 10.8. Our main results about the skill profile of managers are also confirmed for project founders. The coefficients of EXPERIENCE and N_SKILLS are almost identical in the two sets of regressions and the coefficient for HERF is substantially larger than the other coefficients.

Moreover, differently from the previous regressions, the coefficient for TIME_REG is positive and significant, indicating that founders registered earlier to SF.net than non-founders.

10.3.5 Robustness Checks

To check the robustness of our results, we tried alternative classifications of roles.

At the level of individuals, we first built a 7-categories classification in which role 5 (PM and various roles) is splitted in three roles – "PM & Other", "PM & DEV", and "PM & Other & DEV". A six-category classification was also tested whereby role 5 is splitted in two roles – "PM & Other or PM & DEV", and "PM & Other & DEV".

At the level of individual–role pairs, we first employed the dataset on role–individual pairs and used ROLE4 as dependent variable. We also built a three-category classification in which the base category is "No Role"; the second category, "Specialist", includes all roles that perform specialized activities; and the third category, "Generalist", includes roles that imply managerial, administrative, and other support activities.

Table 10.8 Results of the logit estimations. Dependent variable: FOUNDER

Variable	(1)	(2)	(3)	(4)	(5)	(6)
EXPERIENCE	0.04**	0.04*	0.04*	–0.01	–0.01	–0.02
	(0.02)	(0.02)	(0.02)	(0.02)	(0.02)	(0.02)
D_MISSING_SKILLS	–0.65***	–0.43***	–0.79***	–0.59***	–0.47***	–0.68***
	(0.06)	(0.07)	(0.06)	(0.06)	(0.07)	(0.07)
N_SKILLS		0.03***			0.02***	
		(0.00)			(0.00)	
1–HERF			0.46***			0.26***
			(0.07)			(0.07)
D_VIEW_SKILLS				0.05	0.02	0.03
				(0.03)	(0.03)	(0.03)
TIME_REG				0.04***	0.04***	0.04***
				(0.00)	(0.00)	(0.00)
D_MAIL				0.42***	0.41***	0.42***
				(0.03)	(0.03)	(0.03)
D_MAIL_COM				0.08*	0.08**	0.08**
				(0.04)	(0.04)	(0.04)
Constant	0.64***	0.42***	0.32***	–0.19***	–0.31***	–0.35***
	(0.06)	(0.06)	(0.07)	(0.06)	(0.07)	(0.08)
N	66,944	66,944	66,944	66,944	66,944	66,944
Ll	–45,023.9	–44,989.9	–45,000.9	–43,362.8	–43,351	–43,356.3
chi2	1,875.51	1,924.72	1,915.09	5,163.99	5,177.04	5,173.88

Regressions from column (4) to column (6) include dummies for the natural language of the individual (*D_NL*)
*$p<0.10$, **$p<0.05$, ***$p<0.01$. Robust standard errors in parenthesis

The results of estimations using these alternative classifications are very similar to the ones obtained by using ROLE5 as dependent variable.[5]

A potential limitation of our estimations is about the choice of ordered logit models, which is the natural choice for categorical and ordered variables. However, if one thinks of our role categories as distinct choices independent from each other, then multinomial logit estimations should provide a better fit of the data. To check if this model fits our dependent variables, we estimated multinomial logit models on role–individual pair data. We estimated the full multinomial models for all alternatives and the restricted models excluding one alternative, and performed the Hausman test and the seemingly unrelated estimation (SUR) test for testing the assumption of independence of irrelevant alternatives (IIA). Both tests always rejected the IIA assumption.

[5] Results are available upon request from the authors.

These tests then support our choice of ordered logit models.[6] The roles analyzed in this paper can be naturally ordered in terms of managerial complexity and, in all likelihood, they correspond to increasingly higher positions in the team hierarchy. Moreover, over time participants may gain experience in different domains and therefore become able to take more responsibility.

We did not estimate the multinomial logit model on ROLE5, because the assumption of IIA is violated by construction. It is difficult to consider independent an alternative (the fifth category) that combines other alternatives.

10.4 Conclusions

This paper provides novel evidence about OSS entrepreneurs. Our analysis shows that there exist marked differences between project leaders and other project members. These differences are more marked when project managers are also project founders.

Entrepreneurs carry out a larger number of different tasks, such as bug fixing and patch additions to the project software, as compared with "specialists" (including "pure developers"). They also coordinate the job of other contributors by asking for bug or patch reports, and new features. They represent the driving force of OSS projects and have a great influence on the performance of these projects.

For these reasons, it is important to understand which individual characteristics affect the emergence of OSS entrepreneurs. Our paper contributes to the literature by exploring the skill profile of founders and project leaders. We find that it is their skill diversification that distinguishes the entrepreneurs from other project members rather than the level of skills. This finding is in line with Lazear's theory of entrepreneurship, which views entrepreneurs (and top managers) as individuals with balanced skill profiles rather than highly skilled specialists.

The association between skill profile and entrepreneurial roles is robust to control for important individual and project-level characteristics such as size and modularity.

Our results are robust to various controls and do not change significantly when other robustness checks are conducted. However, in future research, we should overcome some limitations imposed by the dataset. Additional individual-level information will be collected from other sources, such as surveys, to understand better the background of project leaders, – e.g., level of education and working experience.

[6] Using ordered probit regressions, results are qualitatively similar. Generalized ordered logit (gologit), for which the proportional odds assumption (POA) is relaxed, produce a certain number of observations with predicted probability less than 0. The reported ologit coefficients have been preferred even in absence of POA, as they represent a sort of compromise between all the categories' coefficients. Notice that they are highly consistent with gologit for N_SKILLS e 1-HERF, but supportive for N_SUBPROJECT and SIZE only for "No-role" and "Other."

Acknowledgments Salvatore Torrisi acknowledges the financial support of the University of Bologna (Progetto strategico Nascita e sviluppo di imprese ad alta tecnologia in Europa (STARTUP).
Francesco Rullani gratefully acknowledges the financial support of Fondazione IRI ("Programma di perfezionamento all'estero in discipline manageriali").

10.5 Appendix. Roles reported in SF.Net

Role	Share (%)
Developer	28.09
Project Manager	10.57
All-Hands Person	3.77
Web Designer	1.02
Tester	0.85
Graphic/Other Designer	0.77
Advisor/Mentor/Consultant	0.58
Doc Writer	0.57
Doc Translator	0.46
Unix Admin	0.42
Analysis/Design	0.34
Packager (.rpm, .deb etc)	0.29
Editorial/Content Writer	0.21
Porter (Cross Platform Devel.)	0.19
Content Management	0.17
Support Manager	0.16
Distributor/Promoter	0.09
Requirements Engineering	0.08
No role	51.37
Total	100.00

Number of observations = 106,823

References

Astebro TB (2006) Does it pay to be a Jack of all trades? Available at SSRN: http://ssrn.com/abstract=925221

Baldwin CY, Clark KB (1997) Managing in an age of modularity. Harvard Bus Rev, September-October: 84–93

Bantel K, Jackson SE (1989) Top management and innovations in banking: does the composition of the top team make a difference? Strategic Manage J 10(Summer special issue):107–124

Baron JN, Hannah MT (2002) Organizational blueprints for success in high-tech start-ups. Calif Manage Rev 44(3):8–36

Bhidé AV (2000) The origin and evolution of new business. Oxford University Press, Oxford

Carbonell P, Rodriguez AI (2006) Designing teams for speedy product development: the moderating effect of technological complexity. J Bus Res 59(2):225–232

Dahlander L (2007) In the club? Human and social capital of the leaders of online user communities. Academy of Management, Best Paper Proceedings

Dalle JM, Jullien N (2003) 'Libre' software: turning fads into institutions? Res Policy 32(11):1–11

Di Bona C, Ockman S, Stone M (eds) (1999) Open sources: voices from the open source revolution. O'Reilly, Sebastopol, CA

Galunic DC, Rodan S (1998) Resource re-combinations in the firm: knowledge structures and the potential for Schumpeterian innovation. Strategic Manage J 19(12):1193–1201

Ghosh RA, David PA (2003). The nature and composition of the Linux kernel developer community: a dynamic analysis. SIEPR-Project NOSTRA Working Paper. Available at http://dxm.org/papers/licks1/

Hambrick DC, Cho TS, Chen M-J (1996) The influence of top management team heterogeneity on firms' competitive moves. Admin Sci Quart 41(4):659–684

Hamilton BH, Nickerson JA, Owan H (2003) Team incentives and worker heterogeneity: an empirical analysis of the impact of teams on productivity and participation. J Polit Econ 1(3):465–497

Harhoff D, Henkel J, von Hippel E (2003) Profiting from voluntary information spillovers: how users benefit by freely revealing their innovations. Res Policy 32(10):1753–1769

Howison J, Crowston K (2004) The perils and pitfalls of mining sourceforge. In: Proceedings of workshop on mining software repositories at the international conference on software engineering (ICSE), Edinburgh, May 25, 2004

Kanawattanachai P, Yoo Y (2002) Dynamic nature of trust in virtual teams. J Strategic Inf Syst 11(3–4):187–213

Kayworth T, Leidner D (2000) The global virtual manager: a prescription for success. Eur Manage J 18(2):183–194

Koch S, Schneider G (2000) Results from software engineering research into open source development projects using public data. Diskussionspapiere zum Tätigkeitsfeld Informationsverarbeitung und Informationswirtschaft, Hans R. Hansen und Wolfgang H. Janko (Hrsg.), Nr. 22, Wirtschaftsuniversität Wien.

Krishnamurthy S (2002) Cave or community? An empirical examination of 100 mature open source projects. First Monday 7(6). Available at http://firstmonday.org/issues/issue7_6/krishnamurthy/index.html.

Laursen K, Mahnke V, Vejrup-Hansen P (2005) Do differences make a difference? The impact of human capital diversity, experience and compensation on firm performance in engineering consulting. Druid working paper No. 05-04, Danish Research Unit for Industrial Dynamics, Copenhagen

Lazear EP (2002) Entrepreneurship. NBER working paper No. 9109, Cambridge: MA

Lazear EP (2004) Balanced skills and entrepreneurship. Am Econ Rev 94(2):208–211

Lerner J, Tirole J (2002) Some simple economics of open source. J Ind Econ 46(2):197–234

Lippman SA, Rumelt RO (1982) Uncertain imitability: an analysis of interfirm differences in efficiency under competition. Bell J Econ 13(2):418–438

Martins LL, Gilson LL, Maynard MT (2004) Virtual teams: what do we know and where do we go from here? J Manage 30(6):805–835

Mateos-Garcia J, Steinmueller WE (2003) The open source way of working: a new paradigm for the division of labour in software development? SPRU - open source movement research INK working paper no. 1., University of Sussex, Brighton

Mockus A, Fielding RT, Herbsleb J (2000) A case study of open source software development: the apache server. In: Proceedings of the 22nd international conference on software engineering, Limerick, Ireland, June 4–11, 2000, pp. 263–272

Raymond ES (2001) The cathedral and the bazaar. Musings on linux and open source by an accidental revolutionary. O'Reilly, Sebastopol, CA

Raymond ES (1999) Linux and open-source success. IEEE Software 16(1):85–89

Schumpeter J (1942) Capitalism, socialism and democracy. Unwin University Books, London

Sutton RI, Hargadon A (1997) Brainstorming groups in context: effectiveness in a product design firm. Admin Sci Quart 42(4):685–718
von Hippel E (2001) Learning from open source software. Sloan Manage Rev 42(4):82–86
Wagner J (2003) Testing Lazear's "Jack-for-all-trades" view of entrepreneurship with German micro data. Appl Econ Lett 10(11):687–689
Wagner J (2006) Are nascent entrepreneurs Jack-of-all trades? A test of Lazear's theory of entrepreneurship with German data. Appl Econ 38(20):2415–2419

Chapter 11
Open Innovation and the Implications for Sustainable Profits*

Richard Reed and Susan F. Storrud-Barnes

Abstract Using economics and strategic management literature, we analyze how the phenomenon of open innovation and its associated intellectual communities have an impact on traditional income streams derived from monopoly, Ricardian, and entrepreneurial rents. In doing so, we find that our existing models of property rights, barriers to competition, organizational cost structures, and innovation capacity require adjustment to account for these phenomena. Open innovation modifies the sources of rents. Traditional entry, distribution and capital barriers decline with declining property rights, as do market power and scale effects. Switching costs will remain unchanged. However, rents from knowledge, experience effects, and more perfect differentiation are expected to increase. Importantly, capturing rents may be more difficult because the source of the innovation remains outside the firm's control.

11.1 Introduction

The last issue of *Time* in 2006 identified the "Person of the Year" as "You." Grossman (2006: 40), who introduced *Time's* cover story and the impact that the World Wide Web is having on society, stated:

R. Reed (✉)
Department of Management and Operations, College of Business and Economics, Washington State University, Pullman, WA, 99164-4736, USA
e-mail: richard_reed@wsu.edu

S.F. Storrud-Barnes
Management and Labor Relations Department, Nance College of Business Administration, Cleveland State University, 2121 Euclid Avenue, BU 436, Cleveland, OH, 44115-2214, USA

* An earlier version of this work was presented at the Strategic Management Society Special Conference on New Frontiers in Entrepreneurship, Catania, Italy, 2007

D.B. Audretsch et al. (eds.), *New Frontiers in Entrepreneurship: Recognizing, Seizing, and Executing, Opportunities*, International Studies in Enterpreneurship,
DOI 10.1007/978-1-4419-0058-6_11,

> "It's a story about community and collaboration on a scale never seen before … It's about the many wresting power from the few and helping one another for nothing and how that will not only change the world, but also change the way the world changes."

He goes on to explain how people have become dissatisfied with using the Web in passive, information-gathering, and recreational ways. They also are doing more than using the Web for purchasing products and services. They are working and being productive:

> "Car companies are running open design contests. Reuters is carrying blog postings alongside its regular new feed. Microsoft is working overtime to fend off user-created Linux. We're looking at an explosion of productivity and innovation, and it's just getting started, as millions of minds that would otherwise have drowned in obscurity get hauled back into the global intellectual economy" (p. 40).

In this work, we look at how those changes are affecting businesses. It has changed the way we do business and the way firms generate income. It has allowed smaller companies to compete more equally with larger companies, it has changed the way the firms achieve operating economies, the way they communicate with suppliers and customers, and it has created new opportunities. We look at what happens when entrepreneurs, either individuals or organizations, tap into that "intellectual economy" by using open innovation and, thus, relinquish their property rights. Open innovation goes beyond things like R&D consortia, where firms jointly develop a product but retain control over the rights (Sakakibara, 2002); and beyond open licensing and copyleft work (Mustonen, 2002) that has accompanied open-source development of computer code (Lerner and Tirole, 2005; von Hippel and von Krogh 2003). Open innovation occurs when something new – a product or service – is designed by an individual or by several individuals who come together in an Internet-based, innovation community. Like the people who are involved in open sourcing, they are not paid for their efforts but, instead, have other motives such as personal need or, simply, the pleasure of being creative. Open innovations in computer hardware are being utilized by companies like IBM and Sun Microsystems (Lamarca 2006). Firms also are using open innovations in clothes design (Hamm 2007), cell phones, white goods, and more (Collins 2007). This approach to innovation is the latest in a series of changes to how businesses innovate. Wind (2006) observed that "Companies are even inviting customers into the lab to become active participants in R & D… [and innovations] now percolate out of communities that involve both customers and firms." The Internet is enabling this latest and largest change.

In 2001, Porter warned that while the Internet was an important technology the notion that the rules about business and competition had become obsolete was not only wrong it was also dangerous because firms still needed strategy. Then popular criteria for success, such as "eyeballs on Internet sites" did not (and still do not) substitute for business plans and profits. Although Porter clearly was right, the societal and business changes that the Internet has wrought means that we can no longer accept our established models of business as sacrosanct. Consequently, more scholars are starting to question our established ways of thinking about strategy. For example, Wind (2006) recently noted that traditional approaches to business – finding raw materials at the best cost and turning them into finished goods with efficient production – have had to be sophisticated with the need to understand outsourcing and networks, to manage knowledge, and to deal with the "empowered" customers. Wind (2006) also admonished that, as the world changes, we should be willing to rethink our models. We agree with that sentiment – our strategy paradigm should not become a core rigidity.

We start with a brief review of the technology – the Internet, the Web, and how they have and are changing business practices. While larger organizations have been successfully utilizing the technology for such things as supply-chain management and business-to-business commerce, its adoption by small- and medium-sized enterprises (SMEs) has been uneven. But, beyond business usage, the Internet enables individuals with a common need or desire for a new product or service to communicate and collaborate on an innovation. As such, the Internet stimulates open innovation, and the sophistication of Web 2.0 provides a catalyst for enticing individuals worldwide into the conversation and thus become part of the open-innovation community. We then discuss open sourcing, which has clear parallels with open innovation. This similarity between open sourcing and open innovation means that we can draw on the established research and thinking on open sourcing to develop our explanation of the likely effects of open innovation. For example, while there is an altruistic aspect to open sourcing – people will give their time to create a good that benefits society – the theoretical and empirical research on the topic explains how there are benefits to be gained by the individuals and businesses that contribute to open-source projects (e.g., Lerner and Tirole 2002, 2005). Thus, per open sourcing, underpinning our arguments on open innovation is the assumption that the profit motive drives businesses to capitalize on the efforts of open-innovation communities. After exploring its effect on the creation of economic rents, we address the implications for the theory and practice of business.

11.2 Contextual Factors

The Internet was in place before the Web appeared – around 1988 and 1991, respectively – with Web browsers appearing around 1993 (Dutta and Roy 2003). The Internet, which is a global network of computers that use defined protocols for transmitting and exchanging data (Cave and Mason 2001), originally was used for e-mail and other communication, but the appearance of web-browsers changed that to what we now see. Thus, today, the Internet and Web are not substantively different and, whether or not it is correct to do so, the terms Internet and Web are now used interchangeably.

It generally is agreed that the Internet has had and will likely persist in having a huge impact on our lives. This technological revolution is not only Schumpeterian in nature but it also is a "sociotechnical" phenomenon that is restricted only by the rate at which society can absorb its use (Dutta and Roy 2003). Worldwide growth in Internet use is exponential (e.g., Dutta and Roy 2003), although usage varies dramatically from country to country (Santora 2006). It was anticipated that by the end of 2005, there would be 765 million users worldwide, with 27% of them in the USA (Daniel and McInerney 2005). By August 2008, the number of users worldwide had increased to nearly 1.5 billion (Internet World Stats 2008).

Despite the dot.com debacle, adoption of the Internet by businesses did not stop "or even pause" (Treese 2006), and now it is an indispensable part of the way we do business. As Goel and Hsieh (2002: 224) noted, "about half the companies in the United States are selling on the Internet." Managers recognized the importance of the Internet early and, as Porter (2001) explained, there was substantial experimentation in its use which meant that, in the short term, market behavior was abnormal – not only were firms willing to subsidize operations at cost or below cost to establish an Internet presence, but both Federal and State Governments were willing to provide subsidies in the form of no tax collection. Porter (2001) had elected to play the role of reality touchstone. He suggested that the Internet alone would not allow firms to generate and sustain a competitive advantage. He argued that the technology opened up access to an industry for newcomers by creating readily accessible markets for all the resources necessary operation – if a firm has not got resources in house, then activities can be outsourced. Not only that, but access to information to compare supplier prices and offerings forces competition and price efficiency on those outsourcing markets. He also provided a list of six principles of strategy that firms need to observe (rather than simply relying on the Internet) and, among other things, they include offering the customer benefits that are different from the competition, being able to perform activities different from the competition, and being willing to trade off some product or service features to be good at other product or service features similar to the competition. (As will later become evident, these three principles still are crucial for firms that elect to use the Internet for accessing open innovation.)

Porter (2001) argued that unless there was evidence of benefits in the form of cost savings or sustainable revenues in the longer term, firms would abandon the technology. That has not happened because of benefits such as the estimated $20 billion in cost savings to GE in 2000–2001 (Kandampully 2003; Welch and Byrne 2001), or Covisint, the pricing and purchasing application developed for auto makers and parts suppliers (Kandampully 2003). In the seven years since Porter's observations, the managerial understanding of the Internet's potential has improved and norms for its use by businesses have emerged. For example, the Internet allows firms to reduce transaction costs by making it "easier for buyers and sellers to search, meet, compare prices, and negotiate" (Berthon, et al., 2003: 554), and its international reach has changed the nature of global-sourcing strategies (Kotabe et al. 1998) and have been getting the marketing message out to customers (Davis and Harveston 2000).

We currently are witnessing the emergence of what is termed Web 2.0. It essentially is still the same architecture and browser combination, but it reflects, in the main, the way society now is using the technology. Treese (2006) identified the main characteristics of Web 2.0 as interactivity, social networking, and tagging (i.e., the process of adding keywords to data for easier retrieval). That means we are now using the technology for such things as the publishing of "blogs," publishing and viewing of "videos," and, perhaps more importantly, it facilitates much greater interactivity among on-line communities, organizations, and organizations and individuals. Web 2.0, thus, is speeding the emergence of open innovation and aiding in getting the user to do some of the work (Quittner 2006).

11.2.1 The Internet and Small Business

By facilitating outsourcing, reduced costs, and easier marketing the Internet diminishes the importance of firm size. For a sample of Italian companies, Bonaccorsi et al. (2006) found that larger companies tended to adopt a mixture of open sourcing and traditional approaches to business, whereas smaller companies preferred to rely totally on open sourcing. In a study of Israeli entrepreneurs, Shoham et al. (2006) found that the Internet was particularly useful in the venture-conception stage. The Internet has allowed SMEs to rethink the way that they compete, including changes in interorganizational relationships between SMEs and their customers (Daniel and McInerney 2005; Lawson-Body and O'Keefe 2006). Lituchy and Rail (2000) studied the impact of the Internet on bed and breakfasts and small inns and found that, generally, these entrepreneurs liked the ability to market their establishments to both domestic and foreign travelers (Davis and Harveston 2000, also noted the impact of the Internet on the internationalization of entrepreneur-led family firms).

On average, the SMEs that use the Internet have revenues almost 40% higher than those that do not (Daniel and McInerney 2005).[1] Another benefit that was revealed by Lituchy and Rail's (2000) sample of SMEs was that the Internet can reduce costs by not having to provide hard-copy advertising materials (e.g., pamphlets). However, the owners and managers of SMEs also perceive problems with the use of the Internet. For example, as Lituchy and Rail (2000) found, the advertising message can get lost in the large number of sites generated by the many other owners of bed and breakfasts and, for small businesses that do not have the necessary skills for maintaining web pages, the unreliability of web services provided by third parties created problems. That, among other things (e.g., no personnel with requisite computer skills, security fears), has made some SMEs reluctant to engage in Internet-based commerce (Daniel and McInerney 2005; Lawson-Body and O'Keefe 2006), which prompted Daniel and McInerney (2005: 183) to state that the Internet remains "an untapped resource and wide-open frontier with vast opportunities for future SME growth." In other words, despite these qualifications and caveats to the benefits of the Internet for SMEs, the changes that are occurring, in not only the technology but also the way that society is using that technology, create opportunities for entrepreneurial activity for these companies (along with their larger competitors).

---

[1] Daniel and McInerney do not infer causality (i.e., the Internet leading to revenues or revenues leading to the Internet use).

11.3 From Open Sourcing to Open Innovation

Open sourcing occurs when a body of computer source code is made publicly available and its users are able to improve the existing code or add new code to better serve their own software needs. The users agree with the provider of the source code to make improvements, but they retain the latitude to pursue whatever improvements they see as being most important (Lerner and Tirole, 2005). It, therefore, not only is effective in allowing software users to have the software they need to deal with their own unique problems but, as Kogut and Metiu (2001: 248) argued, it also is an efficient means of software development and production because it "exploits the distributed intelligence if participants in Internet communities... it avoids the inefficiencies of a strong intellectual property regime... [and] it implements concurrently design and testing of software modules." Apache, Netscape, and Linux exist because of open sourcing. Beyond these classic examples, there also are thousands of other open-source software projects in existence (von Hippel and von Krogh 2003). Any improvements made through open sourcing become public property, and the rights to those improvements are not appropriable (Lerner and Tirole, 2005; von Hippel and von Krogh 2003). As von Hippel and von Krogh 2003) explained, when the original body of material remains protected by property rights and the improvements are in the public domain and not protected, this model of innovation becomes a "private-collective" model rather than the more traditional "private-investment approach" where all property rights are protected. Open sourcing also can include abandoning rights on original material, which results in a model that fully is collective in nature. Similarly, if no original material is provided, any developments made through open sourcing also are collective in nature. These collective models approximate what is happening currently with open innovation.

Open sourcing reduces or eliminates development costs. So does open innovation. Other benefits of open sourcing include reducing or eliminating costs associated with distributing information among workers and guaranteeing peer review of any contributed work, which eliminates agency problems when employees hide their errors (Johnson 2006). These processes that are at work in the open-source communities are similar to those in the open-innovation communities. For example, where Lerner and Tirole (2002) found that the contributors to open-source projects are not all equal insofar as some individuals' contributions are greater or of better quality than others; consequently, they become part of what is perceived as an elite group. Fleming and Waguespack (2007) recently noted a similar phenomenon for open innovation where "leaders" coordinate activities among community members.

Given the lack of remuneration for individuals who become involved in open-source software projects, their contribution is, from an economist's point of view, surprising (Bonaccorsi, et al. 2006; Lerner and Tirole 2002, 2005). However, it has been determined that they get pleasure from the act of writing code, from contributing to the project, from the sense of ownership of the product that is not available when they are employed to write code, from improvement in job performance from being able to use the software in their job, and from enhancements to reputation (Lerner and Tirole, 2005; Mustonen 2003; von Hippel and von Krogh 2003).[2] Beyond the individual's reasons for getting involved in open-source projects, Lerner and Tirole (2005) noted that companies will have their employees contribute to such projects if there are benefits that can be gained by the company; that organizational motivation to use open sourcing also should translate itself to open innovation. Similarly, another benefit Lerner and Tirole (2005) identify for open sourcing is the avoidance of a "patent thicket" with all of its associated costs of applying for, renewing, and defending patents – the costs of which can be substantial (e.g., Grady et al. 1992; Long 2002; Malewicki and Sivakumar 2004; Somaya 2003). Open innovation also avoids patent thickets and costs of defense; it also means forsaking property rights that safeguard revenues.

11.4 Effects on Economic Rents

Sustainable profits – those that cannot be competed away – are economic rents. Rents – their sources, creation, and protection – have been the focus of much strategic research, particularly those dealing with the resource-based view. Mahoney and Pandian (1992) identified three types of rents associated with resource-based theory: monopoly, Ricardian, and entrepreneurial. They explain that monopoly rents arise from barriers to entry that prohibit potential competitors from satisfying the excess demand, Ricardian rents arise from owning scarce and valuable resources, and entrepreneurial rents occur with patenting or the act of bringing to market a new product or service.

Grant (1991) saw monopoly rents accruing from "industry attractiveness" which included monopoly effects and bargaining power, which, in turn, are driven by patents, brands, retaliatory capabilities, market share, firm size, financial resources – and, overarching all of these sources – barriers to entry. Given the nature of this work we separate out patents. Early forms of open innovation (e.g., R & D consortia) kept developments proprietary through extensive patenting but, in this work, where we deal with open innovation in its purest form where there

[2] We can surmise that this shift in perspective from economic assumptions on rationality and utility, maximizing to more behavioral insights on reasons why people become involved in open-source projects is reflective of demographic changes that are occurring as we move from Baby Boomers (and their parents) to Generation Y as the new force-shaping society. Generation Y has grown up in the digital world; they are interconnected, hard-working, value intellectual challenges and successes, along with volunteerism, and are not necessarily driven by money (see, e.g., Eisner's 2005, study that compares and contrasts the characteristics of Baby Boomers, and Generations X and Y). Given those characteristics, it seems probable that open innovation will become more common as Generation Y contributes more of their time and energy to innovation projects via the Internet.

are no secrets and, thus, developments are not proprietary, there are no associated monopoly rents available. There are, however, monopoly rents available from the other entry barriers that prohibit new competition (Mahoney and Pandian 1992). The lists of what constitutes barriers to entry are numerous, overlapping, and long established in the literature: Bain (1954, 1956) identified scale and capital requirements as being important along with product differentiation and absolute cost advantage; Harrigan (1981) used scale, age of assets, and concentration, and found that spare capacity was particularly important; Lieberman (1987) focused on scale and experience effects; Porter (1980) listed economies of scale, capital requirements, differentiation, switching costs, access to distribution channels, and other cost advantages independent of scale, as being sources of barriers to entry. Based mainly on Porter's work, these barriers generally are collapsed into cost advantages of incumbents, product differentiation of incumbents, capital requirements, customer switching costs, access to distribution channels, market power, and government policy (Karakaya and Stahl 1989). We set aside the latter because it is not predictable. As already discussed, there has been tacit governmental support and approval of Internet-based commerce in the form of non-collection of taxes; or, it may be that authorities have simply been slow to respond to the new form of commerce. Whether or not there will be governmental support (or opposition) for open innovation as something that improves consumer welfare is unknowable.

The lists of the sources of Ricardian rents are just as extensive as those for monopoly rents. For example, Hall (1992, 1993) identified the intangible resources of reputation, employee knowhow, culture, networks, and databases as being the main sources of sustainable advantage. Peteraf (1993) required resource heterogeneity and imperfect mobility to be present along with limits to competition (*ex ante* limits from things like acquisition of valuable resources, and *ex post* limits from such things as imperfect imitability). Grant (1991) explained how competitive advantage arises from durable resources that are not readily transparent, transferable, or replicable by competitors, which is similar to Barney's (1991) explanation that resources should be valuable, rare, and difficult to imitate. Also as Grant (1991) noted, being able to capitalize on the benefits that these resources offer means actually being able to appropriate the rents that are created. We have synthesized these insights into two factors: valuable and inimitable resources, and rent appropriability.

The third type of rents, entrepreneurial rents, "are inherently self-destructive due to diffusion of knowledge" (Mahoney and Pandian 1992: 364). Given that open innovation automatically diffuses knowledge, entrepreneurial rents will not exist. Obviously, with open innovation, there still is entrepreneurial activity in the form of commercialization but, as already noted, the protection of intellectual property in the form of patenting of designs, along with competitive issues like rivals, reverse engineering products, or trying to circumvent patents, is eliminated from this study. We thus restrict our discussion on sustained profitability to the effects of open innovation on the sources of monopoly and Ricardian rents.

11.4.1 Monopoly Rents

Although cost advantages of incumbents include both sources of monopoly and Ricardian rents, here we are dealing with the former, and at the forefront, is firm size and the cost advantage and the associated barrier to entry from economies of scale. Economies of scale are "the advantages created within the plant or firm, by reason of the increase in the scale of the plant's production or of the firm's operation" (Marshall 1967: 482). Cost savings are available from specialization and standardization of activities, from the business-level scale effects of "optimal efficient scale of operation" (Bain 1954) – in other words, optimal plant size – and other improvements in size-related efficiencies (Makadok 1999), including corporate-level effects. These cost savings reduce the average cost of production below that of a smaller (potential) new entrant and, if the size differential is sufficient, the price charged by an incumbent may also be reduced to a level below the average cost of a smaller entrant to the industry. Knowledge of that cost advantage deters new entry, which means the incumbent firm does not have to fully reduce prices; the difference is, of course, the monopoly rent.

The majority of thinking on economies of scale was developed before computers, before the Internet, and before the emergence of open sourcing and open innovation. While that does not invalidate the underlying logic on economies of scale, the Internet does make markets more contestable (Goel and Hsieh 2002), as some barriers from economies of scale are eliminated (Goel and Hsieh 2002; Lawson-Body and O'Keefe 2006; Porter 2001). Not only does the Internet provide equal visibility to all, but, as noted earlier, smaller, more-adaptable firms can pursue the benefits of Internet presence to offset larger firms' benefits from size and, thus, as contestability increases, so does industry competition.

Open innovation likely will remain an Internet phenomenon and, therefore, it always will, to some degree, be associated with technological sophistication. Sarker et al. (2006) found that technology-intensive industries had lower barriers to entry for smaller firms (i.e., there were more opportunities), and the survival rate of those firms was higher when there was an alignment between their technological abilities and the industry. Therefore, smaller firms that are willing to embrace and capitalize on Internet-based open innovation not only can adopt an innovation without the costs of developing it, but if the innovation means that the firm can operate with a lower cost structure than the established firms because of things like easier, simpler product design and simpler manufacturing, or use of less expensive materials, entry becomes feasible despite the economies of scale possessed by incumbents. That does not mean, however, that larger firms are disadvantaged completely. Macher and Boerner (2006) examined contract-research organizations in the pharmaceutical industry and found that scale had an effect on firm performance insofar as those with larger numbers of employees were better able to capitalize on knowledge and knowledge spillovers. Further, like open sourcing, open innovation too may reduce transaction costs by eliminating the need for information sharing among employees (Johnson 2006). Therefore, the monopoly rents from scale effects may well be reduced because of the ability of smaller firms to enter the industry and seize the increased opportunities that the technology brings, but they likely will still be available and, principally, will be derived from the scale effects that are attached to the utilization of knowledge (i.e., the input received from the open-innovation community).

The second major source of cost disadvantage for new entrants is experience-curve effects. Like economies of scale, the concept of experience-curve effects also is well established.[3] Preston and Keachie (1964: 105) described the phenomenon as "accumulated production knowhow," which arises from improvements in technique, which implies a learning effect. It also has long been held that while the cost benefits from economies of scale can be significant, they can be even greater from experience (cf. Preston and Keachie 1964). The form of experience effects, thus generally, is held to be $c(x) = ax^{-b}$ (Lieberman 1987), which implies which, unlike economies of scale, there are no diseconomies of experience.[4] In addition to the scale effects from knowledge spillovers, Macher and Boerner's (2006) study showed that experience effects existed in dealing with knowledge, but they had a particularly strong effect on performance when combined with economies of scope. They observed that employees' ability to take ideas from one area and apply them in related areas increased with the experience that firms had at working with knowledge. Participating in a wide array of research projects did not in itself improve knowledge utilization and performance (in fact, it had a detrimental effect on performance), but when combined with experience, the effect was positive. That means the ability to tap into the knowledge of the people who make up the open-innovation community, and then be able to manage it, will make it harder for new entrants to enter an industry successfully. And, given that the experience effects from managing and controlling knowledge are in addition to any benefits from the more traditional experience gains in operations, we would expect that open innovation increases the availability of monopoly rents from barriers to entry based on experience-curve effects.

Differentiation as a barrier to entry is derived from traditional views on marketing and competition. Karakaya and Stahl (1989: 85) explained that "Established firms have brand identification and customer loyalties stemming from past advertising, customer service, product differences, or simply being first into the market." But, with open innovation, marketing likely will change because, among other things, open innovation automatically can build commitment to a product; for example, with open sourcing of computer code, people get "peer recognition" (Lerner and Tirole 2005) and, by inference, they are likely to take ownership of the product they have helped to create. Word-of-mouth recommendations within the open-innovation

---

[3] Convention has it that they were discovered in the 1930s at Wright-Patterson air force base where data analysis revealed that the amount of time required for aircraft production dropped by 10–15% each time production output doubled.

[4] Where c is the marginal cost at output x, a is the cost of the first product, and b is the slope of the experience curve; the greater the value added to a product in the manufacturing process, the greater the potential for cost reductions, and, thus, the larger b becomes.

community will take on a new importance. Not only is it possible to achieve more brand awareness and, thus, better differentiation within virtual communities (Flavian and Guinaliu 2005) but, with open innovation, the product that has been designed to solve an individual's or group of individuals' particular needs is, by definition, perfectly differentiated. Thus, Customers will become locked in and will be less likely to switch to other offerings by new firms to the industry. Differentiation effectively substitutes for some property rights (patents) in deterring entry by bolstering reputation and brand awareness and, therefore, open innovation will increase the rents from barriers to entry, based on differentiation.

Capital requirements are the financial resources that are required to enter and to compete effectively in a market. From surveys of executives, Karakaya and Stahl (1989) and Karakaya (2002) found that capital requirements are the next most important barrier to entry after cost advantages of incumbent firms (see the above discussion on scale and experience effects). But, access to capital is being changed by the Internet. Kandampully (2003) noted that, along with recruiting employees, doing research, and achieving access to foreign customers and suppliers, the Internet also has made it easier to raise capital. Whereas capital-market access remains rooted in the relationship that financial institutions develop with the client, and thus the ability to assess the risk of the projects for which funding is being sought, the Internet has reduced those relational barriers to entry (Kandampully 2003). Further, and compounding those changes, access to capital also may be changed by open innovation because individuals in the open-innovation community who recognize the value of an innovation can be made aware of the financial needs of the organization that elects to produce the new product or service. Through self-interest, those individuals may be willing to adopt the risk that is associated with providing financing for the organization that brings the innovation to market. Such individuals will be "informal or angel investors" (Mason and Harrison 2002; Steier and Greenwood 2000). Although managing angel investors does have drawbacks, they "represent a significant source of venture capital" and that source of capital can go beyond individuals to the full "angel financial network" (Steier and Greenwood 2000: 163) which, in the case of open innovation, may be expected to overlap with the open-innovation community. Thus, open innovation will reduce the monopoly rents from the barriers to entry, based on capital requirements.

Switching costs are "one-time costs facing the buyer of switching from one supplier's product to another's"(Porter, 1980: 10). As Porter (2001) later explained when discussing the issues surrounding the Internet and e-commerce, there had been a misconception that buyers would incur switching costs by learning how to use one firm's site, and therefore, would be reluctant to incur the time and effort to become familiar with another firm's site. Since then, the improvements in both Web technology and site design (all else being equal, such as webmaster skills) means that switching costs have approached zero and that source of rents effectively was eliminated. Again, drawing on the open-source literature, Bonaccorsi et al., (2006) noted that the open sourcing of software does not work well if there are significant switching costs because there is a cost disadvantage to change and customers will not switch if they already are locked into a copyrighted, proprietary program (Mustonen 2003).

That does not mean that open sourcing cannot coexist with traditional approaches to business; for example, the coexistence of Linux and Microsoft. However, if the open-source software is second to the market, then, in the face of high switching costs, it has to provide significant benefits above and beyond the cost of switching, or there has to be a constant source of new customers. If, however, the open-source software is first to market, then the second entrant faces the same problems regardless of how the software was developed. As such, open sourcing confers no additional benefits, nor does it automatically incur penalties. Taking that rationale for software and open sourcing and applying it directly to open innovation, we can deduce that open innovation will not affect monopoly rents from the barriers to entry, based on switching costs.

Much of the thinking on the importance of channels of distribution for the creation of monopoly rents was developed pre-Internet and was based on the distribution of physical products through resellers. It was argued that channels of distribution create barriers to new entry either when incumbent firms control them through vertical integration, or when distributors are satisfied with the products and services provided by established firms (Porter, 1980). A caveat to that rationale arose when Porter (2001) later observed in his discussions about the effects of the Internet that the technology reduces the power of wholesalers and retailers insofar as it allows customers to deal directly with suppliers, which eliminates the need for "middlemen."[5] Also, if no physical product is involved, then, excluding services where the customer is present and the product is consumed as it is produced (e.g., Carmen and Langeard 1980; Czepiel et al. 1985; Flipo 1988), the Internet means that distribution channels as barriers to entry are eliminated. Like switching costs, channels of distribution as barriers to entry may not be affected by open innovation. However, if the open innovation addresses distribution which, given the link between open innovation and the Internet, is likely, then that no-effect scenario no longer holds. It has been shown that within the virtual community, which, in this work, is the open-innovation community, it is possible to increase supply differentiation (Flavian and Guinaliu 2005). Further, as Porter (2001) noted, when buyers can order electronically, there is less need for sales forces which also reduces barriers to entry, particularly for smaller companies. Therefore, open innovation probably will reduce monopoly rents from the barriers to entry, based on distribution channels.

Market power manifests itself in the ability to block new competitors, to control existing competitors (Morris 1996), and to raise prices by restricting output (Gugler and Siebert 2004). Market power is perceived as arising from possession of market share, which has been a major concern of the courts when examining anti-competitive behavior (Cameron and Glick 1996). Whether or not market share is a good indicator of abnormal profits remains unclear (different perspectives on that issue are given by Borenstein 1990; Boulding and Staelin 1990; Mariuzzo et al. 2003) but, here, we adopt the same view as the courts – market power can result in monopoly rents. Daripa and Kapur (2001) and Porter (2001) explained that, because of the ease with

[5] In marketing terms, the Internet has led to disintermediation of middlemen (Wind 2006).

which customers could comparison shop, the Internet was supposed to increase competition among suppliers. However, as Daripa and Kapur (2001: 202) also noted, there is no clear evidence that has been achieved and, instead, "many online markets are advertising-and-technology-intensive, creating a tendency towards growing concentration," which means that some firms are able to acquire market power. Whether or not that translates into higher prices is uncertain – Tellis (1989) found that large, dominant firms in an industry did not abuse market power by increasing prices, in fact their prices tended to be lower. However, other abuses such as exclusive dealing, refusal to supply or late supply, refusing to compensate customers for quality problems, and tardiness in dealing with warranty problems, still constitute abuses that lead to customer dissatisfaction, which manifests itself through complaints, exit, and negative word-of-mouth comments (e.g., Panther and Farquhar 2004; Singh, 1990). While some dissatisfied customers will exit, others will remain, despite the dissatisfaction, particularly if there are high switching costs (Panther, 2004). Thus, it follows that those who leave will seek an alternative, and those who remain will likely seek an alternative, if one with low-switching costs comes along. We, therefore, hypothesize that in the face of market power, and specifically, abuses of power, dissatisfied customers with the requisite skills likely will contribute to open-innovation projects that are aimed at creating an alternative which, in turn, will reduce monopoly rents.[6]

11.4.2 Ricardian Rents

Whereas barriers to entry explain only the rent potential for incumbent firms, a resource perspective embraces both incumbents and new entrants. In the following discussion on valuable and inimitable resources, we draw on the work of Amit and Zott (2001) who examined value creation in *e*-business and developed theory explaining how efficiency, complementarities, novelty, and lock-in are key to explaining the success of firms that incorporate the use of the Internet into their business model. Their work represents a bridge between traditional thinking on the resource-based view and its application to businesses that have developed or acquired the skills and assets necessary for succeeding in an *e*-business and Internet-based world.

On efficiency, they noted that transaction efficiencies are available, not only for the customer but also for firms insofar as they can capitalize on the interconnectivity that exists in virtual markets, and there also are benefits from faster decision making (information is available more readily), streamlined inventory control and supply-chain management, reduced marketing and sales costs, and better scalability (i.e., increased number of customer transactions). Use of the Internet in business requires skills in managing information and knowledge and, as Macher and Boerner

[6] It is arguable that some of the success of Linux has been because of the individuals who objected to Microsoft's dominance of the software industry and perceived market power (real or otherwise).

(2006) showed, those skills (and associated systems) can be honed to further reduce costs. Accessing the ideas of open-innovation communities and being able to work with those groups is not costless (Collins 2007; Lamarca 2006), so having the skills necessary to reduce those costs below those of competitors that also are using open innovation is, by definition, a valuable resource.

Amit and Zott (2001) noted that existing resource-based-theory views include the concept of complementarity among assets as a source of value creation (cf., Amit and Schoemaker 1993). They go on to explain how value can be created by bundling complementary products and they provide examples including a travel-booking business that provides weather, currency, and health information for customers, all of which are complements to the core product, and an Internet-community-building firm that provides complements that are not related to the core (e.g., home-page building, on-line greetings cards, etc). These examples are bundles of services created by firms and, because they create efficiencies for their customers, the tactic has been successful. Because people are nothing if not self serving, it is likely that the individuals involved in open innovation also will tend to produce innovations incorporating bundles of goods. These bundles, and the efficiencies they create for the innovators, will increase differentiation and, consequently, also will increase switching costs. Not only is that valuable for the firm that capitalizes on such an innovation but, by incorporating differentiation, it also is imbued with rarity.

On novelty, Amit and Zott (2001: 508) explained how, among other things, *e*-businesses find "new ways of conducting and aligning commercial transactions… [and] creating value by connecting previously unconnected parties, eliminating inefficiencies in the buying and selling process through adopting innovative transaction methods, capturing latent customer needs (such as haggle-free car purchasing from the convenience of your home), and/or by creating entirely new markets (e.g., auctions for low-ticket items)." The relevance of this for open innovation is clear – novelty not only is incorporated within innovations; open-innovation communities, which will include previously unconnected individuals and groups, also constitute new markets opportunities – and the ability to manage those links and capitalize on the associated market opportunities not only is valuable but also, we surmise, is rare.

Lock-in has more to do with inimitability, and thus sustainability, than value.[7] Amit and Zott (2001) again noted how the resource-based view can be used to address this issue through resources such as brand name, buyer-seller trust, and, we would add, reputation. They explored the existence of switching costs arising from things like familiarity with sites,[8] and the ability to customize and personalize a site enhances those costs to the customer. Of more importance to this work is the

[7] Here we refer to inimitability in a broad sense – the difficulty of imitation – rather than separating the concept into its component parts of causal ambiguity and uncertain imitability (Lippman and Rumelt 1982; Reed and DeFillippi 1990) or trying to resolve the paradox of having them combined (Wilcox King and Zeithaml 2001).

[8] Although, as already established, Porter (2001) questioned the strength of this as a switching cost.

identification of lock-in coming from the virtual markets that help create virtual communities with increased loyalty and transaction frequency. They explained that the interactions between community members become "network generators" as one member of the network has "an effect on the production or utility function of other participants in the network… and *e*-business operations can be designed to harness the power of this lock-in mechanism" (p. 507). This conceptualization of lock-in closely fits our discussion on the effects of differentiation where members contributing to open-source projects are likely to take ownership of the product they have helped to create and, consequently, recommend it to others within the open-source community. In other words, customers are willing to become advocates for a company and recommend its goods or services to others (Wind 2006), and that becomes more important as the number of products available to Web users increases. Branding, thus, takes on a new importance on the Internet (Anonymous 2002; Flavian and Guinaliu 2005). Therefore, drawing together these arguments on value and rareness, accompanying efficiencies, complementarities, novelty, and lock-in, we may expect that open innovation will increase the potential for the creation of Ricardian rents.

Having managed to attract an open-innovation community, and assuming that, as just described, there are Ricardian rents available, the question arises – how does the firm appropriate them? From the literature on open sourcing, it generally is held that firms can benefit from open-source projects when they lag behind the industry leader, when they are small relative to the industry leader, or when they sell complementary products and services (Mustonen 2003; Lerner and Tirole 2005). The first two primarily are tactics for playing catch-up, so it is the latter that currently provides the main source of income. While that approach may work with open licensing, or copyleft where the firm retains rights over original material or design, open innovation provides few safeguards against imitators of complementary products and services. Consequently, firms may have to gamble on customer loyalty and lock-in as the equivalent of a property right. If competitors with a lower cost structure are able to imitate the innovation, which should be easy, given that it is open innovation, then customers may defect despite having emotional capital invested in the innovation.

Grant (1991) explained how the appropriation of Ricardian rents can be difficult if the resources that created the rents are vested in the skills of an individual. That individual becomes powerful and can acquire the rents for himself/herself by bargaining up his/her income. With open innovation, the "elite" members of the open-innovation community hold similar power and may be able to bargain with the firm for special deals (preferential prices, payments, perquisites) that erode the Ricardian (and monopoly) rents. Worse yet, the organization has no control over these individuals because they are not even (powerful) employees and they can defect to competitors taking other, less elite members of the community with them. This scenario fits closely with Amit and Zott's (2001) observation that peer recommendations have a downside because they can turn into a "dangerous downward spiral." Thus, while potential Ricardian rents may be higher, the probability of capturing those rents is reduced.

11.5 Discussion

As more people use the Internet for creative activities rather than passive entertainment, then more innovations will be available for firms to utilize. Research shows that openness to new ideas from the environment improves firm performance (Laursen and Salter 2006), and firms that are not willing to capitalize on the technological and sociological revolution that is producing the explosion of creativity in product and service design, run the risk of falling behind. Open innovation has become a fact of business. Some firms such as IBM, Nokia, and Whirlpool, along with non-profits such as the BBC, already are capitalizing on such creativity (Collins 2007).

We have deduced that open innovation modifies the sources of monopoly rents for industry incumbents. Rents from property rights likely will disappear, and the effect on those from barriers to entry will be mixed; those from capital requirements and distribution will decline, as too will those from market power and from scale effects (and those that remain will come mainly from knowledge scale-effects); whereas those from switching costs will remain unchanged, but those from experience effects and differentiation may increase. Ricardian rents should increase, but they will be more difficult to capture because the source of the innovation – the intellectual capital of the open-innovation community – remains outside the control of the firm. Thus, we can deduce that while our existing models of strategy still work in the face of this new source of innovation, the way we view them will have to be adjusted. That means adjusting our dominant paradigm and rethinking many of our research questions. For example, it has been suggested that open sourcing in low-tech industries may be harmful to performance for established firms. The same may be true for open innovation. Lecocq and Demil (2006) found that an "open systems strategy" (a close relative of open innovation), whereby firms reveal proprietary knowledge to others in the industry (Garud and Kumaraswamy 1993), in a low-tech environment, encouraged new entrants who were better able to cope with the open-systems approach. Many of those entrants were smaller, more adaptable, specialized firms.

Open innovations not only have implications for research, they also have implications for practice. Traditional perspectives on the organization and environment tend to view open systems as a necessary evil (Scott 1992), but open innovation changes what environmental input means to the organization. Instead of being a cost, it becomes a source of revenue. It does, of course, require a willingness to move beyond rational decision-making to the more difficult realm of natural decision-making. Laursen and Salter (2006) found that firm innovation improved as the breadth and depth of searching using external actors and sources increased. While too much searching led to diseconomies and deterioration of performance, the message is clear that being open to new ideas from the environment is superior to a closed, in-house, internal focus on innovation. Thus, the continued growth of open innovation is to be expected because it is in firms' own best interests to foster and support the efforts of open-innovation communities.

Much existing theory still has application to open innovation. For example, the adaptation that accompanies notions of resource dependency still pertains and, perhaps, even more so. There has to be a willingness and desire to adapt not only strategies but also the organization structure and routines. Rindova and Kotha's (2001) call it "morphing" and Scott (1992) refers to it as "morphogenesis." While that may be so for established organizations, new organizations may require more stability and structure to survive – see Sine et al. (2006) work on the survival of firms operating in the Internet economy. Thus, new firms using open innovation may need to adopt a hybrid business model (Bonaccorsi, et al. 2006) whereby open sourcing is combined with some degree of proprietary control. Additionally, to make open innovation work, customer input has to be managed like other knowledge (see Voelpel et al. 2005, description of the management of ShareNet at Siemens A.G.). For established firms this may mean creating new organizational routines (Bonaccorsi, et al. 2006). There also are governance issues to deal with – Demil and Lecoq (2006) use the term "bazaar governance" to convey the fact that there is an openness to open-source communities that is not available in typical market, relational, or hierarchy relationships, or even with open licensing. The same issues need addressing with open innovation.

What emerges from this work is that there is a need to explore the impact of open innovation as it begins to overtake our established ways of thinking and our models of strategy that rest on the assumption that innovations and entrepreneurial activity can be protected by the individual company and thus be exploited for the gain. The Schumpeterian revolution that has occurred with the advent of the Internet, and the way that it is being used by individuals and communities, requires a shift in our dominant paradigm and, thus, our understanding of the way that firms generate and sustain profitability.

References

Amit R, Zott C (2001) Value creation in e-business. Strat Manag J 22:493–520

Amit R, Schoemaker P (1993) Strategic assets and organizational rent. Strat Manag J 14:33–46

Anonymous (2002) When branding met the web. Strategic Direction 18(10):25–28

Bain JS (1954) Economies of scale, concentration, and the condition of entry in twenty manufacturing industries. Am Econ Rev 44:15–39

Bain JS (1956) Barriers to New Competition. Harvard University, Cambridge, MA

Barney JB (1991) Firm resources and sustained competitive advantage. J Manag 17:99–120

Berthon P, Ewing M, Pitt L, Naude P (2003) Understanding B2B and the Web: the acceleration of coordination and motivation. Ind Market Manag 32:553–561

Bonaccorsi A, Giannangeli S, Rossi C (2006) Entry strategies under competing standards: Hybrid business models in the open source software industry. Manag Sci 52:1085–1098

Borenstein S (1990) Airline mergers, airport dominance, and market power. Am Econ Rev 80:400–404

Boulding W, Staelin R (1990) Environment, market share, and market power. Manag Sci 36: 1160–1177

Cameron D, Glick M (1996) Market share and market power in merger and monopolization cases. Manag Decis Econ 17:193–201

Carmen JM, Langeard E (1980) Growth strategies for service firms. Strat Manag J 1:7–22

Cave M, Mason R (2001) The economics of the Internet: Infrastructure and regulation. Oxf Rev Econ Pol 17:188–202

Collins L (2007) Embedding innovation into the firm. Res Tech Manag 50(2):5–6
Czepiel JA, Solomon MR, Surprenant CF, Gutman EG (1985) Service encounters: An overview. In: Czepiel JA, Solomon MR, Surprenant CF (eds) The service encounter: managing employee/customer interaction in the service businesses. Institute of Retail Management, New York University, NY, pp 3–15
Daniel TA, McInerney MS (2005) E-commerce and the "reluctant" small business owner: How technology is changing the business model for small and medium-sized enterprises (SMEs). International Journal of Applied Management and Technology 3:183–206
Daripa A, Kapur S (2001) Pricing on the Internet. Oxf Rev Econ Pol 17:202–216
Davis PS, Harveston PD (2000) Internationalization and organizational growth: The impact of Internet usage and technology involvement among entrepreneur-led family businesses. Fam Bus Rev 13:107–120
Demil B, Lecocq X (2006) Neither market, nor hierarchy nor network: The emergence of bazaar governance. Organ Stud 27:1447–1466
Dutta A, Roy R (2003) Anticipating Internet diffusion. Commun ACM 46(2):66–71
Eisner SP (2005) Managing generation Y. S.A.M. Advanced Management Journal 70(4):4–15
Flavian C, Guinaliu M (2005) The influence of virtual communities on distribution strategies in the internet [*sic*]. Int J Retail Distrib Manag 33:405–425
Fleming L, Waguespack DM (2007) Brokerage, boundary spanning, and leadership in open innovation communities. Organ Sci 18:165–183
Flipo J-P (1988) On the intangibility of services. Serv Indust J 8:286–298
Goel RK, Hsieh EWT (2002) Internet growth and economic theory. Netnomics 4:221–225
Garud R, Kumaraswamy A (1993) Changing competitive dynamics in network industries: An exploration of Sun Microsystems' open systems strategy. Strat Manag J 14:351–369
Grady MF, Alexander JI, Martin DL, Merges RP (1992) Patent law and rent dissipation; Commentaries. Va Law Rev 78:305–381
Grant RM (1991) The resource-based theory of competitive advantage: Implications for strategy formulation. Calif Manag Rev 33(3):114–135
Grossman L (2006) Person of the Year. You. Time, December 25-January 1:40–41
Gugler K, Siebert R (2004) Market power versus efficiency effects of mergers and research joint ventures: evidence from the semiconductor industry. Working Paper 10323. Cambridge, MA: National Bureau of Economic Research
Hall R (1992) The strategic analysis of intangible resources. Strat Manag J 13:135–144
Hall R (1993) A framework linking intangible resources and capabilities to sustainable competitive advantage. Strat Manag J 14:607–618
Hamm S (2007) Radical collaboration: lessons from IBM's innovation factory. *Business Week*, September 10:IN17–IN21
Harrigan K (1981) Barriers to entry and competitive strategies. Strat Manage J 2(4):395–412
Internet World Stats 2008. www.internetworldstats.com.
Johnson JP (2006) Collaboration, peer review and open source software. ScienceDirect 18:477–497
Kandampully J (2003) B2B relationships and networks in the Internet age. Manag Decis 41:443–451
Karakaya F (2002) Barriers to entry in industrial markets. J Bus Ind Market 17:379–388
Karakaya F, Stahl MJ (1989) Barriers to entry and market entry decisions in consumer goods and industrial goods markets. Journal of Marketing 53(2):80–91
Kogut B, Metiu A (2001) Open-source software development and distributed innovation. Oxf Rev Econ Pol 17:248–264
Kotabe M, Murray JY, Javalgi RG (1998) Global sourcing of services and market performance: An empirical investigation. J Int Market 6(4):10–31
Lamarca R (2006) The free range. Mechanical Engineering Design 128(3):26–29
Laursen K, Salter A (2006) Open for innovation: the role of openness in explaining innovation performance among UK manufacturing firms. Strat Manag J 27:131–150
Lawson-Body A, O'Keefe TP (2006) Interorganizational relationships in the context of SMEs' B2B e-commerce. J Electron Commerce Org 4(4):1–28

Lecocq X, Demil B (2006) Strategizing industry structure: the case of open sytems in a low-tech industry. Strat Manag J 27:891–898
Lerner J, Tirole J (2002) Some simple economics of open source. J Ind Econ 50:197–234
Lerner J, Tirole J (2005) The economics of technology sharing: open source and beyond. J Econ Perspect 19:99–120
Lieberman MB (1987) The learning curve, diffusion and competitive strategy. Strat Manag J 8:441–452
Lippman S, Rumelt RP (1982) Uncertain imitability: an analysis of interfirm differences in efficiency under competition. Bell J Econ 13:418–438
Lituchy TR, Rail A (2000) Bed and breakfasts, small inns, and the Internet: The impact of technology on the globalization of small business. J Int Market 8(2):86–97
Long C (2002) Patent signals. Univ Chicago Law Rev 69:625–679
Macher JT, Boerner CS (2006) Experience and scale and scope economies: trade-offs and performance in development. Strat Manag J 27:845–865
Makadok R (1999) Interfirm differences in scale economies and the evolution of market shares. Strat Manag J 20:935–952
Mahoney JT, Pandian RJ (1992) The resource-based view within the conversation of strategic management. Strat Manag J 13:363–380
Malewicki D, Sivakumar K (2004) Patents and product development strategies: A model of antecedents and consequences of patent value. Eur J Innovat Manag 7:5–22
Marshall BV (1967) Comprehensive Economics: Descriptive, Theoretical, and Applied. Longman, London
Mariuzzo F, Walsh PP, Whelan C (2003) Firm size and market power in carbonated soft drinks. Rev Ind Organ 23:283–299
Mason CM, Harrison RT (2002) Is it worth it? The rates of return from information venture capital. Journal of Business Venturing 17:211–236
Morris DJ Jr (1996) Market Power and Business Strategy. Quorum Books, Westport, CT
Mustonen M (2003) Copyleft – the economics of Linux and other open source software. Inf Econ Policy 15:99–121
Panther T, Farquhar JD (2004) Consumer responses to dissatisfaction with financial service providers: An exploration of why some stay while others switch. J of Financial Services Market 8:343–353
Peteraf MA (1993) The cornerstone of competitive advantage: A resource-based view. Strat Manag J 14:179–191
Porter ME (1980) Competitive Strategy: Techniques for Analyzing Industries and Competitors. The Free Press, New York, NY
Porter ME (2001) Strategy and the Internet. Harv Bus Rev 79(3):63–78
Preston LE, Keachie EL (1964) Cost functions and progress functions: an integration. Am Econ Rev 54:100–107
Reed R, DeFillippi RJ (1990) Causal ambiguity, barriers to imitation, and sustainable competitive advantage. Acad Manag Rev 15:88–102
Rindova VP, Kotha S (2001) Continuous "morphing" Competing through dynamic capabilities, form, and function. Acad Manag J 44:1263–1280
Sakakibara M (2002) Formation of R&D Consortia: Industry and Company Effects. Strat Manag J 23(11):1033–1050
Scott WR (1992) Organizations: Rational, Natural, and Open Systems. Prentice Hall, Englewood Cliffs, NJ
Quittner J (2006) Web boom 2.0. Time, December 25-January 1: 75
Santora JC (2006) Crossing the digital divide: do all global citizens have their passports? Academy of Management Perspectives 20(4):118–119
Sarker MB, Echambadi R, Agarwal R, Sen B (2006) The effect of the innovative environment on exit of entrepreneurial firms. Strat Manag J 27:519–539
Shoham S, Baruchson-Arbib S, Guri-Oren O (2006) An exploratory study of Israeli start-up entrepreneur usage of the Internet. Journal of Information Science 32:49–62

Sine WD, Mitsuhashi H, Kirsch DA (2006) Revisiting burns and stalker: formal structure and new venture performance in emerging economic sectors. Acad Manag J 49:121–132
Singh J (1990) Voice, exit, and negative word-of-mouth behaviors: an investigation across three service categories. J of the Academy of Market Science 18(1):1–14
Somaya D (2003) Strategic determinants of decisions not to settle patent litigations. Strat Manag J 24:17–38
Steier L, Greenwood R (2000) Entrepreneurship and the evolution of angel financial networks. Organ Stud 21:163–192
Tellis GJ (1989) The impact of corporate size and strategy on competitive pricing. Strat Manag J 10:569–585
Treese W (2006) Web 2.0: Is it really different? Networker 10(2):15–17
Voelpel SCM, Dous M, Davenport TH (2005) Five steps to creating a global knowledge-sharing system: Siemens' ShareNet. Acad Manag Exec 19(2):9–23
von Hippel E, von Krogh G (2003) Opensource software and the "private-collective" innovation model: Issues for organization science. Organ Sci 14:209–223
Welch J, Byrne JA (2001) Straight from the gut. Warner Business Books, New York
Wilcox King A, Zeithaml CP (2001) Competencies and firm performance: Examining the causal ambiguity paradox. Strat Manag J 22:75–99
Wind Y (2006) Blurring the lines: Is there a need to rethink industrial marketing? J Bus Ind Market 21:474–481

Index

FSC
www.fsc.org
MIX
Papier | Fördert gute Waldnutzung
FSC® C083411

Kolibri 360 GmbH
Ferdinand-Jühlke-Straße 7
99095 Erfurt, Deutschland
produktsicherheit@kolibri360.de